AT HOME with the WORD® 2024

Sunday Scriptures and Scripture Insights

Year B

Sherri Brown

Tat-siong Benny Liew

Krista Chinchilla-Patzke

Edrianne Ezell

Also available in a Large-Print Edition

LTP
LITURGY
TRAINING
PUBLICATIONS

Nihil Obstat
Deacon David Keene, PHD
Chancellor
Archdiocese of Chicago
March 2, 2023

Imprimatur
Most Rev. Robert G. Casey
Vicar General
Archdiocese of Chicago
March 2, 2023

AT HOME WITH THE WORD® 2024 © 2023 Archdiocese of Chicago: Liturgy Training Publications, 3949 South Racine Avenue, Chicago, IL 60609; 800-933-1800; fax: 800-933-7094; email: orders@ltp.org; website: www.LTP.org. All rights reserved.

This book was edited by Mary G. Fox. Michael E. Novak was the production editor, Anna Manhart was the cover designer, Anne Fritzinger was the interior designer, and Matthew B. Clark was the production artist.

The cover art for this year's *At Home with the Word*® is by Cody F. Miller. The interior art is by Kathy Ann Sullivan.

Printed in the United States of America

ISBN: 978-1-61671-692-9

AHW24

Welcome to At Home with the Word® 2024

THE AUTHORS OF THE INTRODUCTIONS

Marielle Frigge, OSB, taught Scripture and theology for thirty-three years at Mount Marty College in Yankton, South Dakota, and is now formation director for Sacred Heart Monastery. Michael Cameron is professor emeritus of Scripture and the history of Christianity at the University of Portland in Oregon

SCRIPTURE READINGS

For each Sunday, you will find the three readings and responsorial psalm from the *Lectionary for Mass*, from which readings are proclaimed in Roman Catholic churches in the United States.

SCRIPTURE INSIGHTS

Two authors have written Scripture Insights for 2024. Sherri Brown, PHD, is associate professor of New Testament at Creighton University, Omaha, Nebraska. Her doctorate in biblical studies is from the Catholic University of America. She is currently writing *Apostle to the Apostles: The Role of Women in the Gospel of John* (Grand Rapids, MI: Baker Academic) and is the author of *Come and See: Discipleship in the Gospel of John* (Mahwah, NJ: Paulist Press, 2022); and *God's Promise: Covenant Relationship in John* (Mahwah, NJ: Paulist Press, 2014). She cowrote the textbooks *Interpreting the Gospels and Letters of John* and *Interpreting the New Testament* with Francis J. Moloney, SDB (Grand Rapids, MI: Eerdmans, 2017, 2019). She wrote the Scripture Insights for Pentecost through the Solemnity of Our Lord Jesus Christ, King of the Universe.

Tat-siong Benny Liew is Class of 1956 Professor in New Testament Studies at the College of the Holy Cross, Worcester, Massachusetts. He is the author of *Politics of Parousia* (Brill, 1999) and *What Is Asian American Biblical Hermeneutics?* (University of Hawaii Press, 2008). In addition, he is the editor of the *Semeia* volume on "The Bible in Asian America" (with Gale Yee; SBL, 2002). He is the executive editor of the academic journal *Biblical Interpretation* (Brill) and the series editor of *T&T Clark's Study Guides to the New Testament* (New York: Bloomsbury). He wrote the Scripture Insights from the First Sunday of Advent through the Seventh Sunday of Easter.

PRACTICE OF FAITH, HOPE, CHARITY

Two authors wrote the Practice of Faith, Hope, or Charity. Krista Chinchilla-Patzke is the faith justice minister at Loyola University Chicago. She earned a master of arts degree in theology and ministry from the School of Theology and Ministry at Boston College. She wrote the Practices for Pentecost Sunday through the Solemnity of Our Lord Jesus Christ, King of the Universe.

Edrianne Ezell, MDIV, a freelance writer, is a former campus minister at the Eastern Illinois University Newman Center, Charleston, Illinois. She earned her master of divinity degree from Weston Jesuit School of Theology and her bachelor of arts in English and studies of religion from the University of Michigan. She wrote the Practices for the First Sunday of Advent through the Seventh Sunday of Easter.

ADDITIONAL DOWNLOADABLE QUESTIONS AND ACTIVITIES

Download additional questions and activities for three audiences: families, Christian initiation groups, and other adult groups. The link http://www.ltp.org/ahw will take you to the *At Home with the Word®* Extra Content page. Click on the desired audience: Adult Faith-Sharing Groups, Christian Initiation Groups, or Families.

WEEKDAY READINGS

See the opening of each liturgical time for a list of Scripture texts read at Mass on weekdays and on feasts falling on weekdays.

ART FOR 2024

On the cover, Cody F. Miller has depicted the Holy Spirit renewing the face of the earth. This is the eighth of several scenes from salvation history to appear on the covers of *At Home with the Word®*. The portrayal is from Psalm 104, from which the responsorial psalm is taken on Pentecost. Inside the book, Kathy Ann Sullivan uses a scratch-board technique to evoke the liturgical seasons, from our ancestors on the Jesse tree to the oil lamps for Ordinary Time in the fall.

Table of Contents

Lent

The Sacred Paschal Triduum

Easter Time

Ordinary Time, Summer

Ordinary Time, Autumn

The Lectionary

By Marielle Frigge, OSB

WHAT IS A LECTIONARY?

The word *lectionary* comes from the Latin word *legere*, "to read," and names a collection of Scripture readings from both the Old and New Testaments that are proclaimed throughout the liturgical year in a particular order. Christian lectionaries were in use already in the fourth century, but before the invention of the printing press in the mid-fifteenth century, readings differed from place to place. Printing allowed for a more standardized lectionary, so that Catholics around the world could hear the same Bible readings at Mass on any given day.

However, in the four centuries before the Second Vatican Council (1963–65), the lectionary had a somewhat limited ability to touch the faith lives of Catholics. Most could not understand what was read because Scripture readings as well as the prayers of the Mass were proclaimed in Latin. Further, because the lectionary of that time used only particular selections from the Bible repeated year after year, Catholics received a restricted exposure to the riches of Scripture.

GIFTS OF THE SECOND VATICAN COUNCIL

After the Second Vatican Council, not only were the biblical readings made available in the language of the people, but the structure of the lectionary was expanded as well. These changes resulted from a fresh understanding of the role of Scripture in the liturgy. Returning to the ancient understanding that Christ is present in the Scriptures, the Council Fathers further emphasized that the Eucharist nourishes God's people at two tables: the proclaimed Word of God and the Eucharistic banquet. For this reason, the revised lectionary includes much more Scripture. Rather than repeating a yearly pattern, it includes a three-year cycle for Sundays and a two-year cycle for weekdays. Through this expanded array of selections, it aims to present the broad sweep of the salvation story, arranged purposefully around the liturgical year with the four major liturgical seasons of Advent, Christmas Time, Lent, and Easter Time punctuating the many weeks of Ordinary Time.

These great liturgical seasons instruct the faithful in the most significant aspects of salvation history. The liturgical year begins with Advent, expressing the ancient longing and hope of God's covenant people for redemption. Christmas Time celebrates the incarnation of the Lord, God's Word of salvation fully present and active in the world, made flesh in Jesus the Christ. During Lent, the Scripture readings call Christians to deeper conversion: to amend their ways of failing to respond to God's saving Word, to cultivate greater intimacy with God, and to rejoice that he never ceases to offer life-changing mercy. These Scriptures about conversion speak powerfully to those preparing for initiation. Easter Time proclaims the paschal mystery, the redeeming death and resurrection of Jesus Christ. That mystery leads us into life in divine Spirit, poured out upon all the faithful at Pentecost, sending us out to serve. In addition to highlighting the liturgical seasons, the lectionary illuminates other key mysteries of Catholic faith in solemnities such as the Most Holy Trinity, the Most Holy Body and Blood of Christ, the Assumption of the Blessed Virgin Mary, and in feasts such as the Presentation of the Lord and the Exaltation of the Holy Cross.

FOUR SUNDAY SCRIPTURE SELECTIONS

At Home with the Word® provides all four Scripture passages of each Sunday: a selection from the Old Testament (except during Easter Time when we hear from Acts of the Apostles); a responsorial psalm or canticle; a New Testament reading from one of the letters, the Acts of the Apostles, or Revelation; and, most important, a Gospel passage. Each year of the three-year cycle draws from a particular Gospel account: Matthew in Year A, Mark in Year B, and Luke in Year C. The Gospel of John, so highly symbolic and profound, is heard in the liturgical seasons. The lectionary includes readings from John on several Sundays of Lent, during the Sacred Paschal Triduum, and most Sundays of Easter Time. Because Mark is the shortest Gospel account, some Sundays of Ordinary Time in Year B use passages from John.

The pattern of today's Catholic lectionary has served as a model for lectionaries of several other Christian churches. As a result, Catholics and many Protestants hear the same Scripture passages proclaimed on Sundays. The biblical Word of God thus draws them closer.

Understanding how the four Scripture passages of each Sunday are related can help us appreciate how the lectionary invites Christians to understand, ponder, and integrate the message of God's Word. The first reading from the Old Testament usually bears some connection to the Gospel passage, often by means of a significant person, event, or image. Rooted in the ancient practice of the Jewish synagogue, the responsorial, which follows the first reading, is usually from a psalm and represents the people's response to God's Word in the first reading. In this way the first two Scripture passages mirror a theme woven throughout the Bible: God always takes the initiative to address humankind, speaking a Word that invites a response from God's people. The responsorial may also illustrate or clarify what the first reading proclaims, or may be related to the liturgical season, and thus is intended to foster meditation on the Word of God.

Frequently the second reading, always from the New Testament, follows the ancient practice of *lectio continua* (Latin for "continuous reading"), so that on each Sunday we hear important selections in order from a particular book. For example, the second reading is often an excerpt from one of the letters of St. Paul, and by continuous reading over several Sundays, the lectionary presents some of his major theological insights in a particular letter.

During Ordinary Time the lectionary presents continuous reading in the Gospels also, allowing us to see each evangelist's distinctive way of unfolding the Gospel story. For example, in Year A, from the Fourteenth Sunday in Ordinary Time to the end of the liturgical year in November, we hear the Gospel of Matthew from chapter 11 through chapter 25. Not every verse of Matthew is included, and occasionally a Sunday solemnity or feast requires a reading from a different Gospel, but continuous reading relates major aspects of Matthew's narrative, just as it does for Mark's in Year B and Luke's in Year C. Over time, through continuous reading, we can become familiar with the particular content and qualities of each Gospel account.

THE LECTIONARY AS A VISUAL SIGN

The lectionary nourishes us with its words proclaimed in the liturgy—the Lord's own voice speaking to his people. It also nourishes us as a visual sign of the Lord's presence among us. The United States Conference of Catholic Bishops reminds Catholics that gestures and physical objects used in liturgy are "signs by which Christians express and deepen their relationship to God" (*Built of Living Stones: Art, Architecture, and Worship,* 23). Although the lectionary's proper place during the liturgy is on the ambo (the special podium from which readings are proclaimed), a part of the lectionary—the Gospel readings—has been made into a separate Book of the Gospels. That book, often richly decorated, may be carried in the entrance procession on Sundays and holydays. It is placed on the altar at the beginning of Mass and then, when the assembly rises to sing the Alleluia, the Gospel reader may processes with the book to the ambo, accompanied by servers holding candles. In response to the deacon or priest's introduction to the Gospel reading, the people respond, signing their forehead, lips, and heart with a small cross. Observing such signs and ceremonies, one could not miss the special reverence we give to the Word of God—especially in the Gospel.

In the bishops' teaching about the ambo, from which the Scriptures are proclaimed, we find an apt crystallization of the Church's conviction about the role of Scripture in the Mass. Urging that the ambo should be of a size and placement that draws attention to the sacred Word, the document says, "Here the Christian community encounters the living Lord in the word of God and prepares itself for the 'breaking of the bread' and the mission to live the word that will be proclaimed" (*Built of Living Stones,* 61).

Introduction to the Gospel according to Mark

By Michael Cameron

In the late 60s of the first century, nearly forty years since the resurrection and ascension of the Lord, he had not yet returned. Jerusalem was under siege by the Romans, and the persecution of Christians in Rome itself was intensifying after the fire of 64. Peter and Paul had died, and few eyewitnesses to Jesus' ministry were left. Christians had told and retold the stories of Jesus' ministry, death, and resurrection over the years, but Christians began to feel the need for written instruction.

In these years, Mark, leaning on the teachings of Peter and others, wrote his Gospel, the earliest one we have. It is likely that he wrote for his suffering community in the environs of Rome. His main concern was to record the basic facts and stay faithful to the tradition, and Mark wrote with a flair for the dramatic and a rich theological sense.

Suffering had thrown Mark's community into a spiritual crisis. The crisis came not because of weak faith, but through a strong faith too focused on the privileges and glory of being the community of the resurrection: being disciples meant enjoying the benefits of Jesus' victory (see 10:35–45). As a counterweight to this, Mark refocused on Jesus' death as the foundation of discipleship (8:31–35). Mark's primary themes of the kingdom of God, the identity of Jesus, and the call to discipleship each undergo dramatic development in the Gospel in light of the cross. For Mark, everything, even Jesus' glorious return, stands in the shadow of his crucifixion. The German New Testament scholar Martin Kähler aptly called the Gospel according to Mark "a passion narrative with an extended introduction."

JESUS PROCLAIMS THE KINGDOM

In Mark's first chapters, Jesus is a messianic figure on the move, proclaiming the nearness of God's kingdom in his words and works. As the Spirit "drove" Jesus into the wilderness after his baptism (1:12), so Jesus charges the early pages of Mark with divine power and urgency. The synagogue exorcism in 1:21–28 demonstrates Jesus' mastery of the spiritual world; the healings that follow in

1:29—2:10 reveal that the kingdom's power lies in redemptive service. Jesus never defines the kingdom of God, but the parables of chapter 4 describe its characteristics. Irresistibly it comes, grows, changes everything, feeds everyone. It heals bodies, repairs hearts, defeats evil, creates community. Nothing stops its relentless coming; not sin (2:7), disease (1:40–45), calamity (4:35–41), or demonic forces (3:22–27). The kingdom emerges as a result of God's action, not humanity's.

The unfeeling religious leaders fail to receive the message (3:1–6). They lack the spiritual eyes and ears to perceive the new in-breaking of God's love in Jesus' ministry and the new turning to God's love that this requires. Paradoxically, Jesus finds this among tax collectors (2:15–17), the sick (1:29–34), and the wretched (5:1–20).

BECOMING DISCIPLES OF JESUS

Initial faith through the miracles is only a first step. The disciples struggle to fulfill the Master's hopes for them. "Do you not yet have faith?" Jesus asks early on (4:40). After Jesus feeds the five thousand, he cares for the disciples by walking to them on the water during their midnight struggle. They merely become frightened. Mark comments, "They had not understood the incident of the loaves. On the contrary, their hearts were hardened" (6:52). Jesus tries again by feeding the four thousand, but their minds are fixed on literal bread. "Do you still not understand?" Jesus asks (8:21).

Peter confesses that Jesus is the Messiah (8:29). But his awareness is only partial, for he needs Jesus to fit his expectations, which definitively exclude suffering. Jesus calls the idea satanic (8:33). Eventually one disciple betrays him, another denies him, and all desert him. Some readers think that Mark's telling of the disciples' failures is his way of disparaging official Christian leadership. But the disciples were later reconciled to the Lord after his resurrection and lived to prove their faith. It is more likely that Mark is encouraging Jesus' followers to take heart from the disciples' example of recovery from failure. With Peter's martyrdom still a recent memory, the story of him denying the Lord would have special power.

CHRIST THE SUFFERING SERVANT

The Son of God has a rich, deep humanity in this Gospel. Mark's Greek word for Jesus' reaction to the plight of the leper in 1:41 might be translated "his heart melted with compassion," the same word used for Jesus' compassion on the crowds.

Jesus insists that his divinity should not be made known (1:44; 3:12; 5:43; 7:36; 8:26, 30), a motif known as the messianic secret. He refuses to be the political messiah that people expected. He reinterpreted honors in terms of his mission as suffering servant, processing into Jerusalem on a humble donkey (11:1–10), not a horse, as a conquering king would. He is anointed by an anonymous woman, not for enthronement but for burial (14:3–9). He wears royal attire and receives homage from the Gentiles, but in mockery (15:16–20). Jesus establishes the new covenant of Jeremiah 31 by becoming the Suffering Servant of Isaiah 53: "This is my blood of the covenant poured out for many" (14:24).

From the beginning the reader knows that Jesus is the Son of God (1:1). Throughout the Gospel the only voices to confess his true identity come from God (1:11; 9:7) and demons (1:24; 3:11; 5:7). Meanwhile, religious leaders call him demon-possessed (3:22), his family thinks he's a lunatic (3:21), and village neighbors complain he's pretentious (6:2–3). To their credit the disciples begin to wonder, "Who then is this?" (4:41). But no human lips confess his true identity—until the end. Stripped of his dignity, his disciples, his life, destitute and utterly alone, Jesus draws his last breath. But at this precise moment the long-awaited confession comes from a Roman centurion: "Truly this man was the Son of God!" (15:39). Jesus' death reveals the identity of God's Son, a living tableau of the disciples' calling to live the Way of the Cross. The Resurrection is proclaimed by disciples who have received a new life after they have lost their lives "for my sake and that of the gospel" (8:35).

Introduction to the Gospel according to John

By Michael Cameron

This Gospel has no year of its own in the lectionary's three-year cycle, but it is strongly represented *every* year during Christmas, Lent, and Easter Time; it also appears in Ordinary Time in Mark for Year B, Sundays 17–21. John shares some features of the first three Gospels (called "synoptic" for "seeing together"). Some stories overlap, characters seen in the synoptics reappear, and John clearly voices the evangelistic, instructional purpose of all the Gospels: that you may believe and receive life in Jesus' name (20:31).

But its vision stands majestically apart, like the eagle that became this Gospel's symbol. It is rooted in the teaching of a mysterious unnamed figure, the "disciple whom Jesus loved" (13:23; 19:26; 20:2; 21:7, 20), who authenticates this Gospel's "testimony" (19:35; 21:24). It uniquely portrays the divine Word acting with God and as God to create all things (1:1–5), taking human flesh to reveal the Father's glory (1:1, 14–18).

John communicates in distinctive ways. The synoptics tell Jesus' story in compact vignettes; John constructs chapter-long dramas (see especially chapters 4, 9, and 11). The first three Gospels contain pithy, memorable sayings about God's kingdom; John's Jesus speaks hypnotically repetitive discourses focused on eternal life (for example, 6:22–59; 10:1–18; chapters 14–17). The synoptics' homespun parables pique curiosity about Jesus' message; the Johannine Jesus poetically develops elements like water (4:7–15), bread (6:25–35), and light (3:19–21; 9:4–5; 12:35–36) into metaphors for contemplating divine truth.

John tells unique stories about Jesus: he changes water into wine (2:1–11), disputes with Nicodemus (3:1–21), engages the Samaritan woman at the well (4:4–26), heals a man born blind (9:1–41), raises dead Lazarus (11:1–45), chides the doubting Thomas (20:24–29), and cooks post-Easter breakfast for the disciples (21:1–14). John also varies details from some familiar synoptic stories, among which Jesus "cleanses the Temple" early in his ministry rather than late (2:13–22); the synoptics' Passover meal ("the Last Supper") is a meal *before*

Passover where Jesus washes the disciples' feet (13:4–15); the synoptic Jesus anguishes before death, but in John goes to the cross with serenity (12:27; 18:11); and unlike the synoptics, John has Jesus die on the day of preparation for Passover when the Passover lambs are sacrificed. These repeated references to Passover heighten the sacrificial symbolism of Jesus' death. Likewise, a strong liturgical symbolism makes Jesus' death the true Passover lamb sacrifice (1:29), his risen body the true Temple (2:21), and his sacramental Body and Blood the true food and drink of Israel's wilderness journey (6:53–58).

John's hallmark strategies of indirectness and double meanings entice characters to move from surface earthly meanings to encoded heavenly meanings. Some catch on, like the woman at the well (4:4–26), but others miss the point, like Nicodemus, (3:3–10), the crowds (7:32–36), and Pilate (18:33–38). This indirectness separates truly committed disciples from the half-hearted window shoppers (2:23–25). Jesus performs "signs" (not "miracles") that lure people up the new ladder of Jacob arching from earth's pictures to heaven's glory (1:51; Genesis 28:12). This imagery of signs ends in a plain revelation about Jesus' divinity not found in the synoptic Gospels. His seven solemn "I AM" statements (6:35; 8:12; 10:7; 10:11; 11:25; 14:6; 15:1) recall God's revelation to Moses as "I AM" (Exodus 3:14) and testify to Jesus as the only source of life. So the inner truth of the blind man seeing is, "I am the light of the world" (9:5), and of the dead man rising, "I am the resurrection and the life" (11:25).

Jesus' signs hint at his divine glory (2:11) to be fully revealed at his "hour" (2:4; 7:30; 8:20; 13:1). Like the disciples, readers put things together only after the resurrection (2:22); then we realize that as Jesus was "lifted up" for crucifixion by the Romans, he was lifted up to glory by his Father (3:14; 8:28; 12:32). He mounted his cross like a king ascending his throne, as Pilate's placard unwittingly proclaimed (19:19–22). The Son's mission was to reunite the world to its source of eternal life in God (3:16; 4:34; 17:4). He died with satisfaction that this work was accomplished, and announced, "It is finished!" (19:30).

In the Gospel according to John, God the Father is unseen and mostly silent, but pervasively present. The Father sent the Son, loves him (5:20; 15:9), bears him witness (5:37; 8:18), glorifies him (8:54), and dwells with him (14:11). The Father grants the Son to have life in himself, to judge the world, and to raise the dead (5:19–30). Father and Son together gave life to the world at creation (1:1–2), and continue to do so (5:17). God the Son in human flesh has "explained" the Father, literally "brought God into the open" (1:18). The Son does this so completely that Jesus says, "Whoever has seen me has seen the Father" (14:9; 12:45).

But divine life emanates from a third mysterious presence, "the Spirit of truth" (14:17). The Father and the Son together send the Spirit (15:26), who teaches the disciples about what Jesus said and who he was (14:26; 16:13). By the Spirit's indwelling, divine life flows through them like a river (7:38–39; 14:17).

John depicts the disciples as fruitful vine branches that the Father lovingly tends (15:1–5). Omitting all other ethical instruction, this Gospel says that the only measure of the disciples' fruitfulness is their love for one another (13:34–35; 15:12–17).

True to character, this Gospel is sometimes one-sided. John's sense of Jesus' real humanity is relatively weak; and though teaching that "salvation is from the Jews" (4:22), it can be hostile toward Judaism (8:21–26, 37–59). John must be balanced by the rest of the New Testament and the Church's later teaching. But its profound spiritual theology of the Word made flesh (1:14) has decisively shaped Christian theology, spirituality, and art, ever since it was written in the late first century.

Introduction to St. Paul and His Letters

By Michael Cameron

PAUL'S CONVERSION

Saul of Tarsus was born about the same time as Jesus, to a pious Jewish family in Tarsus, in the Roman province of Cilicia (modern eastern Turkey). Well educated, and extremely religious, this son of Roman citizens was a member of the strict Pharisees (Philippians 3:5–6). In Christianity's earliest days, he says, "I persecuted the church of God beyond measure and even tried to destroy it" (Galatians 1:14–15). But then came the sudden turning point of his life: just outside Damascus, a brilliant flash of light blinded his eyes, buckled his legs, and altered his mind about God's design for human salvation (Acts 9:1–19). Christ's last known post-resurrection appearance suddenly brought the Pharisee to birth as an apostle, as "one born abnormally" (1 Corinthians 15:8).

Since Moses had said that anyone hanged on a tree was cursed by God, the crucified Christ had been a stumbling block to Saul, the Jew. But God revealed to Paul (Saul's Greek name) the awesome truth that this crucified man was God's power and wisdom (1 Corinthians 1:24). Christ's death and resurrection had turned the page of world history and unleashed the powers and blessings of the age to come. In that knowledge, Paul discounted everything that went before in his life as "rubbish" in comparison to knowing Christ, even his prized Jewish pedigree. Paul's blockbuster insight was that, for Jews and Gentiles alike, saving faith in Jesus Christ alone, not the works of Moses' Law, made one a part of God's people (Philippians 3:5–10).

PAUL'S MISSION AND TEACHINGS

That insight released a mighty energy in Paul to announce Christ to the whole world. So began Paul's thirty-plus-year missionary ministry. He suffered beatings, imprisonments, and repeated brushes with death, but by the mid-60s of the first century, he had planted a network of vibrant Christian communities throughout the eastern Mediterranean basin. Concerned to stay in touch with his churches, to feed them with sound teaching, and to protect them from poachers, he wrote letters that eventually became part of our New Testament. Their profound theology, breathless style, and stirring imagery have kindled and rekindled Christian faith ever since.

Paul never knew the earthly Jesus, and he speaks little of stories familiar to us from the Gospels (though he knew Peter and the Apostles personally, used their traditions, and quotes Jesus' words at the first Eucharist). Paul's thinking flows almost exclusively from the reality of the Lord's death and resurrection—the moment when God's power decisively defeated sin and inaugurated the Age to Come.

Paul explains that event with an outpouring of vivid metaphors. His imagery of "justification" imagines a scene at the judgment day when Christ's death acquits us of breaking the Law of Mount Sinai (Romans 3:21–31). His liturgical concept of "sanctification" pictures Christ giving believers the holiness needed to approach God in purity (1 Corinthians 6:11). Paul connects to economic imagery when he speaks of "redemption," portraying Christ's costly death buying us back from slavery to sin (Romans 3:24; 1 Corinthians 6:20). His political-military picture envisions humanity's ancient and chronic warfare with God brought to an end in "reconciliation" (Romans 5:10–11). He evokes the family with his "adoption" image, conveying our change of status when Christ made us over from slaves to children of God (Romans 8:14–15; Galatians 4:4–7).

Christians behave not according to external laws, Paul teaches, but by the force of the Holy Spirit, who produces in believers the many fruits of the new life (Galatians 5:22–23), the greatest of which is love (1 Corinthians 13:13). The same love of God displayed in Christ's death pours forth into our hearts through the Holy Spirit (Romans 5:5–8). The Spirit remakes us in the image of Christ: "All of us, gazing with unveiled face on the glory of the Lord, are being transformed into the same image from glory to glory, as from the Lord who is the Spirit" (2 Corinthians 3:18).

Christ somehow joined us to himself at his cross so that when he died, we died (2 Corinthians 5:14). Christians "baptized into Christ's death" die to their old selves and rise to newness of life (Romans 6:3–4). In this new humanity, which leaves behind old identities, the oneness of Christ knows "neither Jew nor Greek, slave nor free, male nor female" (Galatians 3:28). All drink of the same Spirit who makes them the mystical "Body of Christ" (1 Corinthians 12:12–27), the Church, whose members offer worship to God while humbly serving one another. In Christ we are "the new creation: the old things have passed away; behold, the new things have come" (2 Corinthians 5:17).

But the new life emerging in Christians conflicts with the world as it is. Paul leaves social change to God while urging Christians to live patiently within the structures of society as they stand until the new age takes over. So slaves do not seek freedom, the unmarried do not seek marriage, and Gentiles do not seek circumcision, because "the world in its present form is passing away" (1 Corinthians 7:17–31).

For the time being we see God, the world, and ourselves in a blur, but one day we will understand everything (1 Corinthians 13:12). Bodily death is pure gain: we depart to "be with Christ" (Philippians 1:23)—Paul does not say more—and await the resurrection of the body, when Christ "will change our lowly body to conform with his glorious body" (Philippians 3:21). We will be radically different, but somehow still ourselves, just as wheat stalks are both different from, and the same as, the tiny seeds they come from (1 Corinthians 15:36–49). When that moment comes, Christ's work will be done, and God will be "all in all" (1 Corinthians 15:28).

But for Paul and his readers, including us, the present remains the time for work. With the hope of the resurrection constantly drawing us on, Paul says, we must "be firm, steadfast, always fully devoted to the work of the Lord, knowing that in the Lord your labor is not in vain" (1 Corinthians 15:58).

Studying and Praying Scripture

By Michael Cameron

A recent study claimed that only 22 percent of American Catholics read the Bible regularly, and just 8 percent are involved in Scripture groups. Not many know how profoundly biblical the Roman Catholic Church has been from her very roots, having "always venerated the divine scriptures as she venerates the Body of the Lord" (*Dei Verbum* [*Dogmatic Constitution on Divine Revelation*], 21). How may Catholics learn to read Scripture? This essay sketches a path for seekers.

PREPARING TO READ

Become an apprentice to the Bible. Ordinary people can reach a good level of understanding, but at a cost: the Bible yields its riches to those who give themselves to the search for understanding. Start by reading daily, even if only for a few minutes. Join a group that reads and discusses Scripture together.

You will need tools. Think of yourself as a prospector for the Bible's gold. Nuggets on the ground are easily picked up, but the really rich veins lie beneath the surface. Digging requires study, commitment, and skills.

Invest in tools that reap the harvest of others' labors. Buy a study Bible with introductions, explanatory notes, and maps. Use another translation for devotional reading and comparison. Get access to a Bible dictionary with detailed information on biblical books, concepts, geography, outlines, customs, and so forth. Bible concordances will help you find all occurrences of particular words. A dictionary of biblical theology will give guidance on major theological ideas. A Bible atlas will give a sense of the locations and movements in the biblical stories. Recent Church documents on the Bible offer rich instruction to seekers.

READING FOR KNOWLEDGE

Get to know historical contexts suggested by a passage. Learn all you can about the Bible's basic story line, its "salvation history," beginning with Israel and continuing in the Church. Salvation by God's grace, obedience to God's will, and judgment on sin are basic to both Old and New Testaments.

Learn about the covenants with Abraham and David that emphasize God's grace. The covenant with Moses presumes God's grace and emphasizes obedience. Both covenant traditions reemerge and are fulfilled in the New Covenant in Jesus, who pours out his life to save all people (grace) but is extremely demanding of his disciples (obedience).

Read entire books of the Bible in order to gain a sense of the "whole cloth" from which the snippets of the Sunday lectionary are cut. Try to imagine what the books meant for their original authors and audiences. Ask how and why a book was put together: What is its structure, outline, main themes, literary forms, overall purpose?

Get to know the Old Testament narratives and psalms, but learn the Gospel accounts especially. The lectionary's yearly focus on Matthew, Mark, or Luke offers an opportunity to learn each one. John is the focus during the Church's special seasons.

READING FOR WISDOM

Read as one who seeks God, like the writer of Psalm 119. Ask what the text is requesting you to believe, do, or hope. Jesus' powerful proclamation in Mark 1:15 gives a strong framework: "This is the time of fulfillment" (now is the time to be attentive and ready to act); "the kingdom of God is at hand" (God is about to speak and act); "repent" (be willing to change your mind and move with fresh direction); "believe in the gospel" (embrace the grace that has already embraced you).

Read books straight through, a self-contained section at a time, carefully, slowly, and meditatively. Stop where natural breaks occur at the end of stories or sequences of thought.

Beware the sense that you already know what a text is going to say. Read attentively, asking what God is teaching you through this text at this minute about your life or about your communities—family, church, work, neighborhood, nation. Trust the Holy Spirit to guide you to what you need.

READING FOR WORSHIP

The goal of reading the Bible is not learning new facts or getting merely private inspiration for living, but entering into deeper communion with God. Allow the Bible to teach you to pray by giving you the words to use in prayer. The psalms are especially apt for this, but any part of the Bible may be prayed. This practice, dating back more than fifteen hundred years, is called *lectio divina*, Latin for "sacred reading."

Read Scripture in relation to the Eucharist. The Bible both prepares for Jesus' real presence and helps us understand it. The same Jesus who healed the lepers, stilled the storm, and embraced the children is present to us in the Word and in the sacrament.

The Bible is a library of spiritual treasures waiting to be discovered. The Church intends that this treasury be "wide open to the Christian faithful" (*Dei Verbum* [*Dogmatic Constitution on Divine Revelation*], 22).

RESOURCES

Brown, Raymond E., ss. *101 Questions and Answers on the Bible*. Mahwah, NJ: Paulist Press, 2003.

Casey, Michael. *Sacred Reading: The Ancient Art of Lectio Divina*. Liguori, MO: Liguori, 1997.

Frigge, Marielle, osb. *Beginning Biblical Studies*. Winona, MN: Anselm Academic, 2013.

Hahn, Scott. *Catholic Bible Dictionary*. New York: Doubleday, 2009.

Magrassi, Mariano. *Praying the Bible*. Collegeville, MN: Liturgical Press, 1998.

New Collegeville Bible Commentary Series. Collegeville, MN: Liturgical Press. (Short books on individual books of the Bible, various dates.)

Paprocki, Joe. *The Bible Blueprint, A Catholic's Guide to Understanding and Embracing God's Word*. Chicago: Loyola Press, 2009.

The Bible Documents: A Parish Resource. Chicago: Liturgy Training Publications, 2001.

The Catholic Study Bible, 3rd Edition. General editor, Donald Senior, cp. New York: Oxford, 2016.

Prayer before Reading the Word

Sustain us, O God,
on our Advent journey
as we go forth to welcome
the One who is to come.

Plant within our hearts
your living Word of promise,
and make haste to help us
as we seek to understand
what we went out to see in the Advent wilderness:
your patience nurturing your saving purpose
    to fulfillment,
your power in Jesus making all things new.

We ask this through our Lord Jesus Christ,
    your Son,
who lives and reigns with you
in the unity of the Holy Spirit,
God, for ever and ever. Amen.

Prayer after Reading the Word

Joy and gladness, O God,
attend the advent of your reign in Jesus,
for whenever the Good News is proclaimed to
    the poor,
feeble limbs are made steady,
and fearful hearts grow strong.

Give us strength for witnessing,
that we may go and tell others what we see
    and hear.
Give us patience for waiting,
until the precious harvest of your Kingdom,
when the return of your Son
will make your saving work complete.

Grant this through our Lord Jesus Christ,
who was, who is, and who is to come,
your Son, who lives and reigns with you
in the unity of the Holy Spirit,
God, for ever and ever. Amen.

Weekday Readings

December 4: *Isaiah 2:1–5; Matthew 8:5–11*

December 5: *Isaiah 11:1–10; Luke 10:21–24*

December 6: *Isaiah 25:6–10a; Matthew 15:29–37*

December 7: *Isaiah 26:1–6; Matthew 7:21, 24–27*

December 8: Solemnity of the Immaculate Conception of the Blessed Virgin Mary

Genesis 3:9–15, 20; Ephesians 1:3–6, 11–12; Luke 1:26–38

December 9: *Isaiah 30:19–21, 23–26; Matthew 9:35—10:1, 5a, 6–8*

December 11: *Isaiah 35:1–10; Luke 5:17–26*

December 12: Feast of Our Lady of Guadalupe

Zechariah 2:14–17; Luke 1:26–38

December 13: *Isaiah 40: 25–31; Matthew 11:28–30*

December 14: *Isaiah 41:13–20; Matthew 11:11–15*

December 15: *Isaiah 48:17–19; Matthew 11:16–19*

December 16: *Sirach 48:1–4, 9–11; Matthew 17:9a, 10–13*

December 18: *Jeremiah 23:5–8; Matthew 1:18–25*

December 19: *Judges 13:2–7, 24–25a; Luke 1:5–25*

December 20: *Isaiah 7:10–14; Luke 1:26–38*

December 21: *Song of Songs 2:8–14 or Zephaniah 3:14–18a; Luke 1:39–45*

December 22: *1 Samuel 1:24–28; Luke 1:46–56*

December 23: *Malachi 3:1–4, 23–24; Luke 1:57–66*

READING I
Isaiah 63:16b–17, 19b; 64:2–7

You, LORD, are our father,
    our redeemer you are named forever.
Why do you let us wander,
        O LORD, from your ways,
    and harden our hearts so that we fear
        you not?
Return for the sake of your servants,
    the tribes of your heritage.
Oh, that you would rend the
        heavens and come down,
    with the mountains quaking before you,
while you wrought awesome
        deeds we could not hope for,
    such as they had not heard of from of old.
No ear has ever heard, no eye ever
        seen, any God but you
    doing such deeds for those who wait for him.
Would that you might meet us doing right,
    that we were mindful of you in our ways!
Behold, you are angry, and we are sinful;
    all of us have become like unclean people,
    all our good deeds are like polluted rags;
we have all withered like leaves,
    and our guilt carries us away like the wind.
There is none who calls upon your name,
    who rouses himself to cling to you;
for you have hidden your face from us
    and have delivered us up to our guilt.
Yet, O LORD, you are our father;
    we are the clay and you the potter:
    we are all the work of your hands.

RESPONSORIAL PSALM
Psalm 80:2–3, 15–16, 18–19 (4)

R. Lord, make us turn to you; let us see your face
    and we shall be saved.

O shepherd of Israel, hearken,
    from your throne upon the cherubim,
        shine forth.
Rouse your power,
    and come to save us.   R.

Once again, O LORD of hosts,
    look down from heaven, and see;
take care of this vine,
    and protect what your right hand has planted,
    the son of man whom you yourself
        made strong.   R.

May your help be with the man of your right hand,
    with the son of man whom you yourself
        made strong.
Then we will no more withdraw from you;
    give us new life, and we will call upon
        your name.   R.

READING II   1 Corinthians 1:3–9

Brothers and sisters: Grace to you and peace from God our Father and the Lord Jesus Christ.

I give thanks to my God always on your account for the grace of God bestowed on you in Christ Jesus, that in him you were enriched in every way, with all discourse and all knowledge, as the testimony to Christ was confirmed among you, so that you are not lacking in any spiritual gift as you wait for the revelation of our Lord Jesus Christ. He will keep you firm to the end, irreproachable on the day of our Lord Jesus Christ. God is faithful, and by him you were called to fellowship with his Son, Jesus Christ our Lord.

GOSPEL   Mark 13:33–37

Jesus said to his disciples: "Be watchful! Be alert! You do not know when the time will come. It is like a man traveling abroad. He leaves home and places his servants in charge, each with his own work, and orders the gatekeeper to be on the watch. Watch, therefore; you do not know when the lord of the house is coming, whether in the evening, or at midnight, or at cockcrow, or in the morning. May he not come suddenly and find you sleeping. What I say to you, I say to all: 'Watch!'"

Practice of Faith

As we begin a new liturgical year, we remember that God, our Father, has enriched us with his Spirit. At times, however, we ignore what God has done for us and wander off on our own path. As you look back at the past year, how have you failed to keep alert and walk in God's ways? ◆ Find a time this Advent season to celebrate the sacrament of reconciliation and to acknowledge your need for God's mercy and guidance. ◆ Reflect on the spiritual gifts you have received from God. Give thanks for these gifts. What can you do to strengthen these gifts or to cultivate new ones? ◆ Today's psalm includes the refrain, "Lord, let us see your face and we shall be saved." Celebrate God's faithfulness by saying this prayer throughout the day, especially while lighting the candle of your Advent wreath. All the passages for this Sunday depict the people's longing to see God's restoration or salvation. We read of difficult experiences, and we read of affirmations of God's faithfulness even though God seems hidden and circumstances seem dire.

Download more questions and activities for families, initiation groups, and other adult groups at http://www.ltp.org/ahw.

Scripture Insights

Mark 13 is an apocalyptic discourse, in which the disciples ask Jesus about "the end," or the reign of God that Jesus declares to be "at hand" (1:15). Jesus states that, in contrast to what false prophets may say (13:5–6, 21–22), those who live in the "end times" must share in the suffering and persecution that he himself will experience, including that of the cross (Mark 13:9–13; see also Mark 8:31–38) because those in power (both in religion and in government) will test their faith in and loyalty to God before God's advent. Jesus also assures his disciples that the Holy Spirit will be with them through all the chaos, conflicts, and catastrophes, so they can turn these afflictions into occasions to demonstrate and share their faith (13:10–11). Furthermore, Jesus tells them that God, out of compassion, will hasten God's advent, though the time of God's advent is known to no one except God (Mark 13:20, 32).

Our specific Markan passage today is the conclusion of this apocalyptic discourse. The disciples are told to "be alert" and to "watch" (13:33, 35). The earlier portion of Mark 13 has clarified that the disciples are not to become idle bystanders or passive observers before God's advent; instead, they are called to a courageous commitment to live out and share their faith. This call to vigilance must be read alongside the insistence that God's advent is unknown (Mark 13:32, 33). We must understand that every moment we live may be the time of God's advent. This makes God's advent always imminent, and Jesus is telling his disciples to develop that continuous sense of imminence.

◆ What is the difference between waiting for something to happen and anticipating something to happen?

◆ What is the difference between hoping to survive a catastrophe and entering into participation in a catastrophe?

◆ Why and how could afflictions become occasions to demonstrate and share one's faith in and loyalty to God?

READING I *Isaiah 40:1–5, 9–11*

Comfort, give comfort to my people,
    says your God.
Speak tenderly to Jerusalem, and proclaim
        to her
    that her service is at an end,
    her guilt is expiated;
indeed, she has received
        from the hand of the LORD
    double for all her sins.

    A voice cries out:
In the desert prepare the way of the LORD!
    Make straight in the wasteland
        a highway for our God!
Every valley shall be filled in,
    every mountain and hill shall be made low;
the rugged land shall be made a plain,
    the rough country, a broad valley.
Then the glory of the LORD shall be revealed,
    and all people shall see it together;
    for the mouth of the LORD has spoken.

Go up onto a high mountain,
    Zion, herald of glad tidings;
cry out at the top of your voice,
    Jerusalem, herald of good news!
Fear not to cry out
    and say to the cities of Judah:
    Here is your God!
Here comes with power
    the Lord GOD,
    who rules by his strong arm;
here is his reward with him,
    his recompense before him.
Like a shepherd he feeds his flock;
    in his arms he gathers the lambs,
carrying them in his bosom,
    and leading the ewes with care.

RESPONSORIAL PSALM
Psalm 85:9–10, 11–12, 13–14 (8)

R. Lord, let us see your kindness,
    and grant us your salvation.

I will hear what God proclaims;
    the LORD—for he proclaims peace to his people.

Near indeed is his salvation to those who
        fear him,
    glory dwelling in our land.   R.

Kindness and truth shall meet;
    justice and peace shall kiss.
Truth shall spring out of the earth,
    and justice shall look down from heaven.   R.

The LORD himself will give his benefits;
    our land shall yield its increase.
Justice shall walk before him,
    and prepare the way of his steps.   R.

READING II *2 Peter 3:8–14*

Do not ignore this one fact, beloved, that with the Lord one day is like a thousand years and a thousand years like one day. The Lord does not delay his promise, as some regard "delay," but he is patient with you, not wishing that any should perish but that all should come to repentance. But the day of the Lord will come like a thief, and then the heavens will pass away with a mighty roar and the elements will be dissolved by fire, and the earth and everything done on it will be found out.

Since everything is to be dissolved in this way, what sort of persons ought you to be, conducting yourselves in holiness and devotion, waiting for and hastening the coming of the day of God, because of which the heavens will be dissolved in flames and the elements melted by fire. But according to his promise we await new heavens and a new earth in which righteousness dwells. Therefore, beloved, since you await these things, be eager to be found without spot or blemish before him, at peace.

GOSPEL *Mark 1:1–8*

The beginning of the gospel of Jesus Christ the Son of God.

As it is written in Isaiah the prophet:

Behold, I am sending my messenger ahead
        of you;
    he will prepare your way.
A voice of one crying out in the desert:
    "Prepare the way of the Lord,
    make straight his paths."

John the Baptist appeared in the desert proclaiming a baptism of repentance for the forgiveness of sins. People of the whole Judean countryside and all the inhabitants of Jerusalem were going out to him and were being baptized by him in the Jordan River as they acknowledged their sins. John was clothed in camel's hair, with a leather belt around his waist. He fed on locusts and wild honey. And this is what he proclaimed: "One mightier than I is coming after me. I am not worthy to stoop and loosen the thongs of his sandals. I have baptized you with water; he will baptize you with the Holy Spirit."

Practice of Hope

Throughout the centuries God has brought about wondrous and surprising change. Whenever God's people felt that he had abandoned them, he always revealed himself, renewing their hope and leading them into a new and better future. ♦ Imagine how people felt as they listened to John the Baptist. Place yourself at the Jordan River. What are people saying to one another? How are they reacting? What do you say and do? In the second reading, we hear of God's patience as we prepare ourselves for God's transformation of heaven and earth. ♦ How is God patient with you? Is there a person toward whom you can show greater patience? What specific, concrete steps can you take to treat that person with greater patience? ♦ What particular change do you need to make in your life "to be found without spot or blemish" (2 Peter 3:14) before the Lord?

Download more questions and activities for families, initiation groups, and other adult groups at http://www.ltp.org/ahw.

Scripture Insights

Today's passages focus on preparation for a special arrival, though each reading characterizes this arrival differently. In Isaiah 40, we see a comforting hope for God's care and deliverance: God promises a "new exodus" for the exiles to leave the oppressive empire of Babylon.

In Psalm 85, the expected arrival of God's salvation is a threefold emphasis on "justice" (Psalm 85:10, 11, 13), which is also the character of "new heavens and a new earth" in 2 Peter 3. In contrast to Psalm 85, however, 2 Peter 3 depicts this "coming of the day of God" with an emphasis not only on transformation but also on destruction and judgment.

In Mark, John the Baptizer is identified as Isaiah's "voice of one crying out in the desert" (1:3) by showing up as the harbinger of Jesus with baptism as a form of purification and preparation for God's people in Jerusalem and Judea (1:5). John's appearance also reminds one of Elijah the prophet. Since a prophet is tasked with calling God's people to repentance in light of God's judgment, we may also understand John's baptism as an expression of repentance.

Although Mark attributes verses two and three to Isaiah, the second verse is from Malachi 3:1. The need for a messenger appears in Malachi 2:17, which notes the acceptance of "evildoers" while asking, "Where is the just God?" Moreover, evil in Malachi 2:17 is portrayed not only as people dismissing God but as being justified in the name of God. In contrast, justice is emphasized in Psalm 85 and 2 Peter 3.

♦ In what ways has injustice been justified in the name of God and religion?

♦ How may today's passages of God's advent as both comfort and judgment be linked with the saying that one should "comfort the afflicted but afflict the comfortable"?

♦ How may we as God's people today participate in the preparation for God's advent?

READING I   *Isaiah 61:1–2a, 10–11*

The spirit of the Lord GOD is upon me,
    because the LORD has anointed me;
he has sent me to bring glad tidings to the poor,
    to heal the brokenhearted,
to proclaim liberty to the captives
    and release to the prisoners,
to announce a year of favor from the LORD
    and a day of vindication by our God.

I rejoice heartily in the LORD,
    in my God is the joy of my soul;
for he has clothed me with a robe of salvation
    and wrapped me in a mantle of justice,
like a bridegroom adorned with a diadem,
    like a bride bedecked with her jewels.
As the earth brings forth its plants,
    and a garden makes its growth spring up,
so will the Lord GOD make justice and praise
    spring up before all the nations.

RESPONSORIAL PSALM   *Luke 1:46–48, 49–50, 53–54 (Isaiah 61:10b)*

R. My soul rejoices in my God.

My soul proclaims the greatness of the LORD;
    my spirit rejoices in God my Savior,
for he has looked upon his lowly servant.
    From this day all generations will call
      me blessed. R.

The Almighty has done great things for me,
    and holy is his Name.
He has mercy on those who fear him
    in every generation. R.

He has filled the hungry with good things,
    and the rich he has sent away empty.
He has come to the help of his servant Israel
    for he has remembered his promise
      of mercy. R.

READING II   *1 Thessalonians 5:16–24*

Brothers and sisters: Rejoice always. Pray without ceasing. In all circumstances give thanks, for this is the will of God for you in Christ Jesus. Do not quench the Spirit. Do not despise prophetic utterances. Test everything; retain what is good. Refrain from every kind of evil.

May the God of peace make you perfectly holy and may you entirely, spirit, soul, and body, be preserved blameless for the coming of our Lord Jesus Christ. The one who calls you is faithful, and he will also accomplish it.

GOSPEL   *John 1:6–8, 19–28*

A man named John was sent from God. He came for testimony, to testify to the light, so that all might believe through him. He was not the light, but came to testify to the light.

And this is the testimony of John. When the Jews from Jerusalem sent priests and Levites to him to ask him, "Who are you?" he admitted and did not deny it, but admitted, "I am not the Christ." So they asked him, "What are you then? Are you Elijah?" And he said, "I am not." "Are you the Prophet?" He answered, "No." So they said to him, "Who are you, so we can give an answer to those who sent us? What do you have to say for yourself?" He said:

"I am *the voice of one crying out in the desert,*
'make straight the way of the Lord,'

as Isaiah the prophet said." Some Pharisees were also sent. They asked him, "Why then do you baptize if you are not the Christ or Elijah or the Prophet?" John answered them, "I baptize with water; but there is one among you whom you do not recognize, the one who is coming after me, whose sandal strap I am not worthy to untie." This happened in Bethany across the Jordan, where John was baptizing.

Practice of Hope

On the Third Sunday of Advent our joy at what God has done for us bursts forth. We rejoice because our celebration of Jesus' birth is simultaneously a celebration of all that God has promised and will accomplish through his Son. ✦ St. Paul thus urges us to rejoice always and give thanks (1 Thessalonians 5:16, 18). Think of times your heart overflowed with joy. Give thanks for such moments. ✦ Pray for those who have lost hope and are filled with sorrow, such as those who have fled their homeland or been unjustly imprisoned. ✦ When John the Baptist urged people to hope in Jesus, he directed attention away from himself. Thank someone in your community who works quietly and diligently to help others without seeking attention or recognition.

Download more questions and activities for families, initiation groups, and other adult groups at http://www.ltp.org/ahw.

Scripture Insights

The song of Mary, traditionally known as the Magnificat, is basically a repetition of Hannah's thanksgiving prayer in 1 Samuel 2 after God answered Hannah's prayer for a child. Not to be missed is the emphasis these words place on how God turns things upside down or right side up. Those who are proud, powerful, and rich, God will scatter, bring down, and send away empty. In contrast, those who are lowly and hungry, God will lift up and fill with good things. Instead of treating all in the same way, in Mary's song God operates with a preferential option for those who are humble and on the margins, such as the young, pregnant, and unwed Mary.

The word *humble* appropriately describes the attitude of John the Baptizer in John 1. Although John could make himself sound more impressive before the religious authorities, he does not make himself the focus of his work. Instead, he confesses that neither his status nor his work is comparable to those of Jesus.

A similar message is found in Isaiah 61, where God's good news and favor are said to be focused upon "the poor," "the brokenhearted," "the captives," and "the prisoners." Isaiah 61 is part of what scholars call Third Isaiah (Isaiah 56–66), written during a time that the exiles began the difficult task of restoration upon their return from Babylon to Palestine. When Luke's Jesus begins his ministry (Luke 4:18–19), he will choose these very words from Isaiah to characterize his ministry.

The passage in 1 Thessalonians 5 suggests that to be "blameless" in God's advent, we must not only pray and give thanks but also know and do what is good by not quenching the Spirit but attending to and carefully discerning what God may want to tell us.

✦ Who are "the poor," "the brokenhearted," "the captives," and "the prisoners" in our society and world today?

✦ How much of what we do today is upholding or challenging the status quo?

✦ What is the difference between a humble ministry of preparation such as John's and the work done by Jesus?

23

READING I
2 Samuel 7:1–5, 8b–12, 14a, 16

When King David was settled in his palace, and the LORD had given him rest from his enemies on every side, he said to Nathan the prophet, "Here I am living in a house of cedar, while the ark of God dwells in a tent!" Nathan answered the king, "Go, do whatever you have in mind, for the LORD is with you." But that night the LORD spoke to Nathan and said: "Go, tell my servant David, 'Thus says the LORD: Should you build me a house to dwell in?

"'It was I who took you from the pasture and from the care of the flock to be commander of my people Israel. I have been with you wherever you went, and I have destroyed all your enemies before you. And I will make you famous like the great ones of the earth. I will fix a place for my people Israel; I will plant them so that they may dwell in their place without further disturbance. Neither shall the wicked continue to afflict them as they did of old, since the time I first appointed judges over my people Israel. I will give you rest from all your enemies. The LORD also reveals to you that he will establish a house for you. And when your time comes and you rest with your ancestors, I will raise up your heir after you, sprung from your loins, and I will make his kingdom firm. I will be a father to him, and he shall be a son to me. Your house and your kingdom shall endure forever before me; your throne shall stand firm forever.'"

RESPONSORIAL PSALM
Psalm 89:2–3, 4–5, 27, 29 (2a)

R. For ever I will sing the goodness of the Lord.

The promises of the LORD I will sing forever;
   through all generations my mouth shall
      proclaim your faithfulness.
For you have said, "My kindness is
      established forever";
   in heaven you have confirmed your
      faithfulness. R.

"I have made a covenant with my chosen one,
   I have sworn to David my servant:
forever will I confirm your posterity
   and establish your throne for
      all generations." R.

"He shall say of me, 'You are my father,
   my God, the Rock, my savior.'
Forever I will maintain my kindness toward him,
   and my covenant with him stands firm." R.

READING II *Romans 16:25–27*

Brothers and sisters: To him who can strengthen you, according to my gospel and the proclamation of Jesus Christ, according to the revelation of the mystery kept secret for long ages but now manifested through the prophetic writings and, according to the command of the eternal God, made known to all nations to bring about the obedience of faith, to the only wise God, through Jesus Christ be glory forever and ever. Amen.

GOSPEL *Luke 1:26–38*

The angel Gabriel was sent from God to a town of Galilee called Nazareth, to a virgin betrothed to a man named Joseph, of the house of David, and the virgin's name was Mary. And coming to her, he said, "Hail, full of grace! The Lord is with you." But she was greatly troubled at what was said and pondered what sort of greeting this might be. Then the angel said to her, "Do not be afraid, Mary, for you have found favor with God.

"Behold, you will conceive in your womb and bear a son, and you shall name him Jesus. He will be great and will be called Son of the Most High, and the Lord God will give him the throne of David his father, and he will rule over the house of Jacob forever, and of his kingdom there will be no end." But Mary said to the angel, "How can this be, since I have no relations with a man?" And the angel said to her in reply, "The Holy Spirit will come upon you, and the power of the Most High will overshadow you. Therefore the child to be born will be called holy, the Son of God." And behold, Elizabeth, your relative, has also conceived a son in her old age, and this is the sixth month for her who was called barren; for nothing will be impossible for God." Mary said, "Behold, I am the handmaid of the Lord. May it be done to me according to your word." Then the angel departed from her.

Practice of Faith

Each reading recalls the promises God has made and fulfilled, from providing an heir to King David to the salvation of all nations in Jesus Christ. Often God seems to fulfill these promises in unexpected ways. ♦ Slowly read through the Gospel passage. Imagine that you are Mary hearing this news or that you are the angel delivering it. Ponder a part of this story that you have not considered. Spend some time renewing your wonder at God's promises. ♦ Look closely at your life. In what ways has God surprised you? How have you responded? Have you always noticed God's surprises? ♦ If you can, share your faith in God's unexpected love by offering to help someone with childcare, housework, or the preparation of a meal.

Download more questions and activities for families, initiation groups, and other adult groups at http://www.ltp.org/ahw.

Scripture Insights

It is best to read today's Lukan passage with the verses preceding it that announce the birth of John. The angel Gabriel's parallel pronouncement of a miraculous birth provides a significant contrast: the miracle of Jesus is a type of miracle that God has never done before. As God has done for Sarai and for Hannah in the Hebrew Scriptures (Genesis 17:15–21; 18:9–14; 21:1–3; 1 Samuel 1:1–20), God will enable yet another married woman (Elizabeth) who has not been able to conceive to finally become pregnant (Luke 1:8–25). The miracle of a woman who is a virgin conceiving, however, does not exist in the Hebrew Scriptures. Not only is the miracle announced to Mary greater than the one announced to Zechariah, it is new.

Our passages from the Old Testament this Sunday portray God's faithfulness to keeping God's promise while the concluding passage from Romans 16 emphasizes God's power and wisdom to bring about God's command and purposes. The birth of Jesus as the promised messiah can be read as affirmation of what these other passages suggest about God. Just as God took David "from the pasture and from the care of the flock to be commander of my people Israel" (2 Samuel 7:8), God, through Gabriel, pronounces "favor" upon a young woman in a small agrarian town of Galilee to send us the messiah. Just as David's life was upended, Mary's life changes dramatically.

One must not forget, however, what this unwed pregnancy may mean for Mary. This "favor" from God inevitably brings her ridicule and, possibly, social ostracism. Is Mary too young to know or anticipate the implications of this pregnancy? Can Mary refuse this "favor" from a powerful angelic being who represents an even more powerful God? Or is she counting on Gabriel's assurance of God's favor and presence with her (Luke 1:28)?

♦ How has your life been changed by divine interruptions that you did not expect?

♦ How have you experienced God's faithfulness and presence during this season of Advent?

♦ What is the difference between doing something in submission and in resignation?

Christmas Time

Prayer before Reading the Word

Almighty God, Creator of all,
whose Word was present with you in
    the beginning
and whose wisdom was placed
at the service of your plan,
enlighten us to know the glorious hope
to which you have called us;
fill us with faith in Jesus and
with love toward all your people,
that we who have seen in Christ
the glory of your Word made flesh
may bear into the world you so love,
the Light no darkness can extinguish:
your Son, our Lord Jesus Christ,
who lives and reigns with you
in the unity of the Holy Spirit,
God, for ever and ever. Amen.

Prayer after Reading the Word

Your Word, O God of ageless glory,
dwelling with you from before time,
has become flesh and lived among us,
and we have seen the glory of your Christ.

Place on our lips the word of salvation,
in our hearts a love that welcomes all,
and, in the depths of our being,
the light of faith and hope,
which the darkness can never overcome.
We ask this through our Lord Jesus Christ,
    your Son,
who lives and reigns with you
in the unity of the Holy Spirit,
God, for ever and ever. Amen.

Weekday Readings

December 26: Feast of St. Stephen, First Martyr
Acts 6:8–10; 7:54–59; Matthew 10:17–22

December 27: Feast of St. John, Apostle and Evangelist
1 John 1:1–4; John 20:1a, 2–8

December 28: Feast of the Holy Innocents, Martyrs
1 John 1:5—2:2; Matthew 2:13–18

December 29: Fifth Day within the Octave of the
    Nativity of the Lord
1 John 2:3–11; Luke 2:22–35

December 30: Sixth Day within the Octave of the
    Nativity of the Lord
1 John 2:12–17; Luke 2:36–40

January 1: Solemnity of Mary, the Holy Mother of God
Numbers 6:22–27; Galatians 4:4–7; Luke 2:16–21

January 2: *1 John 2:22–28; John 1:19–28*

January 3: *1 John 2:29—3:6; John 1:29–34*

January 4: *1 John 3:7–10; John 1:35–42*

January 5: *1 John 3:11–21; John 1:43–51*

January 6: *1 John 5:5–13; Mark 1:7–11 or Luke 3:23–38
    or 3:23, 31–34, 36, 38*

January 8: Feast of the Baptism of the Lord
Isaiah 42:1–4, 6–7 or Isaiah 55:1–11 or Acts 10:34–38
    or 1 John 5:1–9; Mark 1:7–11

READING I *Isaiah 62:1–5*

For Zion's sake I will not be silent,
   for Jerusalem's sake I will not be quiet,
until her vindication shines forth like the dawn
   and her victory like a burning torch.

Nations shall behold your vindication,
   and all the kings your glory;
you shall be called by a new name
   pronounced by the mouth of the LORD.
You shall be a glorious crown in the hand
      of the LORD,
   a royal diadem held by your God.
No more shall people call you "Forsaken,"
   or your land "Desolate,"
but you shall be called "My Delight,"
   and your land "Espoused."
For the LORD delights in you
   and makes your land his spouse.
As a young man marries a virgin,
   your Builder shall marry you;
and as a bridegroom rejoices in his bride
   so shall your God rejoice in you.

RESPONSORIAL PSALM
Psalm 89:4–5, 16–17, 27, 29 (2a)

R. For ever I will sing the goodness of the LORD.

I have made a covenant with my chosen one,
   I have sworn to David my servant:
forever will I confirm your posterity
   and establish your throne for all
      generations. R.

Blessed the people who know the joyful shout;
   in the light of your countenance, O LORD,
      they walk.
At your name they rejoice all the day,
   and through your justice they are exalted. R.

He shall say of me, "You are my father,
   my God, the rock, my savior."
Forever I will maintain my kindness toward him,
   and my covenant with him stands firm. R.

READING II *Acts 13:16–17, 22–25*

When Paul reached Antioch in Pisidia and entered the synagogue, he stood up, motioned with his hand, and said, "Fellow Israelites and you others who are God-fearing, listen. The God of this people Israel chose our ancestors and exalted the people during their sojourn in the land of Egypt. With uplifted arm he led them out of it. Then he removed Saul and raised up David as king; of him he testified, 'I have found David, son of Jesse, a man after my own heart; he will carry out my every wish.' From this man's descendants God, according to his promise, has brought to Israel a savior, Jesus. John heralded his coming by proclaiming a baptism of repentance to all the people of Israel; and as John was completing his course, he would say, 'What do you suppose that I am? I am not he. Behold, one is coming after me; I am not worthy to unfasten the sandals of his feet.'"

GOSPEL *Matthew 1:18–25*

Longer: Matthew 1:1–25

This is how the birth of Jesus Christ came about. When his mother Mary was betrothed to Joseph, but before they lived together, she was found with child through the Holy Spirit. Joseph her husband, since he was a righteous man, yet unwilling to expose her to shame, decided to divorce her quietly. Such was his intention when, behold, the angel of the Lord appeared to him in a dream and said, "Joseph, son of David, do not be afraid to take Mary your wife into your home. For it is through the Holy Spirit that this child has been conceived in her. She will bear a son and you are to name him Jesus, because he will save his people from their sins." All this took place to fulfill what the Lord had said through the prophet:

> *Behold, the virgin shall conceive and bear a son,*
>   *and they shall name him Emmanuel,*

which means "God is with us." When Joseph awoke, he did as the angel of the Lord had commanded him and took his wife into his home. He had no relations with her until she bore a son, and he named him Jesus.

Practice of Charity

At Christmas we celebrate God's continuing devotion to his people. As St. Paul preached at Antioch, God remained with his people from the time of the Exodus, drawing them ever more fully into his light and ever closer to his glory. Today we rejoice in this wondrous gift. Jesus is our savior, our victory, our glorious crown, our bridegroom. ◆ Notice all the ways that light is part of your Christmas celebration. Each time you notice the light, say a prayer of joyful thanks to God. ◆ St. Joseph protected and nurtured the child Jesus. Who has cared for you and protected you? Offer the prayer of St. Joseph for those who raised you and for foster parents and legal guardians. ◆ Today tell someone ways in which that person has delighted you.

Download more questions and activities for families, initiation groups, and other adult groups at http://www.ltp.org/ahw.

Scripture Insights

Unlike Luke's Gospel, Matthew's birth story of Jesus focuses on Joseph rather than on Mary. Joseph is introduced by Matthew as a "righteous" man because of how he responds to the angel's message (1:24–25). Hearing about Mary's immaculate conception and the role of Jesus in God's salvation plan (see Acts 13:16–17, 22–25), Joseph does what the angel tells him without hesitation. In Matthew's Gospel, the "righteous" are those who do the will of God (Matthew 7:21–27).

As the text shows, Joseph's righteousness also relates to what he would do and would not do with his pregnant betrothed before he heard from the angel. Joseph could have taken actions to punish Mary according to the law, yet he simply plans to "divorce her quietly" (Matthew 1:19). According to the parable of the sheep and the goats, we will be judged by what we do or don't do for "these least" ones (Matthew 25:31–46). The will of God that we must carry out in Matthew is to care for those who are weak and defenseless: the hungry, the thirsty, the stranger, the naked, the sick, the imprisoned. Joseph's decision to protect a vulnerable woman is a sign that he is a righteous "sheep." Jesus is Emmanuel, meaning "God is with us" (Matthew 1:22–23), but God's faithful presence (as we see today in the passages from the psalm and from Isaiah) often, in Matthew's view, takes place through human followers of God.

Joseph's plan not to disgrace or punish Mary is reason for him to be called "righteous." When he hears and receives new information from the angel, Joseph is again able to change his decision from divorcing Mary to marrying her. God's plan of salvation always requires human partners who are merciful as well as flexible upon reception of new information.

◆ Who are the "least" ones in our society, and what does the Church do or not do for them?

◆ What is one example in which you have changed your mind about something or someone with the help of new information?

◆ How does our society generally define "righteousness"?

READING I *Genesis 15:1–6; 21:1–3*

Alternate: Sirach 3:2–6, 12–14

The word of the LORD came to Abram in a vision, saying:

"Fear not, Abram!
I am your shield;
I will make your reward very great."

But Abram said, "O Lord GOD, what good will your gifts be, if I keep on being childless and have as my heir the steward of my house, Eliezer?" Abram continued, "See, you have given me no off-spring, and so one of my servants will be my heir." Then the word of the LORD came to him: "No, that one shall not be your heir; your own issue shall be your heir." The Lord took Abram outside and said, "Look up at the sky and count the stars, if you can. Just so," he added, "shall your descendants be." Abram put his faith in the LORD, who credited it to him as an act of righteousness.

The LORD took note of Sarah as he had said he would; he did for her as he had promised. Sarah became pregnant and bore Abraham a son in his old age, at the set time that God had stated. Abraham gave the name Isaac to this son of his whom Sarah bore him.

RESPONSORIAL PSALM
Psalm 105:1–2, 3–4, 6–7, 8–9 (7a, 8a)

Alternate: Psalm 128:1–2, 3, 4–5 (see 1)

R. The Lord remembers his covenant forever.

Give thanks to the LORD, invoke his name;
    make known among the nations his deeds.
Sing to him, sing his praise,
    proclaim all his wondrous deeds. R.

Glory in his holy name;
    rejoice, O hearts that seek the LORD!
Look to the LORD in his strength;
    constantly seek his face. R.

You descendants of Abraham, his servants,
    sons of Jacob, his chosen ones!
He, the LORD, is our God;
    throughout the earth his judgments prevail. R.

He remembers forever his covenant
    which he made binding for a
        thousand generations
which he entered into with Abraham
    and by his oath to Isaac. R.

READING II *Hebrews 11:8, 11–12, 17–19*

Alternate: Colossians 3:12–21 or 3:12–17

Brothers and sisters: By faith Abraham obeyed when he was called to go out to a place that he was to receive as an inheritance; he went out, not knowing where he was to go. By faith he received power to generate, even though he was past the normal age—and Sarah herself was sterile—for he thought that the one who had made the promise was trustworthy. So it was that there came forth from one man, himself as good as dead, descendants as numerous as the stars in the sky and as countless as the sands on the seashore.

By faith Abraham, when put to the test, offered up Isaac, and he who had received the promises was ready to offer his only son, of whom it was said, "Through Isaac descendants shall bear your name." He reasoned that God was able to raise even from the dead, and he received Isaac back as a symbol.

GOSPEL *Luke 2:22–40*

Shorter: Luke 2:22, 39–40

When the days were completed for their purification according to the law of Moses, they took him up to Jerusalem to present him to the Lord, just as it is written in the law of the Lord, *Every male that opens the womb shall be consecrated to the Lord,* and to offer the sacrifice of *a pair of turtledoves or two young pigeons,* in accordance with the dictate in the law of the Lord.

Now there was a man in Jerusalem whose name was Simeon. This man was righteous and devout, awaiting the consolation of Israel, and the Holy Spirit was upon him. It had been revealed to him by the Holy Spirit that he should not see death before he had seen the Christ of the Lord. He came in the Spirit into the temple; and when the parents brought in the child Jesus to perform the custom of the law in regard to him, he took him into his arms and blessed God, saying:

"Now, Master, you may let your servant go
    in peace, according to your word,
for my eyes have seen your salvation,
    which you prepared in sight of all the peoples,
a light for revelation to the Gentiles,
    and glory for your people Israel."

The child's father and mother were amazed at what was said about him; and Simeon blessed them and said to Mary his mother, "Behold, this child is destined for the fall and rise of many in Israel, and to be a sign that will be contradicted—and you yourself a sword will pierce—so that the thoughts of many hearts may be revealed." There was also a prophetess, Anna, the daughter of Phanuel, of the tribe of Asher. She was advanced in years, having lived seven years with her husband after her marriage, and then as a widow until she was eighty-four. She never left the temple, but worshiped night and day with fasting and prayer. And coming forward at that very time, she gave thanks to God and spoke about the child to all who were awaiting the redemption of Jerusalem.

When they had fulfilled all the prescriptions of the law of the Lord, they returned to Galilee, to their own town of Nazareth. The child grew and became strong, filled with wisdom; and the favor of God was upon him.

Practice of Faith

The faith of Abraham and Sarah and Simeon and Anna is a testimony that strengthens ours. ♦ Call or visit someone who suffered the death of a loved one this past year. ♦ Offer to be a liturgical minister. ♦ Before you go to sleep tonight, pray the prayer of Simeon from today's Gospel.

Download more questions and activities for families, initiation groups, and other adult groups at http://www.ltp.org/ahw.

Scripture Insights

Joseph and Mary offer in the Temple for Jesus' birth "a pair of turtledoves or two young pigeons." Such an offering is prescribed in Leviticus 12 for the poor who cannot afford a lamb or a sheep. From this, we can deduce that Luke's Jesus is born into a poor family. The image of the newborn Jesus lying in a manger is consistent with this picture. Given the less-than-desirable circumstances of Jesus' birth, it may be difficult for the couple to hold on to the angel's pronouncement to Mary about Jesus (1:30–33), especially given Simeon's words to Mary that "you yourself a sword will pierce" (Luke 2:35).

Abraham and Sarah held onto God's faithful promise to them of descendants and land. Both were advanced in age, but they went out, "dwelling in tents" and "not knowing where" they were going (Hebrews 11:8, 9). Unlike Simeon, who was able to see the messiah before his death (Luke 2:26), they died seeing neither the promised multiplication of descendants nor the promised land. Defining faith as "the realization of what is hoped for and evidence of things not seen," Hebrews 11 was written to encourage a community wavering in their faith.

We witness God's faithfulness in these passages. We also see the need for our response in faith, and that faith requires endurance and action. Just as Abraham and Sarah made the move out of Ur (Genesis 15:7), Joseph and Mary offer a sacrifice out of their limited means and, by faith in what they have heard from Simeon and Anna (as well as from the angel Gabriel and the shepherds), they do the hard work of raising and parenting Jesus.

♦ What challenges keep you, your parish, or society from seeing a way forward?

♦ Whose example do you lean on when your faith wavers?

♦ How do you imagine God's faithfulness?

READING I *Isaiah 60:1–6*

Rise up in splendor, Jerusalem!
    Your light has come,
    the glory of the Lord shines upon you.
See, darkness covers the earth,
    and thick clouds cover the peoples;
but upon you the LORD shines,
    and over you appears his glory.
Nations shall walk by your light,
    and kings by your shining radiance.
Raise your eyes and look about;
    they all gather and come to you:
your sons come from afar,
    and your daughters in the arms of
        their nurses.

Then you shall be radiant at what you see,
    your heart shall throb and overflow,
for the riches of the sea shall be emptied out
        before you,
    the wealth of nations shall be brought to you.
Caravans of camels shall fill you,
    dromedaries from Midian and Ephah;
all from Sheba shall come
    bearing gold and frankincense,
    and proclaiming the praises of the LORD.

RESPONSORIAL PSALM
Psalm 72:1–2, 7–8, 10–11, 12–13 (see 11)

R. Lord, every nation on earth will adore you.

O God, with your judgment endow the king,
    and with your justice, the king's son;
he shall govern your people with justice
    and your afflicted ones with judgment. R.

Justice shall flower in his days,
    and profound peace, till the moon be no more.
May he rule from sea to sea,
    and from the River to the ends of the earth. R.

The kings of Tarshish and the Isles shall offer gifts;
    the kings of Arabia and Seba shall bring tribute.
All kings shall pay him homage,
    all nations shall serve him. R.

For he shall rescue the poor when he cries out,
    and the afflicted when he has
        no one to help him.
He shall have pity for the lowly and the poor;
    the lives of the poor he shall save. R.

READING II *Ephesians 3:2–3a, 5–6*

Brothers and sisters: You have heard of the stewardship of God's grace that was given to me for your benefit, namely, that the mystery was made known to me by revelation. It was not made known to people in other generations as it has now been revealed to his holy apostles and prophets by the Spirit: that the Gentiles are coheirs, members of the same body, and copartners in the promise in Christ Jesus through the gospel.

GOSPEL *Matthew 2:1–12*

When Jesus was born in Bethlehem of Judea, in the days of King Herod, behold, magi from the east arrived in Jerusalem, saying, "Where is the newborn king of the Jews? We saw his star at its rising and have come to do him homage." When King Herod heard this, he was greatly troubled, and all Jerusalem with him. Assembling all the chief priests and the scribes of the people, he inquired of them where the Christ was to be born. They said to him, "In Bethlehem of Judea, for thus it has been written through the prophet:

And you, Bethlehem, land of Judah,
    are by no means least among the rulers
        of Judah;
since from you shall come a ruler,
    who is to shepherd my people Israel."

Then Herod called the magi secretly and ascertained from them the time of the star's appearance. He sent them to Bethlehem and said, "Go and search diligently for the child. When you have found him, bring me word, that I too may go and do him homage." After their audience with the king they set out. And behold, the star that they had seen at its rising preceded them, until it came and stopped over the place where the child was. They were overjoyed at seeing the star, and on entering the house they saw the child with Mary his mother. They prostrated themselves and did him homage. Then they opened their treasures and offered him gifts of gold, frankincense, and myrrh. And having been warned in a dream not to return to Herod, they departed for their country by another way.

Practice of Charity

Little is known about the mysterious visitors who arrive in Jerusalem seeking the newborn king. They caused quite a stir there and probably also in Bethlehem when they found Mary and Joseph. ◆ Imagine being in the house when the Magi arrive. How do they interact with Mary and Joseph? In what ways might each person, with their different backgrounds, have treated the others with loving kindness? The story of the Magi along with the other readings reminds us that we don't have to compete for God's love. God offers love freely and abundantly. ◆ Look at a map of the world or picture one in your head and pray for people from different countries. ◆ Is there someone you can honor with the gift of your presence? Perhaps you know someone in the hospital or a nursing home whose day you would brighten with a visit.

Download more questions and activities for families, initiation groups, and other adult groups at http://www.ltp.org/ahw.

Scripture Insights

The "magi from the east" (Matthew 2:1) follow a star to welcome Jesus as the "newborn king of the Jews" (Matthew 2:2). Since Persia was to the east of Palestine, these were most likely priests of Zoroastrianism, the imperial religion of Persia. Zoroastrian priests of the time were known for their ability to read the stars, as these magi can do. Following the star to Jerusalem, they encounter King Herod and the chief priests and scribes in Jerusalem. The scribes appear because Herod does not know the answer to the Magi's question regarding the birthplace of the promised messiah (Matthew 2:4).

Unlike the Magi who, despite being Gentiles and priests of a foreign religion, travel a great distance to pay "homage" to the Jewish messiah with precious gifts (Matthew 2:9–11; see also Isaiah 60:1–6; Ephesians 3:2–3a, 5–6), this second group—notwithstanding being Jewish, possessing scriptural knowledge about their promised messiah, and being told about the birth of Jesus—do not care enough to make a trip out of Jerusalem. Instead, they stay put and ask the foreigners to return with a report. The text tells us early that something is not right with this group of people: they are troubled by Jesus' birth (Matthew 2:3).

One can also contrast what these two groups of people know and do not know. While the Magi know the time of Jesus' birth through their observation of the star, they do not know the location of the birth. In contrast, the chief priests and scribes know where the messiah is to be born, but they do not know when. Only when these two groups of people from different religious traditions share what they know are the Magi able to find Jesus.

◆ On what basis do we tend to evaluate people of other faiths and of our Church today?

◆ How can people of different religious traditions work together today? What greater truths may we learn from such interreligious collaboration?

◆ In what ways do we fail to do the right things despite having the right knowledge?

33

Prayer before Reading the Word

Not to the wise and powerful of this world,
O God of all blessedness,
but to those who are poor in spirit
do you reveal in Jesus
the righteousness of your kingdom.

Gathered here,
like the disciples on the mountain,
we long to listen as Jesus, the teacher, speaks.
By the power of his word
refashion our lives
in the pattern of the Beatitudes.

We ask this through our Lord Jesus Christ,
    your Son,
who lives and reigns with you
in the unity of the Holy Spirit,
God, for ever and ever. Amen.

Prayer after Reading the Word

God of all the nations,
we proclaim your wisdom and your power
in the mystery of Christ's cross.
We have heard Christ's call
and it compels us to follow.

Let the truth of the Gospel
break the yoke of our selfishness.
Let the cross draw us and all people
to the joy of salvation.

We ask this through our Lord Jesus Christ,
    your Son,
who lives and reigns with you
in the unity of the Holy Spirit,
God, for ever and ever. Amen.

Weekday Readings

January 9: *1 Samuel 1:9–20; Mark 1:21–28 or 1 Samuel 1:1–8 and 1:9–20; Mark 1:14–20 and 1:21–28*
January 10: *1 Samuel 3:1–10, 19–20; Mark 1:29–39*
January 11: *1 Samuel 4:1–11; Mark 1:40–45*
January 12: *1 Samuel 8:4–7, 10–22a; Mark 2:1–12*
January 13: *1 Samuel 9:1–4, 17–19; 10:1a; Mark 2:13–17*

January 15: *1 Samuel 15:16–23; Mark 2:18–22*
January 16: *1 Samuel 16:1–13; Mark 2:23–28*
January 17: *1 Samuel 17:32–33, 37, 40–51; Mark 3:1–6*
January 18: *1 Samuel 18:6–9; 19:1–7; Mark 3:7–12*
January 19: *1 Samuel 24:3–21; Mark 3:13–19*
January 20: *2 Samuel 1:1–4, 11–12, 19, 23–27; Mark 3:20–21*

January 22: *2 Samuel 5:1–7, 10; Mark 3:22–30*
January 23: *2 Samuel 6:12b–15, 17–19; Mark 3:31–35*
January 24: *2 Samuel 7:4–17; Mark 4:1–20*
January 25: Feast of the Conversion of St. Paul the Apostle
Acts 22:3–16 or Acts 9:1–22; Mark 16:15–18
January 26: *2 Timothy 1:1–8 or Titus 1:1–5; Mark 4:26–34*
January 27: *2 Samuel 12:1–7a, 10–17; Mark 4:35–41*

January 29: *2 Samuel 15:13–14, 30; 16:5–13; Mark 5:1–20*
January 30: *2 Samuel 18:9–10, 14b, 24–25a, 30—19:3; Mark 5:21–43*
January 31: *2 Samuel 24:2, 9–17; Mark 6:1–6*
February 1: *1 Kings 2:1–4, 10–12; Mark 6:7–13*
February 2: Feast of the Presentation of the Lord
Malachi 3:1–4; Hebrews 2:14–18; Luke 2:22–40 or 2:22–32
February 3: *1 Kings 3:4–13; Mark 6:30–34*

February 5: *1 Kings 8:1–7, 9–13; Mark 6:53–56*
February 6: *1 Kings 8:22–23, 27–30; Mark 7:1–13*
February 7: *1 Kings 10:1–10; Mark 7:14–23*
February 8: *1 Kings 11:4–13; Mark 7:24–30*
February 9: *1 Kings 11:29–32; 12:19; Mark 7:31–37*
February 10: *1 Kings 12:26–32; 13:33–34; Mark 8:1–10*

February 12: *James 1:1–11; Mark 8:11–13*
February 13: *James 1:12–18; Mark 8:14–21*

Reading I *1 Samuel 3:3b–10, 19*

Samuel was sleeping in the temple of the LORD where the ark of God was. The LORD called to Samuel, who answered, "Here I am." Samuel ran to Eli and said, "Here I am. You called me." "I did not call you," Eli said. "Go back to sleep." So he went back to sleep. Again the LORD called Samuel, who rose and went to Eli. "Here I am," he said. "You called me." But Eli answered, "I did not call you, my son. Go back to sleep."

At that time Samuel was not familiar with the LORD, because the LORD had not revealed anything to him as yet. The LORD called Samuel again, for the third time. Getting up and going to Eli, he said, "Here I am. You called me." Then Eli understood that the LORD was calling the youth. So he said to Samuel, "Go to sleep, and if you are called, reply, 'Speak, LORD, for your servant is listening.'" When Samuel went to sleep in his place, the LORD came and revealed his presence, calling out as before, "Samuel, Samuel!" Samuel answered, "Speak, for your servant is listening."

Samuel grew up, and the LORD was with him, not permitting any word of his to be without effect.

Responsorial Psalm
Psalm 40:2, 4, 7–8, 8–9, 10 (8a, 9a)

R. Here am I, Lord; I come to do your will.

I have waited, waited for the LORD,
   and he stooped toward me and heard my cry.
And he put a new song into my mouth,
   a hymn to our God. R.

Sacrifice or offering you wished not,
   but ears open to obedience you gave me.
Holocausts or sin-offerings you sought not;
   then said I, "Behold I come." R.

"In the written scroll it is prescribed for me,
to do your will, O my God, is my delight,
   and your law is within my heart!" R.

I announced your justice in the vast assembly;
   I did not restrain my lips, as you,
      O LORD, know. R.

Reading II
1 Corinthians 6:13c–15a, 17–20

Brothers and sisters: The body is not for immorality, but for the Lord, and the Lord is for the body; God raised the Lord and will also raise us by his power.

Do you not know that your bodies are members of Christ? But whoever is joined to the Lord becomes one Spirit with him. Avoid immorality. Every other sin a person commits is outside the body, but the immoral person sins against his own body. Do you not know that your body is a temple of the Holy Spirit within you, whom you have from God, and that you are not your own? For you have been purchased at a price. Therefore glorify God in your body.

Gospel *John 1:35–42*

John was standing with two of his disciples, and as he watched Jesus walk by, he said, "Behold, the Lamb of God." The two disciples heard what he said and followed Jesus. Jesus turned and saw them following him and said to them, "What are you looking for?" They said to him, "Rabbi"—which translated means Teacher—, "where are you staying?" He said to them, "Come, and you will see." So they went and saw where Jesus was staying, and they stayed with him that day. It was about four in the afternoon. Andrew, the brother of Simon Peter, was one of the two who heard John and followed Jesus. He first found his own brother Simon and told him, "We have found the Messiah"—which is translated Christ. Then he brought him to Jesus. Jesus looked at him and said, "You are Simon the son of John; you will be called Cephas"—which is translated Peter.

Practice of Hope

Eli instructed Samuel to tell the Lord, "Speak, for your servant is listening." Too often we say, "Listen, Lord, for your servant is speaking." ◆ Choose a day this week to turn off the television and your cell phone, and to avoid all social media. Find a quiet place to listen to the Lord. If you aren't sure how to listen for God, read slowly through one of the readings several times, then note a word or phrase that catches your attention. Ponder this word or phrase. Notice the thoughts and feelings that emerge within you. What response does God offer you? ◆ St. Paul assures us that our bodies are part of the Body of Christ and are, therefore, sacred. How do you treat your body? Do you get sufficient exercise and sleep? Do you eat healthy foods? ◆ What changes might you need to make to honor your body?

Download more questions and activities for families, initiation groups, and other adult groups at http://www.ltp.org/ahw.

Scripture Insights

Our Gospel passage today takes place after John's witness to Jesus (John 1:19–28) and John's identification of Jesus as "the Lamb of God, who takes away the sin of the world" (1:29–34). In this passage, we see Jesus beginning his ministry and the disciples coming to join him in his mission. His first two disciples, Andrew and an anonymous person, were initially disciples of John the Baptizer. They only follow Jesus because of John's testimony. Jesus asks them a pointed question when he sees that they are following him: "What are you looking for?" (1:38). Instead of answering Jesus' question, the men acknowledge Jesus as "rabbi," and ask where he is staying, thus seemingly suggesting their desire to simply be with Jesus. The word *stay*, both in the Greek and in the biblical translation used for the lectionary, is repeated three times in two verses. Moreover, it is the same verb that Jesus will use when he pronounces later in John 15: "Remain in me as I remain in you" (15:4).

After that question, Jesus issues them an authoritative invitation (the Greek for *come* is an imperative) and gives them a promise (literally in the Greek, "You will see"). Notice how this passage is replete with reference to "watching," "looking," or "seeing" (1:36, 38, 39, 42). By "staying" or "remaining" with Jesus, Andrew sees that Jesus is the messiah. Just as John the Baptizer has done, Andrew proceeds to give a testimony about Jesus to his brother, Simon. The text puts much emphasis on Andrew's initiative: he seeks Simon out and then he brings Simon to Jesus (1:41–42). Like John the Baptizer, Andrew does not focus on himself (he uses the first-person plural, "we," in 1:41) but focuses instead on pointing others to Jesus.

◆ How and to whom can you be a witness for Jesus today?

◆ What does it take to "stay" or "remain" with Jesus?

◆ How has Christ changed your vision? What has he enabled you to see and see differently?

READING I *Jonah 3:1–5, 10*

The word of the LORD came to Jonah, saying: "Set out for the great city of Nineveh, and announce to it the message that I will tell you." So Jonah made ready and went to Nineveh, according to the LORD's bidding. Now Nineveh was an enormously large city; it took three days to go through it. Jonah began his journey through the city, and had gone but a single day's walk announcing, "Forty days more and Nineveh shall be destroyed," when the people of Nineveh believed God; they proclaimed a fast and all of them, great and small, put on sackcloth.

When God saw by their actions how they turned from their evil way, he repented of the evil that he had threatened to do to them; he did not carry it out.

RESPONSORIAL PSALM
Psalm 25:4–5, 6–7, 8–9 (4a)

R. Teach me your ways, O Lord.

Your ways, O LORD, make known to me;
    teach me your paths,
guide me in your truth and teach me,
    for you are God my savior.   R.

Remember that your compassion, O LORD,
    and your love are from of old.
In your kindness remember me,
    because of your goodness, O LORD.   R.

Good and upright is the LORD;
    thus he shows sinners the way.
He guides the humble to justice
    and teaches the humble his way.   R.

READING II *1 Corinthians 7:29–31*

I tell you, brothers and sisters, the time is running out. From now on, let those having wives act as not having them, those weeping as not weeping, those rejoicing as not rejoicing, those buying as not owning, those using the world as not using it fully. For the world in its present form is passing away.

GOSPEL *Mark 1:14–20*

After John had been arrested, Jesus came to Galilee proclaiming the gospel of God: "This is the time of fulfillment. The kingdom of God is at hand. Repent, and believe in the gospel."

As he passed by the Sea of Galilee, he saw Simon and his brother Andrew casting their nets into the sea; they were fishermen. Jesus said to them, "Come after me, and I will make you fishers of men." Then they abandoned their nets and followed him. He walked along a little farther and saw James, the son of Zebedee, and his brother John. They too were in a boat mending their nets. Then he called them. So they left their father Zebedee in the boat along with the hired men and followed him.

Practice of Faith

When Jonah warned the people of Nineveh of God's impending punishment, they promptly repented. When Jesus summoned the Galilean fishermen to participate in the proclamation of God's kingdom, they promptly joined him. When we hear St. Paul urging the Christians in Corinth not to become preoccupied by worldly concerns, we hear that same invitation to ask ourselves if we are truly living as God intends or if we need to make changes in our lives. ◆ Scrutinize your life. What do you spend time on? What do you spend money on? ◆ When Jesus called his first disciples, they immediately left everything behind. Is there something in your life you need to walk away from completely? ◆ Do you know someone who might join you in making meaningful life changes? Talk with that person about how you can support each other.

Download more questions and activities for families, initiation groups, and other adult groups at http://www.ltp.org/ahw.

Scripture Insights

John the Baptizer's preparation for the way of Jesus involves participation in Jesus' way. Like Jesus, John the Baptizer is arrested by the authorities (1:14). Jesus' arrival in Mark is about the coming of God's reign (1:15). The time has come for all other kingdoms or empires to end. We need to trust this Good News by orienting ourselves to a different direction and renouncing all existing forms of dominion (the Greek word translated as *repent* means a changing or a transformation of the mind). Because Jesus' way is not the way of those in power, preparing or following Jesus' way inevitably involves conflict. What we prepare for and follow is the way of the cross. John the Baptizer will be beheaded (Mark 6:14–29).

Jesus' early disciples illustrate what Paul suggests in 1 Corinthians 7:29–31. In contrast to Jonah, who took his time responding to God's call before he finally carried God's message to Nineveh in Jonah 3, they respond to Jesus' call immediately—and they not only drop their usual business but also leave their family. Work and family are structures that support or conventions that govern our lives over time. Mark and Paul tell us that the coming of God's reign requires us to renounce our ties to, and our dependence on, ways that sustain our lives over time because Jesus' way is not a way to ensure the continuation of one's life through property or progeny. It is the way of the cross.

Psalm 25 and Jonah 3 remind us of God's love and mercy. The way of the cross does not mean that God wills or wants us to suffer and die as if God were a sadist. God only calls us to live by God's reign, but the cross may become inevitable because there are those who prefer the perpetuation of the status quo to the coming of God's reign.

◆ What do we have to lose, or what are we afraid of losing today?

◆ How do we reconcile God's love and mercy with Jesus' cross?

◆ What causes us to procrastinate and keeps us from embracing a sense of urgency?

READING I *Deuteronomy 18:15–20*

Moses spoke to all the people, saying: "A prophet like me will the LORD, your God, raise up for you from among your own kin; to him you shall listen. This is exactly what you requested of the LORD, your God, at Horeb on the day of the assembly, when you said, 'Let us not again hear the voice of the LORD, our God, nor see this great fire any more, lest we die.' And the LORD said to me, 'This was well said. I will raise up for them a prophet like you from among their kin, and will put my words into his mouth; he shall tell them all that I command him. Whoever will not listen to my words which he speaks in my name, I myself will make him answer for it. But if a prophet presumes to speak in my name an oracle that I have not commanded him to speak, or speaks in the name of other gods, he shall die.'"

RESPONSORIAL PSALM
Psalm 95:1–2, 6–7, 7–9 (8)

R. If today you hear his voice, harden not
　　your hearts.

Come, let us sing joyfully to the LORD;
　let us acclaim the rock of our salvation.
Let us come into his presence with thanksgiving;
　let us joyfully sing psalms to him.　R.

Come, let us bow down in worship;
　let us kneel before the LORD who made us.
For he is our God,
　and we are the people he shepherds,
　　the flock he guides.　R.

Oh, that today you would hear his voice:
　"Harden not your hearts as at Meribah,
　as in the day of Massah in the desert,
where your fathers tempted me;
　they tested me though they had seen
　　my works."　R.

READING II *1 Corinthians 7:32–35*

Brothers and sisters: I should like you to be free of anxieties. An unmarried man is anxious about the things of the Lord, how he may please the Lord. But a married man is anxious about the things of the world, how he may please his wife, and he is divided. An unmarried woman or a virgin is anxious about the things of the Lord, so that she may be holy in both body and spirit. A married woman, on the other hand, is anxious about the things of the world, how she may please her husband. I am telling you this for your own benefit, not to impose a restraint upon you, but for the sake of propriety and adherence to the Lord without distraction.

GOSPEL *Mark 1:21–28*

Then they came to Capernaum, and on the sabbath Jesus entered the synagogue and taught. The people were astonished at his teaching, for he taught them as one having authority and not as the scribes. In their synagogue was a man with an unclean spirit; he cried out, "What have you to do with us, Jesus of Nazareth? Have you come to destroy us? I know who you are—the Holy One of God!" Jesus rebuked him and said, "Quiet! Come out of him!" The unclean spirit convulsed him and with a loud cry came out of him. All were amazed and asked one another, "What is this? A new teaching with authority. He commands even the unclean spirits and they obey him." His fame spread everywhere throughout the whole region of Galilee.

Practice of Hope

Jesus' expulsion of the demon is a powerful reminder of the truth of his teaching. We who believe in him commit ourselves to that same struggle against evil. ◆ In what ways do you yield to evil? How have you resisted evil? Pray for the courage to withstand whatever evils confront you. ◆ As Jesus exercised his teaching authority, people saw that he fulfilled God's promise to send a great prophet to speak on his behalf. Who speaks truly for God today? How can you too speak in ways that help others believe that God's goodness prevails over evil? ◆ For St. Paul, who thought Christ would come again at any moment, marriage was a distraction from serving God. Today we celebrate how marriage can strengthen commitment to the Lord. Reflect on your close relationships. Do they lead you toward or away from God?

Download more questions and activities for families, initiation groups, and other adult groups at http://www.ltp.org/ahw.

Scripture Insights

Unlike the teaching of the religious authorities that comes across as trite and hollow, the teaching of Mark's Jesus not only astonishes the people but is also affirmed by a miracle he performs. This miracle extends the contrast between the authority of Jesus and that of the religious authorities (Mark 1:22). While the unclean spirit recognizes Jesus as "the Holy One of God" and knows that Jesus comes to "destroy" all demonic powers (1:24), it does not have the same worry regarding the religious authorities, who are undoubtedly present in the synagogue. Deuteronomy 18:20–22 warns about prophets who speak presumptuously in the name of God, but we will need to be careful here, given not only the warning of Deuteronomy 18 but also the long history of anti-Judaism within the Christian traditions and the reality of the Holocaust. We can avoid this problem if we remember that the one who announces Jesus as coming from God in the Markan passage today is the unclean spirit (1:24). Open confessions of Jesus do not guarantee that the confessor is not influenced or possessed by the demonic.

Even though the passage ends by repeating the people's amazement and the connection between Jesus' teaching and authority, it does not give us the contents of Jesus' teaching (1:21–22, 27). Instead, it tells us that the people are responding to the fact that a person possessed by a demon is now made whole. The Old Testament Scriptures today also suggest that validation should come from one's work more than one's word. In contrast to the unclean spirit who confesses but torments a person, Jesus tells the unclean spirit to be quiet and restores the person's freedom by delivering him from a demonic power (1:25–26).

◆ How do you evaluate if an idea or a teaching, whether new or old, is of God or not?

◆ What do we think should characterize the work of God?

◆ What might be some examples of religious structures and authorities harboring demonic powers and influences?

READING I *Job 7:1–4, 6–7*

Job spoke, saying:
  Is not man's life on earth a drudgery?
    Are not his days those of hirelings?
  He is a slave who longs for the shade,
    a hireling who waits for his wages.
  So I have been assigned months of misery,
    and troubled nights have been allotted to me.
  If in bed I say, "When shall I arise?"
    then the night drags on;
    I am filled with restlessness until the dawn.
  My days are swifter than a weaver's shuttle;
    they come to an end without hope.
  Remember that my life is like the wind;
    I shall not see happiness again.

RESPONSORIAL PSALM
Psalm 147:1–2, 3–4, 5–6 (see 3a)

R. Praise the Lord, who heals the brokenhearted.
  or: Alleluia.

Praise the LORD, for he is good;
  sing praise to our God, for he is gracious;
  it is fitting to praise him.
The LORD rebuilds Jerusalem;
  the dispersed of Israel he gathers.   R.

He heals the brokenhearted
  and binds up their wounds.
He tells the number of the stars;
  he calls each by name.   R.

Great is our Lord and mighty in power;
  to his wisdom there is no limit.
The LORD sustains the lowly;
  the wicked he casts to the ground.   R.

READING II
1 Corinthians 9:16–19, 22–23

Brothers and sisters: If I preach the gospel, this is no reason for me to boast, for an obligation has been imposed on me, and woe to me if I do not preach it! If I do so willingly, I have a recompense, but if unwillingly, then I have been entrusted with a stewardship. What then is my recompense? That, when I preach, I offer the gospel free of charge so as not to make full use of my right in the gospel.

Although I am free in regard to all, I have made myself a slave to all so as to win over as many as possible. To the weak I became weak, to win over the weak. I have become all things to all, to save at least some. All this I do for the sake of the gospel, so that I too may have a share in it.

GOSPEL *Mark 1:29–39*

On leaving the synagogue Jesus entered the house of Simon and Andrew with James and John. Simon's mother-in-law lay sick with a fever. They immediately told him about her. He approached, grasped her hand, and helped her up. Then the fever left her and she waited on them.

When it was evening, after sunset, they brought to him all who were ill or possessed by demons. The whole town was gathered at the door. He cured many who were sick with various diseases, and he drove out many demons, not permitting them to speak because they knew him.

Rising very early before dawn, he left and went off to a deserted place, where he prayed. Simon and those who were with him pursued him and on finding him said, "Everyone is looking for you." He told them, "Let us go on to the nearby villages that I may preach there also. For this purpose have I come." So he went into their synagogues, preaching and driving out demons throughout the whole of Galilee.

Practice of Charity

Although the Book of Job doesn't explain suffering, the text invites us to talk with God about the pain we see and might be dealing with. As we hear in the Gospel passage, our loving God cares about our health and well-being. ◆ Bring into your mind the times you have suffered physically or mentally. Talk openly with God about how you feel about your suffering. ◆ Spend some time praying for people you know who are in pain. Offer them your loving compassion. Send a card or a note to one of those people, telling them you are keeping the individual in your prayers. ◆ St. Paul writes that, as a symbol of God's freely given love, he refuses to accept financial support for his ministry. This week look for signs of God's love and celebrate them at the end of each day.

Download more questions and activities for families, initiation groups, and other adult groups at http://www.ltp.org/ahw.

Scripture Insights

Once again, we see Jesus in today's Markan passage setting a person free from bondage. After having freed a man from an unclean spirit (1:21–28), Jesus restores a woman (Simon's mother-in-law) from the torment and paralysis of fever to health (1:30–31). As the psalmist declares, God's greatness is in God's goodness and graciousness, particularly to those who are wounded and in need (Psalm 147:1–6).

Just as the healing performed by Mark's Jesus seems to be instantaneous, the service of Peter's mother-in-law also seems to be immediate. As soon as she has experienced the healing touch of Jesus, she goes to work. Note that her service here is extended to everyone present and not limited to Jesus, who has cured her.

Similarly, we see Jesus healing all kinds of people with various problems (1:32–34). One of the signs of the coming of God's reign (1:15) is the release of humans from the bondage of sickness and possession by demons, or what today we may call bondage of the body and of the mind.

Mark's Gospel makes a point of showing that Jesus is not concerned with bringing attention to himself. As he did with the unclean spirit, Jesus would not allow the demons who knew him to reveal his identity or talk about him (1:34). Instead of basking in the praise and thanks of those whom he has cured, he withdraws to a "deserted place" and then departs from Galilee, even though he has gained the attention of all the people there (Mark 1:21, 35–39). We see a similar message by Paul in today's reading from 1 Corinthians 9. Rather than boasting and seeking attention for himself, Paul emphasizes service to others. We also see this in the example of Peter's mother-in-law.

◆ What kinds of things keep humanity in bondage today?

◆ What makes service or ministry to others difficult or challenging?

◆ What kinds of service or ministry can you extend to other people today?

READING I *Leviticus 13:1–2, 44–46*

The LORD said to Moses and Aaron, "If someone has on his skin a scab or pustule or blotch which appears to be the sore of leprosy, he shall be brought to Aaron, the priest, or to one of the priests among his descendants. If the man is leprous and unclean, the priest shall declare him unclean by reason of the sore on his head.

"The one who bears the sore of leprosy shall keep his garments rent and his head bare, and shall muffle his beard; he shall cry out, 'Unclean, unclean!' As long as the sore is on him he shall declare himself unclean, since he is in fact unclean. He shall dwell apart, making his abode outside the camp."

RESPONSORIAL PSALM
Psalm 32:1–2, 5, 11 (7)

R. I turn to you, Lord, in time of trouble,
  and you fill me with the joy of salvation.

Blessed is he whose fault is taken away,
  whose sin is covered.
Blessed the man to whom the LORD imputes
    not guilt,
  in whose spirit there is no guile.   R.

Then I acknowledged my sin to you,
  my guilt I covered not.
I said, "I confess my faults to the LORD,"
  and you took away the guilt of my sin.   R.

Be glad in the LORD and rejoice, you just;
  exult, all you upright of heart.   R.

READING II *1 Corinthians 10:31—11:1*

Brothers and sisters, whether you eat or drink, or whatever you do, do everything for the glory of God. Avoid giving offense, whether to the Jews or Greeks or the church of God, just as I try to please everyone in every way, not seeking my own benefit but that of the many, that they may be saved. Be imitators of me, as I am of Christ.

GOSPEL *Mark 1:40–45*

A leper came to Jesus and kneeling down begged him and said, "If you wish, you can make me clean." Moved with pity, he stretched out his hand, touched him, and said to him, "I do will it. Be made clean." The leprosy left him immediately, and he was made clean. Then, warning him sternly, he dismissed him at once.

He said to him, "See that you tell no one anything, but go, show yourself to the priest and offer for your cleansing what Moses prescribed; that will be proof for them."

The man went away and began to publicize the whole matter. He spread the report abroad so that it was impossible for Jesus to enter a town openly. He remained outside in deserted places, and people kept coming to him from everywhere.

Practice of Charity

In Jesus' day people with certain skin conditions had to live apart from the community, which only added to their suffering. Imagine being someone in such circumstances. ✦ How do you take care of your basic needs? Do you form relationships with others who have similar ailments? How do healthy people treat you? ✦ Who in your community might feel outcast or lonely because of a physical disability or a mental illness? Do such people make you feel uncomfortable? Ask Christ to cleanse you of whatever keeps you from treating others with dignity and love. ✦ After Jesus heals him, the leper doesn't return to his former life. Have you changed because of the good things God has done for you, or have you returned to your usual way of living? As Lent approaches, consider what you can do to live more fully "for the glory of God" (1 Corinthians 10:31).

Download more questions and activities for families, initiation groups, and other adult groups at http://www.ltp.org/ahw.

Scripture Insights

A leper is considered unclean and forced to experience a kind of social death (Leviticus 13). When a leper comes to Jesus for help, his words, surprisingly, express an uncertainty not about Jesus' ability to heal, but about Jesus' desire to help him. Some ancient manuscripts have Jesus, therefore, being moved with "anger" rather than "pity" in Mark 1:41, because this leper's experience of religion and society has caused him to doubt Jesus' commitment to meet human needs and to enable human wholeness. To make a point about his good will, Jesus cures the leper specifically through touch (Mark 1:41), even though touching a leper may risk sharing a leper's uncleanness and marginalization.

Jesus then tells the cleansed leper to "say nothing to anyone," but to show himself to the priest and, "as a testimony," to follow the law's prescription for a purification (Mark 1:43–44; see also Leviticus 14). By committing the leper to silence, Jesus is clearly seeking to contain testimony about his own identity. He would prefer that the testimony be about the coming of God's reign (Mark 1:15). Jesus is focused on making the work of God known rather than making himself known. Paul is not mistaken when he tells the Corinthians in today's reading that they will be emulating his imitation of Christ if they seek to glorify God and not their own advantage.

Surprisingly, the leper ignores Jesus' command to keep things silent. Because of this, Jesus' movement is restricted: he has to remain "in deserted places" (Mark 1:45). Just as John baptized in the desert (1:2–4) and Jesus was tested by the devil in the desert before beginning his public ministry (Mark 1:12–13), perhaps God's movement can only be forged at the margins.

✦ In what ways might the Church have caused people to question God's commitment to human wholeness and flourishing?

✦ How may we demonstrate our solidarity with those who have been marginalized?

✦ Why are creativity and change often found at the margins or among the marginalized?

Lent

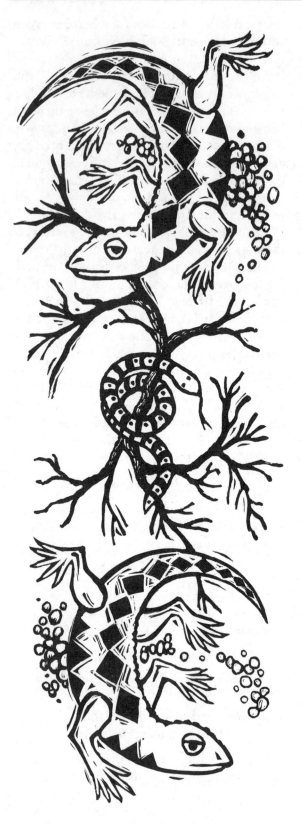

Prayer before Reading the Word

To Abraham and Sarah you called out,
O God of mystery,
inviting them to journey to a land of promise.
To us also you call out,
inviting us to pass through Lent to Easter's glory.
Open our ears, therefore, to listen to Jesus,
the Beloved Son in whom you are well pleased,
so that, embracing the mystery of the cross,
we may come to the holy mountain,
    to immortal life,
and a share in Christ's transfigured glory.
We ask this through our Lord Jesus Christ,
    your Son,
who lives and reigns with you
in the unity of the Holy Spirit,
God, for ever and ever. Amen.

Prayer after Reading the Word

O God, the living fountain of new life,
to the human race, parched with thirst,
you offer the living water of grace
that springs up from the rock,
our Savior Jesus Christ.
Grant your people the gift of the Spirit,
that we may learn to profess our faith
with courage and conviction
and announce with joy
the wonders of your saving love.
We ask this through our Lord Jesus Christ,
    your Son,
who lives and reigns with you
in the unity of the Holy Spirit,
God, for ever and ever. Amen.

Weekday Readings

February 14: Ash Wednesday
Joel 2:12–18; 2 Corinthians 5:20—6:2; Matthew 6:1–6, 16–18
February 15: *Deuteronomy 30:15–20; Luke 9:22–25*
February 16: *Isaiah 58:1–9a; Matthew 9:14–15*
February 17: *Isaiah 58:9b–14; Luke 5:27–32*

February 19: *Leviticus 19:1–2, 11–18; Matthew 25:31–46*
February 20: *Isaiah 55:10–11; Matthew 6:7–15*
February 21: *Jonah 3:1–10; Luke 11:29–32*
February 22: Feast of the Chair of St. Peter the Apostle
1 Peter 5:1–4; Matthew 16:13–19
February 23: *Ezekiel 18:21–28; Matthew 5:20–26*
February 24: *Deuteronomy 26:16–19; Matthew 5:43–48*

February 26: *Daniel 9:4b–10; Luke 6:36–38*
February 27: *Isaiah 1:10, 16–20; Matthew 23:1–12*
February 28: *Jeremiah 18:18–20; Matthew 20:17–28*
February 29: *Jeremiah 17:5–10; Luke 16:19–31*
March 1: *Genesis 37:3–4, 12–13a, 17b–28a; Matthew 21:33–43, 45–46*
March 2: *Micah 7:14–15, 18–20; Luke 15:1–3, 11–32*

March 4: *2 Kings 5:1–15ab; Luke 4:24–30*
March 5: *Daniel 3:25, 34–43; Matthew 18:21–35*
March 6: *Deuteronomy 4:1, 5–9; Matthew 5:17–19*
March 7: *Jeremiah 7:23–28; Luke 11:14–23*
March 8: *Hosea 14:2–10; Mark 12:28–34*
March 9: *Hosea 6:1–6; Luke 18:9–14*

March 11: *Isaiah 65:17–21; John 4:43–54*
March 12: *Ezekiel 47:1–9, 12; John 5:1–16*
March 13: *Isaiah 49:8–15; John 5:17–30*
March 14: *Exodus 32:7–14; John 5:31–47*
March 15: *Wisdom 2:1a, 12–22; John 7:1–2, 10, 25–30*
March 16: *Jeremiah 11:18–20; John 7:40–53*

March 18: *Daniel 13:1–9, 15–17, 19–30, 33–62 or 13:41c–62; John 8:1–11*
March 19: Solemnity of St. Joseph, Spouse of the Blessed Virgin Mary
2 Samuel 7:4–5a, 12–14a, 16; Romans 4:13, 16–18, 22; Matthew 1:16, 18–21, 24a or Luke 2:41–51a
March 20: *Daniel 3:14–20, 91–92, 95; John 8:31–42*
March 21: *Genesis 17:3–9; John 8:51–59*
March 22: *Jeremiah 20:10–13; John 10:31–42*
March 23: *Ezekiel 37:21–28; John 11:45–56*

March 25: *Isaiah 42:1–7; John 12:1–11*
March 26: *Isaiah 49:1–6; John 13:21–33, 36–38*
March 27: *Isaiah 50:4–9a; Matthew 26:14–25*

READING I *Genesis 9:8–15*

God said to Noah and to his sons with him: "See, I am now establishing my covenant with you and your descendants after you and with every living creature that was with you: all the birds, and the various tame and wild animals that were with you and came out of the ark. I will establish my covenant with you, that never again shall all bodily creatures be destroyed by the waters of a flood; there shall not be another flood to devastate the earth." God added: "This is the sign that I am giving for all ages to come, of the covenant between me and you and every living creature with you: I set my bow in the clouds to serve as a sign of the covenant between me and the earth. When I bring clouds over the earth, and the bow appears in the clouds, I will recall the covenant I have made between me and you and all living beings, so that the waters shall never again become a flood to destroy all mortal beings."

RESPONSORIAL PSALM
Psalm 25:4–5, 6–7, 8–9 (see 10)

R. Your ways, O Lord, are love and truth to
   those who keep your covenant.

Your ways, O LORD, make known to me;
   teach me your paths.
Guide me in your truth and teach me,
   for you are God my savior. R.

Remember that your compassion, O LORD,
   and your love are from of old.
In your kindness remember me,
   because of your goodness, O LORD. R.

Good and upright is the LORD,
   thus he shows sinners the way.
He guides the humble to justice,
   and he teaches the humble his way. R.

READING II *1 Peter 3:18–22*

Beloved: Christ suffered for sins once, the righteous for the sake of the unrighteous, that he might lead you to God. Put to death in the flesh, he was brought to life in the Spirit. In it he also went to preach to the spirits in prison, who had once been disobedient while God patiently waited in the days of Noah during the building of the ark, in which a few persons, eight in all, were saved through water. This prefigured baptism, which saves you now. It is not a removal of dirt from the body but an appeal to God for a clear conscience, through the resurrection of Jesus Christ, who has gone into heaven and is at the right hand of God, with angels, authorities, and powers subject to him.

GOSPEL *Mark 1:12–15*

The Spirit drove Jesus out into the desert, and he remained in the desert for forty days, tempted by Satan. He was among wild beasts, and the angels ministered to him.

   After John had been arrested, Jesus came to Galilee proclaiming the gospel of God: "This is the time of fulfillment. The kingdom of God is at hand. Repent, and believe in the gospel."

Practice of Hope

The flood that covered the earth mirrored the evil that had spread across it. Such sin still permeates the earth and can feel overwhelming. ◆ Reflect on the promise God made to Noah and the earth. What promise can you make back to God? In what specific, concrete ways can you care for the earth and its inhabitants? ◆ During his time in the desert, Jesus committed himself to opposing evil in all its forms. Schedule a time to go to confession this week. Acknowledge the ways you have ignored opportunities to make life-giving choices. ◆ Celebrate God's gift of creation by spending time in nature or learning more about a particular species or ecosystem.

Download more questions and activities for families, initiation groups, and other adult groups at http://www.ltp.org/ahw.

Scripture Insights

The "wilderness" or "desert" in biblical literature signifies a liminal or in-between place. After their liberation from Egypt, the Hebrews wandered in the "wilderness" for forty years. Without the structure and security of society, they had to depend on God for the essentials of food and water. It was in the wilderness that they learned how to trust God and become God's people.

After his baptism Jesus is driven into the desert (Mark 1:12), where he is tested by the devil, accompanied by wild beasts, and attended by the angels (Mark 1:13). Perhaps Jesus also must spend time (forty days) in this ambivalent space to prepare for his ministry.

Just as Jesus needs to prepare before beginning his public ministry, we need to repent for the coming of God's reign (Mark 1:14–15). We see this not only in the words of Jesus but also in the authorities' decision to arrest John the Baptizer and, as 1 Peter 3:18 reminds us, in the experience of Noah and the suffering of Jesus. The passage in 1 Peter 3 continues to remind us of God's patience and love. Although most people refused to respond to Noah's call to repentance, God's salvation still came to Noah's family despite its small number. As the psalmist declares in our passage today, God is good and God's love is steadfast. The question is whether we are willing to learn God's ways.

God's covenant with Noah in Genesis 9 also shows that God's reign has to do with an affirmation of life that is not limited to human life. The phrase "every living creature" (9:10, 12, 15, 16) and the phrase "every mortal being" (9:15 twice, 16, 17) are each repeated four times in this chapter, not to mention one appearance of "all creatures" (9:11). As if these repetitions are not enough, the text further spells out "the birds, and the various tame and wild animals" (9:10; see also 9:2).

◆ How and why might human conventions and social structures keep us from seeing and participating in the in-breaking of the holy?

◆ Of what do you need to repent this Lent?

◆ What would affirmation of all life forms on earth imply?

READING I
Genesis 22:1–2, 9a, 10–13, 15–18

God put Abraham to the test. He called to him, "Abraham!" "Here I am!" he replied. Then God said: "Take your son Isaac, your only one, whom you love, and go to the land of Moriah. There you shall offer him up as a holocaust on a height that I will point out to you."

When they came to the place of which God had told him, Abraham built an altar there and arranged the wood on it. Then he reached out and took the knife to slaughter his son. But the LORD's messenger called to him from heaven, "Abraham, Abraham!" "Here I am!" he answered. "Do not lay your hand on the boy," said the messenger. "Do not do the least thing to him. I know now how devoted you are to God, since you did not withhold from me your own beloved son." As Abraham looked about, he spied a ram caught by its horns in the thicket. So he went and took the ram and offered it up as a holocaust in place of his son.

Again the LORD's messenger called to Abraham from heaven and said: "I swear by myself, declares the LORD, that because you acted as you did in not withholding from me your beloved son, I will bless you abundantly and make your descendants as countless as the stars of the sky and the sands of the seashore; your descendants shall take possession of the gates of their enemies, and in your descendants all the nations of the earth shall find blessing—all this because you obeyed my command."

RESPONSORIAL PSALM
Psalm 116:10, 15, 16–17, 18–19 (9)

R. I will walk before the Lord,
   in the land of the living.

I believed, even when I said,
   "I am greatly afflicted."
Precious in the eyes of the LORD
   is the death of his faithful ones. R.

O LORD, I am your servant;
   I am your servant, the son of your handmaid;
   you have loosed my bonds.
To you will I offer sacrifice of thanksgiving,
   and I will call upon the name of the LORD. R.

My vows to the LORD I will pay
   in the presence of all his people,
in the courts of the house of the LORD,
   in your midst, O Jerusalem. R.

READING II *Romans 8:31b–34*

Brothers and sisters: If God is for us, who can be against us? He who did not spare his own Son but handed him over for us all, how will he not also give us everything else along with him?

Who will bring a charge against God's chosen ones? It is God who acquits us, who will condemn? Christ Jesus it is who died—or, rather, was raised—who also is at the right hand of God, who indeed intercedes for us.

GOSPEL *Mark 9:2–10*

Jesus took Peter, James, and John and led them up a high mountain apart by themselves. And he was transfigured before them, and his clothes became dazzling white, such as no fuller on earth could bleach them. Then Elijah appeared to them along with Moses, and they were conversing with Jesus. Then Peter said to Jesus in reply, "Rabbi, it is good that we are here! Let us make three tents: one for you, one for Moses, and one for Elijah." He hardly knew what to say, they were so terrified. Then a cloud came, casting a shadow over them; from the cloud came a voice, "This is my beloved Son. Listen to him." Suddenly, looking around, they no longer saw anyone but Jesus alone with them.

As they were coming down from the mountain, he charged them not to relate what they had seen to anyone, except when the Son of Man had risen from the dead. So they kept the matter to themselves, questioning what rising from the dead meant.

Practice of Faith

Jesus' sudden transformation bewilders his closest disciples, who would be able to make sense of it only after Jesus' resurrection. ◆ What memorable experience of God have you had? How has your understanding of that moment changed over time? How does that moment sustain you during difficult times? ◆ Once the disciples understood what Jesus' transfiguration meant, they might have recalled it when they needed the strength to persevere in the face of adversity. Spend time in adoration of the Blessed Sacrament this week. Gaze upon Christ, who gave himself for you and intercedes for you. ◆ Abraham acknowledges that Isaac, like all of God's promises, is a gift, undeserved and unearned. Consider all that you claim as yours. Do you have something that someone else needs? What would it cost you to give some of what you have away?

Download more questions and activities for families, initiation groups, and other adult groups at http://www.ltp.org/ahw.

Scripture Insights

Our Markan passage today alludes to Jesus' resurrection. Although the lectionary text begins with movement, the biblical passage from which the reading is taken starts with a temporal reference ("After six days," Mark 9:2), and ends with repeated references to being risen/rising "from the dead" (Mark 9:9, 10). Peter, James, and John not only witnessed Jesus' transfiguration (Mark 9:2), they also saw Jesus raising Jairus' deceased daughter (Mark 5:21–24, 35–43).

The Old Testament Scriptures promise that God will send a new prophet who is like Moses or like Elijah (Deuteronomy 18:15; 34:10; Malachi 3:23), so their appearance and conversation with Jesus may point to Jesus as that promised prophet. The presence of Moses and Elijah can also be seen as referring to a coming prophet because there is no tomb for either of them, so their appearance speaks again to the resurrection.

In Mark's telling, Peter proposes to build "three tents" because he is terrified (Mark 9:5–6). Peter's response to Jesus' first passion prediction in Mark's Gospel caused Jesus to rebuke him and address him as "Satan" (Mark 8:31–33). Just as Peter's earlier folly did not disqualify him from seeing Jesus' transfiguration, this mistake will not result in his abandonment.

Instead of speaking nonsense out of fear, Peter should "listen" to what Jesus tells him (Mark 9:7): namely, Jesus' prediction of his death and resurrection (Mark 9:9–10). As Peter's failure in Mark 8 shows, the way of the cross is difficult to accept, but death must come before resurrection. This may also explain Jesus' command for silence, including in this passage: Peter, James, and John are not to say anything about Jesus' transfiguration until after Jesus' resurrection. Otherwise, Jesus might be mistaken for one who comes in glory and power without the cross.

◆ What would the way of the cross mean today?

◆ What do we as a Church tend to say or do out of fear and terror?

◆ In what ways could we be following a Christ without the way of the cross?

READING I *Exodus 20:1–17*

Shorter: Exodus 20:1–3, 7–8, 12–17

In those days, God delivered all these commandments: "I, the LORD, am your God, who brought you out of the land of Egypt, that place of slavery. You shall not have other gods besides me. You shall not carve idols for yourselves in the shape of anything in the sky above or on the earth below or in the waters beneath the earth; you shall not bow down before them or worship them. For I, the LORD, your God, am a jealous God, inflicting punishment for their fathers' wickedness on the children of those who hate me, down to the third and fourth generation; but bestowing mercy down to the thousandth generation on the children of those who love me and keep my commandments.

"You shall not take the name of the LORD, your God, in vain. For the LORD will not leave unpunished the one who takes his name in vain.

"Remember to keep holy the sabbath day. Six days you may labor and do all your work, but the seventh day is the sabbath of the LORD, your God. No work may be done then either by you, or your son or daughter, or your male or female slave, or your beast, or by the alien who lives with you. In six days the LORD made the heavens and the earth, the sea and all that is in them; but on the seventh day he rested. That is why the LORD has blessed the sabbath day and made it holy.

"Honor your father and your mother, that you may have a long life in the land which the LORD, your God, is giving you. You shall not kill. You shall not commit adultery. You shall not steal. You shall not bear false witness against your neighbor. You shall not covet your neighbor's house. You shall not covet your neighbor's wife, nor his male or female slave, nor his ox or ass, nor anything else that belongs to him."

RESPONSORIAL PSALM
Psalm 19:8, 9, 10, 11 (John 6:68c)

R. Lord, you have the words of everlasting life.

The law of the LORD is perfect,
    refreshing the soul;
the decree of the LORD is trustworthy,
    giving wisdom to the simple.   R.

The precepts of the LORD are right,
    rejoicing the heart;
the command of the LORD is clear,
    enlightening the eye.   R.

The fear of the LORD is pure,
    enduring forever;
the ordinances of the LORD are true,
    all of them just.   R.

They are more precious than gold,
    than a heap of purest gold;
sweeter also than syrup
    or honey from the comb.   R.

READING II *1 Corinthians 1:22–25*

Brothers and sisters: Jews demand signs and Greeks look for wisdom, but we proclaim Christ crucified, a stumbling block to Jews and foolishness to Gentiles, but to those who are called, Jews and Greeks alike, Christ the power of God and the wisdom of God. For the foolishness of God is wiser than human wisdom, and the weakness of God is stronger than human strength.

GOSPEL *John 2:13–25*

Since the Passover of the Jews was near, Jesus went up to Jerusalem. He found in the temple area those who sold oxen, sheep, and doves, as well as the money changers seated there. He made a whip out of cords and drove them all out of the temple area, with the sheep and oxen, and spilled the coins of the money changers and overturned their tables, and to those who sold doves he said, "Take these out of here, and stop making my Father's house a marketplace." His disciples recalled the words of Scripture, *Zeal for your house will consume me.* At this the Jews answered and said to him, "What sign can you show us for doing this?" Jesus answered and said to them, "Destroy this temple and in three days I will raise it up." The Jews said, "This temple has been under construction for forty-six years, and you will raise it up in three days?" But he was speaking about the temple of his body. Therefore, when he was raised from the dead, his disciples remembered that he had said this, and they came to believe the Scripture and the word Jesus had spoken.

While he was in Jerusalem for the feast of Passover, many began to believe in his name when they saw the signs he was doing. But Jesus would not trust himself to them because he knew them all, and did not need anyone to testify about human nature. He himself understood it well.

Practice of Faith

By doing things such as temporarily stopping the worship in the Jerusalem temple, Jesus reoriented worship around himself. ◆ What in your life do you need Jesus to stop and tear down so that you may worship him more fully? Pray for the wisdom to see your life as he does. ◆ The third part of the *Catechism of the Catholic Church* includes a study of the Ten Commandments. Choose one of the commandments and read more about it. Both the Ten Commandments and Jesus' teaching bind God's people together so that they will be one in how they pray and live. ◆ Is there someone in your faith community with whom you are at odds? Could you meet that person in a comfortable venue, honor that person's perspective, and come to some mutual understanding?

Download more questions and activities for families, initiation groups, and other adult groups at http://www.ltp.org/ahw.

Scripture Insights

Jesus' cleansing of the temple in John's Gospel is dramatic and violent. After turning over the tables of the moneychangers, he makes a whip to drive out the sheep and the cattle (John 2:15). The animals are there to be sacrificed, and this necessitates money exchange because Jewish people would come to the temple from various parts of the Roman Empire to observe the Passover. Jesus' action is during a high season of the religion and a peak season for the business, so he is doing this at the worst possible time from the perspective of those in charge.

Jesus causes this commotion because God's house has been turned into a marketplace. What is supposed to be about faith in and commitment to God becomes a business. It's little wonder that Jesus would not entrust himself to those who say they believe (John 2:23–25). Although the religious leaders may allow, endorse, or even promote this activity, they cannot defend this malpractice from one who demands true worship.

Jesus is then asked to validate his actions with a sign (John 2:18), which is not a viable basis according to both John and Paul (John 2:23–35; 1 Corinthians 1:22–25). In response, Jesus talks about his upcoming death and resurrection, even though the people who hear his words have trouble understanding what he means (John 2:19–21).

Twice in this passage, John talks about the disciples remembering (John 2:17, 22). They remember a verse from Psalm 69 and realize that Jesus is motivated by his "zeal for [God's] house" (John 2:17; see also Psalm 69:9). This verse in Psalm 69 is surrounded by references to the psalmist's struggles because of enemies seeking to destroy and kill the psalmist (Psalm 69:2–8, 10–21, 29). The zeal that "consume[s]" Jesus (John 2:17), as the following dialogue between Jesus and "the Jews" who oppose him shows, carries the sense of possession and destruction. ("The Jews" are in quotation marks to signify that opponents of Jesus should not be equated with the Jewish people.)

◆ In what ways is faith commercialized?

◆ What memories strengthen your faith today?

◆ What conditions do you bring to your encounters with God?

READING I *Exodus 17:3–7*

In those days, in their thirst for water, the people grumbled against Moses, saying, "Why did you ever make us leave Egypt? Was it just to have us die here of thirst with our children and our livestock?" So Moses cried out to the LORD, "What shall I do with this people? A little more and they will stone me!" The LORD answered Moses, "Go over there in front of the people, along with some of the elders of Israel, holding in your hand, as you go, the staff with which you struck the river. I will be standing there in front of you on the rock in Horeb. Strike the rock, and the water will flow from it for the people to drink." This Moses did, in the presence of the elders of Israel. The place was called Massah and Meribah, because the Israelites quarreled there and tested the LORD, saying, "Is the LORD in our midst or not?"

RESPONSORIAL PSALM
Psalm 95:1–2, 6–7, 8–9 (8)

R. If today you hear his voice, harden not
    your hearts.

Come, let us sing joyfully to the LORD;
    let us acclaim the Rock of our salvation.
Let us come into his presence with thanksgiving;
    let us joyfully sing psalms to him. R.

Come, let us bow down in worship;
    let us kneel before the LORD who made us.
For he is our God,
    and we are the people he shepherds, the flock
        he guides. R.

Oh, that today you would hear his voice:
    "Harden not your hearts as at Meribah,
        as in the day of Massah in the desert.
Where your fathers tempted me;
    they tested me though they had seen
        my works." R.

READING II *Romans 5:1–2, 5–8*

Brothers and sisters: Since we have been justified by faith, we have peace with God through our Lord Jesus Christ, through whom we have gained access by faith to this grace in which we stand, and we boast in hope of the glory of God.

And hope does not disappoint, because the love of God has been poured out into our hearts through the Holy Spirit who has been given to us. For Christ, while we were still helpless, died at the appointed time for the ungodly. Indeed, only with difficulty does one die for a just person, though perhaps for a good person one might even find courage to die. But God proves his love for us in that while we were still sinners Christ died for us.

GOSPEL
John 4:5–15, 19b–26, 39a, 40–42
Longer: John 4:5–42

Jesus came to a town of Samaria called Sychar, near the plot of land that Jacob had given to his son Joseph. Jacob's well was there. Jesus, tired from his journey, sat down there at the well. It was about noon.

A woman of Samaria came to draw water. Jesus said to her, "Give me a drink." His disciples had gone into the town to buy food. The Samaritan woman said to him, "How can you, a Jew, ask me, a Samaritan woman, for a drink?"—For Jews use nothing in common with Samaritans.—Jesus answered and said to her, "If you knew the gift of God and who is saying to you, 'Give me a drink,' you would have asked him and he would have given you living water." The woman said to him, "Sir, you do not even have a bucket and the cistern is deep; where then can you get this living water? Are you greater than our father Jacob, who gave us this cistern and drank from it himself with his children and his flocks?" Jesus answered and said to her, "Everyone who drinks this water will be thirsty again; but whoever drinks the water I shall give will never thirst; the water I shall give will become in him a spring of water welling up to eternal life." The woman said to him, "Sir, give me this water, so that I may not be thirsty or have to keep coming here to draw water.

"I can see that you are a prophet. Our ancestors worshiped on this mountain; but you people say that the place to worship is in Jerusalem." Jesus said to her, "Believe me, woman, the hour is coming when you will worship the Father neither on this mountain nor in Jerusalem. You people worship what you do not understand; we worship what we understand, because salvation is from the Jews. But the hour is coming, and is now here, when true worshipers will worship the Father in Spirit and truth; and indeed the Father seeks such people to worship him. God is Spirit, and those who worship him must worship in Spirit and truth." The woman said to him, "I know that the Messiah is coming, the one called the Christ; when he comes, he will tell us everything." Jesus said to her, "I am he, the one who is speaking with you."

Many of the Samaritans of that town began to believe in him. When the Samaritans came to him, they invited him to stay with them; and he stayed there two days. Many more began to believe in him because of his word, and they said to the woman, "We no longer believe because of your word; for we have heard for ourselves, and we know that this is truly the savior of the world."

Practice of Faith

In today's Gospel Jesus refers to the Spirit as water. ♦ Choose a day to thank God for water each time you use it. ♦ Learn about places deprived of clean water, such as situations featured in the children's book *Drop by Drop*, by the United States Conference of Catholic Bishops' Department of Justice, Peace, and Human Development. A video version is at www.usccb.org/resources/drop-drop-abridged -video-version. ♦ Consider participating in or starting an initiative to provide clean water to others. Make sure your efforts fit the needs of those you want to help.

Download more questions and activities for families, initiation groups, and other adult groups at http://www.ltp.org/ahw.

Scripture Insights

The Samaritan woman's multiple husbands may be the result of deaths, divorces, or the practice of levirate marriage. Coming to draw water around "noon" (John 4:6) may contrast Nicodemus' coming to Jesus "by night" (John 3:2).

Just as the ambiguity of the Greek language confuses Nicodemus—"being born from above" in the Greek may mean being born again (John 3:3–4)—the Samaritan woman initially mistakes Jesus' "living water," since the Greek may also mean "flowing water," such as a river or a stream (John 4:10–12). John 7:37–39 explains that "living water" refers to the Holy Spirit.

This passage might also point to Jesus as the messianic bridegroom. In some biblical traditions, a man and a woman meeting at a well signifies that a betrothal is about to occur (see Genesis 24:1–51; 29:1–12; Exodus 2:15–21). References to the woman's husbands may be metaphors for the multiple deities of the Samaritans, thus making Jesus the seventh but true deity for the Samaritan woman and her people. The discussion between them at Jacob's well is, then, theological (John 4:19–24). The woman gradually changes her view of Jesus: from just a(nother) Jewish man (John 4:9) to "a prophet" (John 4:19) to possibly "the Messiah" (John 4:29). Then she does what other disciples have done (John 1:40–42, 45): she introduces Samaritans to Jesus as "truly the Savior of the world" (John 4:28–30, 39–42).

♦ If the references to husbands are metaphorical in John 4, how would you interpret the mentioning of the sixth man?

♦ How would you compare and contrast the interaction between the Israelites and Moses and the interaction between the Samaritan woman and Jesus?

♦ How can we develop our theological literacy and improve our theological understandings?

READING I
2 Chronicles 36:14–16, 19–23

In those days, all the princes of Judah, the priests, and the people added infidelity to infidelity, practicing all the abominations of the nations and polluting the LORD's temple which he had consecrated in Jerusalem.

Early and often did the LORD, the God of their fathers, send his messengers to them, for he had compassion on his people and his dwelling place. But they mocked the messengers of God, despised his warnings, and scoffed at his prophets, until the anger of the LORD against his people was so inflamed that there was no remedy. Their enemies burnt the house of God, tore down the walls of Jerusalem, set all its palaces afire, and destroyed all its precious objects. Those who escaped the sword were carried captive to Babylon, where they became servants of the king of the Chaldeans and his sons until the kingdom of the Persians came to power. All this was to fulfill the word of the LORD spoken by Jeremiah: "Until the land has retrieved its lost sabbaths, during all the time it lies waste it shall have rest while seventy years are fulfilled."

In the first year of Cyrus, king of Persia, in order to fulfill the word of the LORD spoken by Jeremiah, the LORD inspired King Cyrus of Persia to issue this proclamation throughout his kingdom, both by word of mouth and in writing: "Thus says Cyrus, king of Persia: All the kingdoms of the earth the LORD, the God of heaven, has given to me, and he has also charged me to build him a house in Jerusalem, which is in Judah. Whoever, therefore, among you belongs to any part of his people, let him go up, and may his God be with him!"

RESPONSORIAL PSALM
Psalm 137:1–2, 3, 4–5, 6 (6ab)

R. Let my tongue be silenced, if I ever forget you!

By the streams of Babylon
  we sat and wept
  when we remembered Zion.
On the aspens of that land
  we hung up our harps. R.

For there our captors asked of us
  the lyrics of our songs,
and our despoilers urged us to be joyous:
  "Sing for us the songs of Zion!" R.

How could we sing a song of the LORD
  in a foreign land?
If I forget you, Jerusalem,
  may my right hand be forgotten! R.

May my tongue cleave to my palate
  if I remember you not,
if I place not Jerusalem
  ahead of my joy. R.

READING II *Ephesians 2:4–10*

Brothers and sisters: God, who is rich in mercy, because of the great love he had for us, even when we were dead in our transgressions, brought us to life with Christ—by grace you have been saved—, raised us up with him, and seated us with him in the heavens in Christ Jesus, that in the ages to come he might show the immeasurable riches of his grace in his kindness to us in Christ Jesus. For by grace you have been saved through faith, and this is not from you; it is the gift of God; it is not from works, so no one may boast. For we are his handiwork, created in Christ Jesus for the good works that God has prepared in advance, that we should live in them.

GOSPEL *John 3:14–21*

Jesus said to Nicodemus: "Just as Moses lifted up the serpent in the desert, so must the Son of Man be lifted up, so that everyone who believes in him may have eternal life."

For God so loved the world that he gave his only Son, so that everyone who believes in him might not perish but might have eternal life. For God did not send his Son into the world to condemn the world, but that the world might be saved through him. Whoever believes in him will not be condemned, but whoever does not believe has already been condemned, because he has not believed in the name of the only Son of God. And this is the verdict, that the light came into the world, but people preferred darkness to light, because their works were evil. For everyone who does wicked things hates the light and does not come toward the light, so that his works might not be exposed. But whoever lives the truth comes to the light, so that his works may be clearly seen as done in God.

Practice of Hope

Although Jesus came to save the world, "people preferred darkness to light" and ultimately condemned God's Son, the Light of the World, to death. ◆ What have you said and done that you don't want brought into the light? Bring these things before God and confess your need for God's grace. Remember that you are God's handiwork, saved through faith. ◆ Like Jesus, some people have been wrongly condemned. Learn more about the Innocence Project (innocenceproject.org) and the work being done to exonerate people who were wrongly convicted. ◆ Gather close friends or family members for a prayer service at night. Ask everyone to bring a candle and a Scripture passage that speaks about God's light. Invite each person to express gratitude for the ways in which we need light. Conclude by inviting all to offer their petitions for God's light to remain with us.

Download more questions and activities for families, initiation groups, and other adult groups at http://www.ltp.org/ahw.

Scripture Insights

In the verses prior to today's reading from John 3, Jesus explains to Nicodemus that a different kind of birth is needed to enter God's kingdom (3:3). Now, Jesus refers to a story involving Moses (Numbers 21:4–9) as he presents the gift of eternal life that is available through his death and resurrection (John 3:14–15). Just as the Israelites had to look at a snake that Moses lifted up—that is, confronting and acknowledging their sin—to be saved, we have to be willing to let Jesus expose our evil deeds to avoid God's judgment of condemnation (John 3:19–20). Jesus, the life and light of the world when the world was first created (John 1:1–5), comes again to impart to the world life and light (8:12; 11:25). Nicodemus might come to Jesus "at night" (John 3:2), but Jesus is "the light [that] came into the world" (John 3:19).

Jesus tells us concretely how much and in what manner God loves the world that God has created: God gives us God's only Son (John 3:16–17). God's gift of salvation is given to us even "when we were dead in our transgressions" (Ephesian 2:4–5). After all, it is "the sin of the world" that led to Jesus' incarnation and then crucifixion (John 1:29). In other words, the judgment of condemnation discussed by John is really a self-condemnation because one is not willing to look to Jesus and acknowledge one's wrongdoing.

God sent Jesus out of love, but we have the choice to embrace the light to receive life or embrace our fears to hide in the night.

◆ Read the beginning of John 3. There, Jesus speaks with an individual called Nicodemus, but a few of the second person pronouns ("you") are in the plural rather than the singular (John 3:7, 11, 12). Why?

◆ What connections can you make between the Old Testament passages and the New Testament passages for this Sunday?

◆ What might the light of Christ expose about our lives individually and collectively as a society that we would rather hide?

READING I *1 Samuel 16:1b, 6–7, 10–13a*

The LORD said to Samuel: "Fill your horn with oil, and be on your way. I am sending you to Jesse of Bethlehem, for I have chosen my king from among his sons."

As Jesse and his sons came to the sacrifice, Samuel looked at Eliab and thought, "Surely the LORD's anointed is here before him." But the LORD said to Samuel: "Do not judge from his appearance or from his lofty stature, because I have rejected him. Not as man sees does God see, because man sees the appearance but the LORD looks into the heart." In the same way Jesse presented seven sons before Samuel, but Samuel said to Jesse, "The LORD has not chosen any one of these." Then Samuel asked Jesse, "Are these all the sons you have?" Jesse replied, "There is still the youngest, who is tending the sheep." Samuel said to Jesse, "Send for him; we will not begin the sacrificial banquet until he arrives here." Jesse sent and had the young man brought to them. He was ruddy, a youth handsome to behold and making a splendid appearance. The LORD said, "There—anoint him, for this is the one!" Then Samuel, with the horn of oil in hand, anointed David in the presence of his brothers; and from that day on, the spirit of the LORD rushed upon David.

RESPONSORIAL PSALM
Psalm 23:1–3a, 3b–4, 5, 6 (1)

R. The Lord is my shepherd;
   there is nothing I shall want.

The LORD is my shepherd; I shall not want.
   In verdant pastures he gives me repose;
beside restful waters he leads me;
   he refreshes my soul. R.

He guides me in right paths
   for his name's sake.
Even though I walk in the dark valley
   I fear no evil; for you are at my side
with your rod and your staff
   that give me courage. R.

You spread the table before me
   in the sight of my foes;
you anoint my head with oil;
   my cup overflows. R.

Only goodness and kindness follow me
   all the days of my life;
and I shall dwell in the house of the LORD
   for years to come. R.

READING II *Ephesians 5:8–14*

Brothers and sisters: You were once darkness, but now you are light in the Lord. Live as children of light, for light produces every kind of goodness and righteousness and truth. Try to learn what is pleasing to the Lord. Take no part in the fruitless works of darkness; rather expose them, for it is shameful even to mention the things done by them in secret; but everything exposed by the light becomes visible, for everything that becomes visible is light. Therefore, it says:
   "Awake, O sleeper,
   and arise from the dead,
   and Christ will give you light."

GOSPEL *John 9:1, 6–9, 13–17, 34–38*

Longer: John 9:1–41

As Jesus passed by he saw a man blind from birth. He spat on the ground and made clay with the saliva, and smeared the clay on his eyes, and said to him, "Go wash in the Pool of Siloam"—which means Sent—. So he went and washed, and came back able to see.

His neighbors and those who had seen him earlier as a beggar said, "Isn't this the one who used to sit and beg?" Some said, "It is," but others said, "No, he just looks like him." He said, "I am."

They brought the one who was once blind to the Pharisees. Now Jesus had made clay and opened his eyes on a sabbath. So then the Pharisees also asked him how he was able to see. He said to them, "He put clay on my eyes, and I washed, and now I can see." So some of the Pharisees said, "This man is not from God, because he does not keep the sabbath." But others said, "How can a sinful man do such signs?" And there was a division among them. So they said to the blind man again, "What do you have to say about him, since he opened your eyes?" He said, "He is a prophet."

They answered and said to him, "You were born totally in sin, and are you trying to teach us?" Then they threw him out.

When Jesus heard that they had thrown him out, he found him and said, "Do you believe in the Son of Man?" He answered and said, "Who is he, sir, that I may believe in him?" Jesus said to him, "You have seen him, and the one speaking with you is he." He said, "I do believe, Lord," and he worshiped him.

Practice of Faith

Our second reading is a foretaste of the Easter Vigil, with its service of light and sacraments of initiation. ◆ Pray for those preparing to enter the Church this Easter. In John's Gospel, blindness is a metaphor for not understanding who Jesus is and not believing in him. ◆ Learn more about Jesus by focusing on an aspect of his life that you don't often think about, such as healer, teacher, or prophet. Your parish library might have some books on Jesus, such as *Jesus of Nazareth*, by Pope Benedict XVI (New York: Doubleday, 2007). ◆ There are people in our midst who have much to offer, like David, but are too often overlooked. Open your eyes to these people by volunteering at a local soup kitchen or a home for those with special needs. Those whom we help in some way often help us to see Christ more clearly and to deepen our relationship with him.

Download more questions and activities for families, initiation groups, and other adult groups at http://www.ltp.org/ahw.

Scripture Insights

Today's Gospel passage is both a story of healing and a story of controversy. Jesus' healing of a person born blind brings about disagreements among the blind person's neighbors and among the Pharisees regarding the identity of the blind person and of Jesus (John 9:8–9, 16).

This blind man is known to his neighbors as a beggar (John 9:8). He is just a poor person without any other pedigree or importance, but Jesus sees his need and takes the initiative to help him.

The religious authorities repeatedly charge that Jesus' healing act is violating the sabbath (John 9:14, 16). They see Jesus as a threat because he is challenging one of their holiest and most treasured traditions. Unlike them, Jesus thinks and acts in a way that values human needs and well-being over religious rites or regulations, even if the person in question is ordinary and poor. Jesus' identity becomes crucial because it raises the question of whether the religious authorities or Jesus represents God's will.

The passages from 1 Samuel and from Ephesians for today both suggest that we need to discern God's will to know what pleases God. The author of Ephesians further suggests that we can discern this by the work or fruit that becomes visible. Just as the psalmist affirms "the goodness and kindness" of God (Psalm 23:1–6), "light produces every kind of goodness and righteousness and truth" (Ephesians 5:8–14).

◆ Why does John's Gospel make a point to not only specify the name of the pool to which the person born blind should go but also translates the meaning of that pool's name (John 9:7)?

◆ How may we evaluate Jesus' healing of the man born blind and the divided response of the religious authorities in John 9 and how that divided response is related to what the author of Ephesians called "the light [that] produces every kind of goodness and righteousness and truth" (Ephesians 5:9)?

◆ How might the Church have chosen rites or regulations over human needs and welfare?

March 17, 2024 FIFTH SUNDAY OF LENT

READING I *Jeremiah 31:31–34*

The days are coming, says the LORD, when I will make a new covenant with the house of Israel and the house of Judah. It will not be like the covenant I made with their fathers the day I took them by the hand to lead them forth from the land of Egypt; for they broke my covenant, and I had to show myself their master, says the LORD. But this is the covenant that I will make with the house of Israel after those days, says the LORD. I will place my law within them and write it upon their hearts; I will be their God, and they shall be my people. No longer will they have need to teach their friends and relatives how to know the LORD. All, from least to greatest, shall know me, says the LORD, for I will forgive their evildoing and remember their sin no more.

RESPONSORIAL PSALM
Psalm 51:3–4, 12–13, 14–15 (12a)

R. Create a clean heart in me, O God.

Have mercy on me, O God, in your goodness;
  in the greatness of your compassion wipe out
    my offense.
Thoroughly wash me from my guilt
  and of my sin cleanse me. R.

A clean heart create for me, O God,
  and a steadfast spirit renew within me.
Cast me not out from your presence,
  and your Holy Spirit take not from me. R.

Give me back the joy of your salvation,
  and a willing spirit sustain in me.
I will teach transgressors your ways,
  and sinners shall return to you. R.

READING II *Hebrews 5:7–9*

In the days when Christ Jesus was in the flesh, he offered prayers and supplications with loud cries and tears to the one who was able to save him from death, and he was heard because of his reverence. Son though he was, he learned obedience from what he suffered; and when he was made perfect, he became the source of eternal salvation for all who obey him.

GOSPEL *John 12:20–33*

Some Greeks who had come to worship at the Passover Feast came to Philip, who was from Bethsaida in Galilee, and asked him, "Sir, we would like to see Jesus." Philip went and told Andrew; then Andrew and Philip went and told Jesus. Jesus answered them, "The hour has come for the Son of Man to be glorified. Amen, amen, I say to you, unless a grain of wheat falls to the ground and dies, it remains just a grain of wheat; but if it dies, it produces much fruit. Whoever loves his life loses it, and whoever hates his life in this world will preserve it for eternal life. Whoever serves me must follow me, and where I am, there also will my servant be. The Father will honor whoever serves me.

"I am troubled now. Yet what should I say? 'Father, save me from this hour'? But it was for this purpose that I came to this hour. Father, glorify your name." Then a voice came from heaven, "I have glorified it and will glorify it again." The crowd there heard it and said it was thunder; but others said, "An angel has spoken to him." Jesus answered and said, "This voice did not come for my sake but for yours. Now is the time of judgment on this world; now the ruler of this world will be driven out. And when I am lifted up from the earth, I will draw everyone to myself." He said this indicating the kind of death he would die.

Practice of Charity

In Jeremiah's day, covenants were formal agreements or treaties between individuals or nations. Parts of the covenants between nations were often cut onto stone and prominently displayed. ◆ Think of formal agreements that you have signed. You have probably also pledged your support and love in many unwritten contracts. Choose one of these covenants, write down the part that is most meaningful to you, and display it in your home. ◆ God promises to write his law upon our hearts. Ask God to write upon your heart. What words does God place within you? ◆ As we hear in the second reading, Jesus felt fear and sorrow at his approaching death, but he offered his life out of love for his Father and for us. Others have followed in his footsteps. Learn more about a Christian martyr. How did this person also reveal and participate in God's love?

Download more questions and activities for families, initiation groups, and other adult groups at http://www.ltp.org/ahw.

Scripture Insights

Right after the religious leaders' comment that "[t]he world has gone after him [Jesus]" (John 12:19), some Greeks who have come to Jerusalem for the Passover want to see Jesus (John 12:20–21). Earlier in the Gospel of John, some have wondered if Jesus intends to go to the "dispersion among the Greeks to teach the Greeks" (John 7:35).

It is unclear if the Greeks get to see Jesus. Philip and Andrew inform Jesus of the Greeks' desire to see him, and then Jesus speaks to "them," which may or may not include the Greeks.

Jesus focuses on his imminent death by crucifixion (John 12:32–33), which brings about eternal salvation (Hebrews 5:7–9). Moreover, he states that death will be inevitable for his true followers so they must repudiate their self-preservation and self-interest (John 12:24–26). Setting an example for his followers, he says that he won't ask God to spare him from death (John 12:27).

Death is inevitable because Jesus comes, as Jeremiah 31 suggests, to inaugurate a new age of God's reign that challenges and drives out the ruler of this world (John 12:31). This understandably provokes the most desperate and violent reaction from those who represent and support the ruler of this world. The deaths of Jesus and his followers will become a judgment of—and paradoxically, a victory over—this worldly ruler.

When a voice from heaven interrupts Jesus' speech, Jesus says that the voice is not for him but for those to whom he is speaking (John 12:28–30). Perhaps that is why the audience to whom Jesus is speaking remains ambiguous, because it includes readers of John's Gospel. If we lose the one who is the source of life, we will surely be losing our lives.

◆ What other significance may be implied by the coming of the Greeks in this passage (see John 12:32 and Isaiah 56:3–8)?

◆ What is the significance that the statement by the heavenly voice is not for Jesus, but for those to whom Jesus is speaking (John 12:28–30)?

◆ In what ways are we supporting or resisting the ruler of this world today?

READING I *Ezekiel 37:12–14*

Thus says the Lord GOD: O my people, I will open your graves and have you rise from them, and bring you back to the land of Israel. Then you shall know that I am the LORD, when I open your graves and have you rise from them, O my people! I will put my spirit in you that you may live, and I will settle you upon your land; thus you shall know that I am the LORD. I have promised, and I will do it, says the LORD.

RESPONSORIAL PSALM
Psalm 130:1–2, 3–4, 5–6, 7–8 (7)

R. With the Lord there is mercy and fullness
   of redemption.

Out of the depths I cry to you, O LORD;
   LORD, hear my voice!
Let your ears be attentive
   to my voice in supplication. R.

If you, O LORD, mark iniquities,
   LORD, who can stand?
But with you is forgiveness,
   that you may be revered. R.

I trust in the LORD;
   my soul trusts in his word.
More than sentinels wait for the dawn,
   let Israel wait for the LORD. R.

For with the LORD is kindness
   and with him is plenteous redemption;
and he will redeem Israel
   from all their iniquities. R.

READING II *Romans 8:8–11*

Brothers and sisters: Those who are in the flesh cannot please God. But you are not in the flesh; on the contrary, you are in the spirit, if only the Spirit of God dwells in you. Whoever does not have the Spirit of Christ does not belong to him. But if Christ is in you, although the body is dead because of sin, the spirit is alive because of righteousness. If the Spirit of the One who raised Jesus from the dead dwells in you, the One who raised Christ from the dead will give life to your mortal bodies also, through his Spirit dwelling in you.

GOSPEL *John 11:3–7, 17, 20–27, 33b–45*
Longer: John 11:1–45

The sisters of Lazarus sent word to Jesus, saying, "Master, the one you love is ill." When Jesus heard this he said, "This illness is not to end in death, but is for the glory of God, that the Son of God may be glorified through it." Now Jesus loved Martha and her sister and Lazarus. So when he heard that he was ill, he remained for two days in the place where he was. Then after this he said to his disciples, "Let us go back to Judea."

When Jesus arrived, he found that Lazarus had already been in the tomb for four days. When Martha heard that Jesus was coming, she went to meet him; but Mary sat at home. Martha said to Jesus, "Lord, if you had been here, my brother would not have died. But even now I know that whatever you ask of God, God will give you." Jesus said to her, "Your brother will rise." Martha said, "I know he will rise, in the resurrection on the last day." Jesus told her, "I am the resurrection and the life; whoever believes in me, even if he dies, will live, and everyone who lives and believes in me will never die. Do you believe this?" She said to him, "Yes, Lord. I have come to believe that you are the Christ, the Son of God, the one who is coming into the world."

He became perturbed and deeply troubled, and said, "Where have you laid him?" They said to him, "Sir, come and see." And Jesus wept. So the Jews said, "See how he loved him." But some of them said, "Could not the one who opened the eyes of the blind man have done something so that this man would not have died?"

So Jesus, perturbed again, came to the tomb. It was a cave, and a stone lay across it. Jesus said, "Take away the stone." Martha, the dead man's sister, said to him, "Lord, by now there will be a stench; he has been dead for four days." Jesus said to her, "Did I not tell you that if you believe you will see the glory of God?" So they took away the stone. And Jesus raised his eyes and said, "Father,

I thank you for hearing me. I know that you always hear me; but because of the crowd here I have said this, that they may believe that you sent me." And when he had said this, he cried out in a loud voice, "Lazarus, come out!" The dead man came out, tied hand and foot with burial bands, and his face was wrapped in a cloth. So Jesus said to them, "Untie him and let him go."

Now many of the Jews who had come to Mary and seen what he had done began to believe in him.

Practice of Charity

By raising Lazarus from the dead, Jesus reveals the new life he brings. ♦ Each day this week, pray for those who have died. Remember especially those who died with no one to mourn them. ♦ Jesus gave up his own life out of a deep love for Lazarus and all people. Others followed in his footsteps. Learn more about a Christian martyr. How did this person also reveal and participate in God's love? ♦ When we die, our loved ones will mourn. Relieve some of their burden by preparing your will. Is there anything else you should put in place in the event of your death?

Download more questions and activities for families, initiation groups, and other adult groups at http://www.ltp.org/ahw.

Scripture Insights

Having just escaped the religious authorities' attempt to arrest him, Jesus is in retreat across the Jordan when the news about Lazarus' illness in Bethany reaches him (John 10:39—11:3, 7–8, 16). Lazarus has been buried for four days by the time Jesus arrives (John 11:17).

The passage mentions Jesus' love for Lazarus and his sisters (John 11:3, 5). It also uses a particular verb that expresses emotion, even anger—translated as "perturbed" in English—twice (John 11:33, 38), not to mention an explicit reference to Jesus himself weeping (John 11:35–36). Because of his raising of Lazarus, the religious authorities decide that they must eliminate Jesus (John 11:46–57). This story about Lazarus foreshadows, then, Jesus' death and resurrection. The cross of Jesus is related to a story that arguably expresses his love and gift of life in a most concrete way.

In response to Martha's words, which limit resurrection to "the last day," Jesus declares, "I am the resurrection and the life" (John 11:21–26). The phrase "and the life" emphasizes Jesus' gift not only as an otherworldly promise but also as a this-worldly reality. Since this phrase "and the life" is missing in some ancient Greek manuscripts, one may wonder if some ancient scribes were repeating Martha's mistake by placing a narrow focus on resurrection as something for the future. Although this story of love and resurrection begins as a story of grief (because Jesus did not get to Bethany earlier), it affirms that abundant life is available through Jesus right here and right now, even when things look dead and when Jesus seems absent (see John 14:15–27; Romans 8:8–11).

♦ This story about the three siblings and Jesus seem to link love closely with death. Where do you see these connections, and how may we understand these connections?

♦ Psalm 130 presents a waiting for God in hope. How is that similar to or different from Martha's focus on only a future "resurrection"?

♦ What feels dry and dead in this season of your life and your community's life?

March 24, 2024

Gospel at procession with palms: Mark 11:1–10 or John 12:12–16

READING I *Isaiah 50:4–7*

The Lord GOD has given me
   a well-trained tongue,
that I might know how to speak to the weary
   a word that will rouse them.
Morning after morning
   he opens my ear that I may hear;
and I have not rebelled,
   have not turned back.
I gave my back to those who beat me,
   my cheeks to those who plucked my beard;
my face I did not shield
   from buffets and spitting.

The Lord GOD is my help,
   therefore I am not disgraced;
I have set my face like flint,
   knowing that I shall not be put to shame.

RESPONSORIAL PSALM *Psalm 22:8–9, 17–18, 19–20, 23–24 (2a)*

R. My God, my God, why have you
   abandoned me?

All who see me scoff at me;
   they mock me with parted lips,
      they wag their heads:
"He relied on the LORD; let him deliver him,
   let him rescue him, if he loves him."   R.

Indeed, many dogs surround me,
   a pack of evildoers closes in upon me;
they have pierced my hands and my feet;
   I can count all my bones.   R.

They divide my garments among them,
   and for my vesture they cast lots.
But you, O LORD, be not far from me;
   O my help, hasten to aid me.   R.

I will proclaim your name to my brethren;
   in the midst of the assembly I will praise you:
"You who fear the LORD, praise him;
   all you descendants of Jacob, give glory to him;
   revere him, all you descendants of Israel!"   R.

READING II *Philippians 2:6–11*

Christ Jesus, though he was in the form of God,
  did not regard equality with God
  something to be grasped.
Rather, he emptied himself,
  taking the form of a slave,
  coming in human likeness;
  and found human in appearance,
he humbled himself,
  becoming obedient to the point of death,
  even death on a cross.
Because of this, God greatly exalted him
  and bestowed on him the name
  which is above every name,
  that at the name of Jesus
  every knee should bend,
  of those in heaven and on earth and under
    the earth,
  and every tongue confess that
Jesus Christ is Lord,
  to the glory of God the Father.

GOSPEL *Mark 14:1—15:47*

Shorter: Mark 15:1–39

The Passover and the Feast of Unleavened Bread were to take place in two days' time. So the chief priests and the scribes were seeking a way to arrest him by treachery and put him to death. They said, "Not during the festival, for fear that there may be a riot among the people."

When he was in Bethany reclining at table in the house of Simon the leper, a woman came with an alabaster jar of perfumed oil, costly genuine spikenard. She broke the alabaster jar and poured it on his head. There were some who were indignant. "Why has there been this waste of perfumed oil? It could have been sold for more than three hundred days' wages and the money given to the poor." They were infuriated with her. Jesus said, "Let her alone. Why do you make trouble for her? She has done a good thing for me. The poor you will always have with you, and whenever you wish you can do good to them, but you will not always have me. She has done what she could. She has anticipated anointing my body for burial. Amen, I say to you, wherever the gospel is proclaimed to the whole world, what she has done will be told in memory of her."

Then Judas Iscariot, one of the Twelve, went off to the chief priests to hand him over to them. When they heard him they were pleased and promised to pay him money. Then he looked for an opportunity to hand him over.

On the first day of the Feast of Unleavened Bread, when they sacrificed the Passover lamb, his disciples said to him, "Where do you want us to go and prepare for you to eat the Passover?" He sent two of his disciples and said to them, "Go into the city and a man will meet you, carrying a jar of water. Follow him. Wherever he enters, say to the master of the house, 'The Teacher says, "Where is my guest room where I may eat the Passover with my disciples?"' Then he will show you a large upper room furnished and ready. Make the preparations for us there." The disciples then went off, entered the city, and found it just as he had told them; and they prepared the Passover.

When it was evening, he came with the Twelve. And as they reclined at table and were eating, Jesus said, "Amen, I say to you, one of you will betray me, one who is eating with me." They began to be distressed and to say to him, one by one, "Surely it is not I?" He said to them, "One of the Twelve, the one who dips with me into the dish. For the Son of Man indeed goes, as it is written of him, but woe to that man by whom the Son of Man is betrayed. It would be better for that man if he had never been born."

While they were eating, he took bread, said the blessing, broke it, and gave it to them, and said, "Take it; this is my body." Then he took a cup, gave thanks, and gave it to them, and they all drank from it. He said to them, "This is my blood of the covenant, which will be shed for many. Amen, I say to you, I shall not drink again the fruit of the vine until the day when I drink it new in the kingdom of God." Then, after singing a hymn, they went out to the Mount of Olives.

Then Jesus said to them, "All of you will have your faith shaken, for it is written:

I will strike the shepherd,
and the sheep will be dispersed.

But after I have been raised up, I shall go before you to Galilee." Peter said to him, "Even though all should have their faith shaken, mine will not be." Then Jesus said to him, "Amen, I say to you, this very night before the cock crows twice you will deny me three times." But he vehemently replied, "Even though I should have to die with you, I will not deny you." And they all spoke similarly.

Then they came to a place named Gethsemane, and he said to his disciples, "Sit here while I pray." He took with him Peter, James, and John, and began to be troubled and distressed. Then he said to them, "My soul is sorrowful even to death. Remain here and keep watch." He advanced a little and fell to the ground and prayed that if it were possible the hour might pass by him; he said, "Abba, Father, all things are possible to you. Take this cup away from me, but not what I will but what you will." When he returned he found them asleep. He said to Peter, "Simon, are you asleep? Could you not keep watch for one hour? Watch and pray that you may not undergo the test. The spirit is willing but the flesh is weak." Withdrawing again, he prayed, saying the same thing. Then he returned once more and found them asleep, for they could not keep their eyes open and did not know what to answer him. He returned a third time and said to them, "Are you still sleeping and taking your rest? It is enough. The hour has come. Behold, the Son of Man is to be handed over to sinners. Get up, let us go. See, my betrayer is at hand."

Then, while he was still speaking, Judas, one of the Twelve, arrived, accompanied by a crowd with swords and clubs who had come from the chief priests, the scribes, and the elders. His betrayer had arranged a signal with them, saying, "The man I shall kiss is the one; arrest him and lead him away securely." He came and immediately went over to him and said, "Rabbi." And he kissed him. At this they laid hands on him and arrested him. One of the bystanders drew his sword, struck the high priest's servant, and cut off his ear. Jesus said to them in reply, "Have you come out as against a robber, with swords and clubs, to seize me? Day after day I was with you teaching in the temple area, yet you did not arrest me; but that the Scriptures may be fulfilled." And they all left him and fled. Now a young man followed him wearing nothing but a linen cloth about his body. They seized him, but he left the cloth behind and ran off naked.

They led Jesus away to the high priest, and all the chief priests and the elders and the scribes came together. Peter followed him at a distance into the high priest's courtyard and was seated with the guards, warming himself at the fire. The chief priests and the entire Sanhedrin kept trying to obtain testimony against Jesus in order to put him to death, but they found none. Many gave false witness against him, but their testimony did not agree. Some took the stand and testified falsely against him, alleging, "We heard him say, 'I will destroy this temple made with hands and within three days I will build another not made with hands.'" Even so their testimony did not agree. The high priest rose before the assembly and questioned Jesus, saying, "Have you no answer? What are these men testifying against you?" But he was silent and answered nothing. Again the high priest asked him and said to him, "Are you the Christ, the son of the Blessed One?" Then Jesus answered, "I am;

and 'you will see the Son of Man
    seated at the right hand of the Power
    and coming with the clouds of heaven.'"

At that the high priest tore his garments and said, "What further need have we of witnesses? You have heard the blasphemy. What do you think?" They all condemned him as deserving to die. Some began to spit on him. They blindfolded him and struck him and said to him, "Prophesy!" And the guards greeted him with blows.

While Peter was below in the courtyard, one of the high priest's maids came along. Seeing Peter warming himself, she looked intently at him and said, "You too were with the Nazarene, Jesus." But he denied it saying, "I neither know nor understand what you are talking about." So he went out into the outer court. Then the cock crowed. The maid saw him and began again to say to the bystanders, "This man is one of them." Once again he denied it. A little later the bystanders said to Peter once more, "Surely you are one of them; for you too are a Galilean." He began to curse and to swear, "I do not know this man about whom you are talking." And immediately a cock crowed a second time. Then Peter remembered the word that Jesus had said to him, "Before the cock crows twice you will deny me three times." He broke down and wept.

As soon as morning came, the chief priests with the elders and the scribes, that is, the whole Sanhedrin held a council. They bound Jesus, led him away, and handed him over to Pilate. Pilate questioned him, "Are you the king of the Jews?"

He said to him in reply, "You say so." The chief priests accused him of many things. Again Pilate questioned him, "Have you no answer? See how many things they accuse you of." Jesus gave him no further answer, so that Pilate was amazed.

Now on the occasion of the feast he used to release to them one prisoner whom they requested. A man called Barabbas was then in prison along with the rebels who had committed murder in a rebellion. The crowd came forward and began to ask him to do for them as he was accustomed. Pilate answered, "Do you want me to release to you the king of the Jews?" For he knew that it was out of envy that the chief priests had handed him over. But the chief priests stirred up the crowd to have him release Barabbas for them instead. Pilate again said to them in reply, "Then what do you want me to do with the man you call the king of the Jews?" They shouted again, "Crucify him." Pilate said to them, "Why? What evil has he done?" They only shouted the louder, "Crucify him." So Pilate, wishing to satisfy the crowd, released Barabbas to them and, after he had Jesus scourged, handed him over to be crucified.

The soldiers led him away inside the palace, that is, the praetorium, and assembled the whole cohort. They clothed him in purple and, weaving a crown of thorns, placed it on him. They began to salute him with, "Hail, King of the Jews!" and kept striking his head with a reed and spitting upon him. They knelt before him in homage. And when they had mocked him, they stripped him of the purple cloak, dressed him in his own clothes, and led him out to crucify him.

They pressed into service a passer-by, Simon, a Cyrenian, who was coming in from the country, the father of Alexander and Rufus, to carry his cross.

They brought him to the place of Golgotha—which is translated Place of the Skull—. They gave him wine drugged with myrrh, but he did not take it. Then they crucified him and divided his garments by casting lots for them to see what each should take. It was nine o'clock in the morning when they crucified him. The inscription of the charge against him read, "The King of the Jews."

With him they crucified two revolutionaries, one on his right and one on his left. Those passing by reviled him, shaking their heads and saying, "Aha! You who would destroy the temple and rebuild it in three days, save yourself by coming down from the cross." Likewise the chief priests, with the scribes, mocked him among themselves and said, "He saved others; he cannot save himself. Let the Christ, the King of Israel, come down now from the cross that we may see and believe." Those who were crucified with him also kept abusing him.

At noon darkness came over the whole land until three in the afternoon. And at three o'clock Jesus cried out in a loud voice, *"Eloi, Eloi, lema sabachthani?"* which is translated, "My God, my God, why have you forsaken me?" Some of the bystanders who heard it said, "Look, he is calling Elijah." One of them ran, soaked a sponge with wine, put it on a reed and gave it to him to drink saying, "Wait, let us see if Elijah comes to take him down." Jesus gave a loud cry and breathed his last.

[Here all kneel and pray for a short time.]

The veil of the sanctuary was torn in two from top to bottom. When the centurion who stood facing him saw how he breathed his last he said, "Truly this man was the Son of God!" There were also women looking on from a distance. Among them were Mary Magdalene, Mary the mother of the younger James and of Joses, and Salome. These women had followed him when he was in Galilee and ministered to him. There were also many other women who had come up with him to Jerusalem.

When it was already evening, since it was the day of preparation, the day before the sabbath, Joseph of Arimathea, a distinguished member of the council, who was himself awaiting the kingdom of God, came and courageously went to Pilate and asked for the body of Jesus. Pilate was amazed that he was already dead. He summoned the centurion and asked him if Jesus had already died. And when he learned of it from the centurion, he gave the body to Joseph. Having bought a linen cloth, he took him down, wrapped him in the linen cloth, and laid him in a tomb that had been hewn out of the rock. Then he rolled a stone against the entrance to the tomb. Mary Magdalene and Mary the mother of Joses watched where he was laid.

Practice of Charity

Jesus' passion and death is ultimately a love story. ◆ As you move through this story, imagine being with Jesus. How does he seem to you at each stage of his passion? Do you ask him anything? If so, how does he reply? ◆ Many people pray the Stations of the Cross during Lent and Holy Week. How much do you know about the history of the stations and the ancient practice of pilgrimage? You can read more at https://www.vatican.va/news _services/liturgy/documents/ns_lit_doc_via-crucis _en.html. Your parish may have informative resources on the stations. ◆ If you know someone in your community who is grieving the death of a loved one, ask that person if a visit from you would be welcome to share stories and memories. You could also offer to pray the Rosary together.

Download more questions and activities for families, initiation groups, and other adult groups at http://www.ltp.org/ahw.

Scripture Insights

The context of the Passover underscores the mission of Jesus: to deliver humans from oppressive power. We see this conflict between Jesus and established power in spatial terms. Jesus is in Bethany, his preferred home base even after his arrival in Jerusalem, the center of power for Jews (Mark 11:1, 11, 12). Furthermore, he is at the home of an outcast in Bethany: "Simon the leper" (Mark 14:3).

At Simon's house, an anonymous woman anoints Jesus, who explicitly associates this gesture with his burial, thus signifying that the divine reign he inaugurates is by means of death rather than domination (see Philippians 2:6–11).

Jesus states that the woman's act will be told "in memory of her" wherever the Gospel is proclaimed (Mark 14:9), even or especially when her name is unknown. Discipleship means putting oneself aside to be in solidarity with the outcast to help bring about liberation. Although we know the names of several disciples in these two chapters, the Gospel is not told "in memory of" them because their actions are for personal gain or for self-preservation.

Betrayed, denied, or abandoned by his male disciples (see also Mark 13:12), Jesus cries out to God by quoting from the beginning of Psalm 22 (Mark 15:34; Psalm 22:2). When the soldiers parcel out Jesus' clothing by casting lots (Mark 15:24) and when those passing by mock the crucified Jesus (Mark 15:29), Mark's Gospel is also referring to Psalm 22 (see Psalm 22:18 and 22:6–8, respectively). Although this psalm focuses on the experience of one who has been abandoned, it concludes by affirming God's rescue (Psalm 22:19–24).

◆ How may we prevent a reading of Mark 14:4–7 as a license for not addressing poverty?

◆ What exactly did the Roman centurion see that led him to utter an unexpected confession of faith in Mark 15:39?

◆ What is the difference between self-promotion, self-preservation, self-effacement, self-denial, and acting against self-interest?

Holy Thursday brings to an end the forty days of Lent, which make up the season of anticipation of the great Three Days. Composed of prayer, almsgiving, fasting, and the preparation of the catechumens for baptism, the season of Lent is now brought to a close, and the Three Days begin as we approach the liturgy of Holy Thursday evening. As those to be initiated into the Church have prepared themselves for their entrance into the fullness of life, so have we been awakening in our hearts, minds, and bodies our own entrances into the life of Christ, experienced in the life of the Church.

The Sacred Paschal Triduum (Latin for "three days") is the center, the core, of the entire year for Christians. These Three Days mark the mystery around which our entire lives are played out. Adults in the community are invited to plan ahead so that the whole time from Thursday night until Easter Sunday is free of social engagements, free of entertainment, and free of meals except for the most basic nourishment. We measure these days—indeed, our very salvation in the life of God—in step with the catechumens themselves; we are revitalized as we support them along the way and participate in their initiation rites.

We are asked to fast on Good Friday and to continue fasting, if possible, all through Holy Saturday as strictly as we can so that we come to the Easter Vigil hungry and full of excitement, parched and longing to feel the sacred water of the font on our skin. We pare down distractions on Good Friday and Holy Saturday so that we may be free for prayer and anticipation, for reflection, preparation, and silence. The Church is getting ready for the great night of the Easter Vigil.

As one who has been initiated into the Church, as one whose life has been wedded to this community gathered at the table, you should anticipate the Triduum with concentration and vigor. With you, the whole Church knows that our presence for the liturgies of the Triduum is not just an invitation. Everyone is needed. We pull out all the stops for these days. As humans, wedded to humanity by the joys and travails of life and grafted onto the body of the Church by the sanctifying waters of Baptism, we lead the new members into new life in this community of faith.

To this end, the Three Days are seen not as three distinct liturgies, but as one movement. These days have been connected liturgically from the early days of the Christian Church. As members of this community, we should be personally committed to preparing for and attending the Triduum and its culmination in the Easter Vigil of Holy Saturday.

The Church proclaims the direction of the Triduum with the opening antiphon of Holy Thursday, which comes from Paul's Letter to the Galatians (6:14). With this verse the Church sets a spiritual environment into which we as committed Christians enter the Triduum:

We should glory in the Cross
of our Lord Jesus Christ,
in whom is our salvation, life and resurrection,
through whom we are saved and delivered.

HOLY THURSDAY

On Thursday evening we enter into this Triduum together. Whether presider, lector, preacher, greeter, altar server, minister of the Eucharist, decorator, or person in the remote corner in the last pew of the church, we begin, as always, by hearkening to the Word of God. These are the Scriptures for the liturgy of Holy Thursday:

Exodus 12:1–8, 11–14
Ancient instructions for the meal of the Passover.

1 Corinthians 11:23–26
Eat the bread and drink the cup until the return of the Lord.

John 13:1–15
Jesus washes the feet of the disciples.

Then the priest, like Jesus, does something strange: he washes feet. Jesus gave us this image of what the Church is supposed to look like, feel like, act like. Our position—whether as observer, washer or washed, servant or served—may be difficult. Yet we learn from the discomfort, from the awkwardness.

Then we celebrate the Eucharist. Because it is connected to the other liturgies of the Triduum on Good Friday and Holy Saturday night, the evening liturgy of Holy Thursday has no ending. Whether we stay to pray awhile or leave, we are now in the quiet, peace, and glory of the Triduum.

GOOD FRIDAY

We gather quietly in community on Friday and again listen to the Word of God:

Isaiah 52:13—53:12
The servant of the Lord was crushed for our sins.

Hebrews 4:14–16; 5:7–9
The Son of God learned obedience through his suffering.

John 18:1—19:42
The passion of Jesus Christ.

After the homily, we pray at length for all the world's needs: for the Church; for the pope, the clergy and all the baptized; for those preparing for initiation; for the unity of Christians; for Jews; for non-Christians; for atheists; for all in public office; and for those in special need.

Then there is another once-a-year event: the holy cross is held up in our midst, and we come forward one by one to do reverence with a kiss, bow, or genuflection. This communal reverence of an instrument of torture recalls the painful price, in the past and today, of salvation, the way in which our redemption is wrought, the scourging and humiliation of Jesus Christ that bring direction and life back to a humanity that is lost and dead. During the adoration of the cross, we sing not only of the sorrow, but of the glory of the cross by which we have been saved.

Again, we bring to mind the words of Paul (Galatians 6:14), on which last night's entrance antiphon is loosely based: "May I never boast except in the cross of our Lord Jesus Christ, through which the world has been crucified to me, and I to the world."

We continue in fasting and prayer and vigil, in rest and quiet, through Saturday. This Saturday for us is God's rest at the end of creation. It is Christ's repose in the tomb. It is Christ's visit with the dead.

EASTER VIGIL

Hungry now, pared down to basics, lightheaded from vigilance and full of excitement, we, the already baptized, gather in darkness and light a new fire. From this blaze we light a great candle that will make this night bright for us and will burn throughout Easter Time.

We hearken again to the Word of God with some of the most powerful narratives and proclamations of our tradition:

Genesis 1:1—2:2
The creation of the world.

Genesis 22:1–18
The sacrifice of Isaac.

Exodus 14:15—15:1
The crossing of the Red Sea.

Isaiah 54:5–14
You will not be afraid.

Isaiah 55:1–11
Come, come to the water.

Baruch 3:9–15, 32—4:4
Walk by the light of wisdom.

Ezekiel 36:16–17a, 18–28
The Lord says: I will sprinkle water.

Romans 6:3–11
United with him in death.

Year A: Matthew 28:1–10, Year B: Mark 16:1–7, Year C: Luke 24:1–12
Jesus has been raised.

After the readings, we call on our saints to stand with us as we go to the font and the priest celebrant blesses the waters. The chosen of all times and all places attend to what is about to take place. The elect renounce evil, profess the faith of the Church, and are baptized and anointed.

All of us renew our baptismal promises. These are the moments when death and life meet, when we reject evil and make our promises to God. All of this is in the communion of the Church. So together we go to the table and celebrate the Easter Eucharist.

Easter Time

Prayer before Reading the Word

God of all creation,
whose mighty power raised Jesus from the dead,
be present to this community of disciples
whom you have called to the hope
of a glorious inheritance among the saints.
As we hear the Word that brings salvation,
make our hearts burn within us,
that we may recognize Christ crucified and risen,
who opens our hearts to
      understand the Scriptures,
who is made known to us in the breaking
      of the bread,
and who lives and reigns with you
in the unity of the Holy Spirit,
God, for ever and ever. Amen.

Prayer after Reading the Word

O God of Easter glory,
gather your baptized people
around the teaching of the apostles,
devoted to the life we share in the Church,
devoted to the breaking of the bread.
Make us so embrace the name of Christ,
that we glorify you in the world
and bear witness to your Word
made known to us by Jesus,
our Passover and our peace,
who lives and reigns with you
in the unity of the Holy Spirit,
God, for ever and ever. Amen.

Weekday Readings

April 1: Monday within the Octave of Easter
Acts 2:14, 22–33; Matthew 28:8–15
April 2: Tuesday within the Octave of Easter
Acts 2:36–41; John 20:11–18
April 3: Wednesday within the Octave of Easter
Acts 3:1–10; Luke 24:13–35
April 4: Thursday within the Octave of Easter
Acts 3:11–26; Luke 24:35–48
April 5: Friday within the Octave of Easter
Acts 4:1–12; John 21:1–14
April 6: Saturday within the Octave of Easter
Acts 4:13–21; Mark 16:9–15

April 8: Solemnity of the Annunciation of the Lord
Isaiah 7:10–14; 8:10; Hebrews 10:4–10; Luke 1:26–38
April 9: Acts 4:32–37; John 3:7b–15
April 10: *Acts 5:17–26; John 3:16–21*
April 11: *Acts 5:27–33; John 3:31–36*
April 12: *Acts 5:34–42; John 6:1–15*
April 13: *Acts 6:1–7; John 6:16–21*

April 15: *Acts 6:8–15; John 6:22–29*
April 16: *Acts 7:51—8:1a; John 6:30–35*
April 17: *Acts 8:1b–8; John 6:35–40*
April 18: *Acts 8:26–40; John 6:44–51*
April 19: *Acts 9:1–20; John 6:52–59*
April 20: *Acts 9:31–42; John 6:60–69*

April 22: *Acts 11:1–18; John 10:1–10*
April 23: *Acts 11:19–26; John 10:22–30*
April 24: *Acts 12:24—13:5a; John 12:44–50*
April 25: Feast of St. Mark, Evangelist
1 Peter 5:5b–14; Mark 16:15–20
April 26: *Acts 13:26–33; John 14:1–6*
April 27: *Acts 13:44–52; John 14:7–14*

April 29: *Acts 14:5–18; John 14:21–26*
April 30: *Acts 14:19–28; John 14:27–31a*
May 1: *Acts 15:1–6; John 15:1–8*
May 2: *Acts 15:7–21; John 15:9–11*
May 3: Feast of Sts. Philip and James, Apostles
1 Corinthians 15:1–8; John 14:6–14
May 4: *Acts 16:1–10; John 15:18–21*

May 6: *Acts 16:11–15; John 15:26—16:4a*
May 7: *Acts 16:22–34; John 16:5–11*
May 8: *Acts 17:15, 22—18:1; John 16:12–15*
May 9: Solemnity of the Ascension of the Lord
   [Ecclesiastical Provinces of Boston, Hartford,
   New York, Newark, Omaha, and Philadelphia]
Acts 1:1–11; Ephesians 1:17–23 or Ephesians 4:1–13 or
   4:1–7, 11–13; Mark 16:15–20
(If the Ascension of the Lord is celebrated on the following
   Sunday, then):
May 9: *Acts 18:1–8; John 16:16–20*
May 10: *Acts 18:9–18; John 16:20–23*
May 11: *Acts 18:23–28; John 16:23b–28*

May 13: *Acts 19:1–8; John 16:29–33*
May 14: Feast of St. Matthias, Apostle
Acts 1:15–17, 20–26; John 15:9–17
May 15: *Acts 20:28–38; John 17:11b–19*
May 16: *Acts 22:30; 23:6–11; John 17:20–26*
May 17: *Acts 25:13b–21; John 21:15–19*
May 18: *Acts 28:16–20, 30–31; John 21:20–25*

READING I *Acts 10:34a, 37–43*

Peter proceeded to speak and said: "You know what has happened all over Judea, beginning in Galilee after the baptism that John preached, how God anointed Jesus of Nazareth with the Holy Spirit and power. He went about doing good and healing all those oppressed by the devil, for God was with him. We are witnesses of all that he did both in the country of the Jews and in Jerusalem. They put him to death by hanging him on a tree. This man God raised on the third day and granted that he be visible, not to all the people, but to us, the witnesses chosen by God in advance, who ate and drank with him after he rose from the dead. He commissioned us to preach to the people and testify that he is the one appointed by God as judge of the living and the dead. To him all the prophets bear witness, that everyone who believes in him will receive forgiveness of sins through his name."

RESPONSORIAL PSALM
Psalm 118:1–2, 16–17, 22–23 (24)

R. This is the day the Lord has made;
    let us rejoice and be glad.

or: Alleluia.

Give thanks to the LORD, for he is good,
    for his mercy endures forever.
Let the house of Israel say,
    "His mercy endures forever." R.

"The right hand of the LORD
        has struck with power;
    the right hand of the LORD is exalted.
I shall not die, but live,
    and declare the works of the LORD." R.

The stone which the builders rejected
    has become the cornerstone.
By the LORD has this been done;
    it is wonderful in our eyes. R.

READING II *Colossians 3:1–4*

Alternate: 1 Corinthians 5:6b–8

Brothers and sisters: If then you were raised with Christ, seek what is above, where Christ is seated at the right hand of God. Think of what is above, not of what is on earth. For you have died, and your life is hidden with Christ in God. When Christ your life appears, then you too will appear with him in glory.

GOSPEL *John 20:1–9*

Alternates: Mark 16:1–7; or at an afternoon or evening Mass: Luke 24:13–35

On the first day of the week, Mary of Magdala came to the tomb early in the morning, while it was still dark, and saw the stone removed from the tomb. So she ran and went to Simon Peter and to the other disciple whom Jesus loved, and told them, "They have taken the Lord from the tomb, and we don't know where they put him." So Peter and the other disciple went out and came to the tomb. They both ran, but the other disciple ran faster than Peter and arrived at the tomb first; he bent down and saw the burial cloths there, but did not go in. When Simon Peter arrived after him, he went into the tomb and saw the burial cloths there, and the cloth that had covered his head, not with the burial cloths but rolled up in a separate place. Then the other disciple also went in, the one who had arrived at the tomb first, and he saw and believed. For they did not yet understand the Scripture that he had to rise from the dead.

Practice of Hope

Imagine that you have come to Jesus' tomb and found it empty. Describe your surroundings. Is anyone with you? What have you experienced the past few days? How have you felt? Spend some time gazing into the tomb. What do you think and feel now? Offer a prayer beside the tomb. ◆ At Mass during the Easter season we hear from the Acts of the Apostles. Read the introduction to this book in a Catholic Bible or choose one of the apostles and discover what Church tradition tells us this person said and did after Jesus' resurrection. ◆ Although many people think of Easter as being only one day, Catholics celebrate this solemnity for a whole week before continuing into the Easter season. ◆ Try to go to daily Mass at least once this week. Let the readings renew your hope for salvation.

Download more questions and activities for families, initiation groups, and other adult groups at http://www.ltp.org/ahw.

Scripture Insights

Acts 10 emphasizes our roles as witnesses to share the Good News of Jesus' resurrection, but there are times when we struggle to understand the meaning of the empty tomb.

Not only is the word *tomb* repeated seven times in today's Gospel reading, but the gloomy mood is already set with Mary Magdalene going to the tomb "while it was still dark" (John 20:1).

Mary Magdalene sees the open tomb and concludes that some people have removed Jesus' body, so she runs to inform Peter and the "other disciple whom Jesus loved" (John 20:1–2), who may represent Gentile or Johannine Christianity, or everyone who is loved by Jesus. When Peter and the beloved disciple take turns to enter the empty tomb, they only see linen wrappings and a face cloth, which is neatly "rolled up in a separate place" (John 20:7). This signals that the empty tomb is not a result of theft or robbery.

Upon entering the empty tomb, the beloved disciple "saw and believed" (John 20:8), but we are not told exactly what he believed. Things become even more baffling when we next read that "they did not yet understand the Scripture that he had to rise from the dead" (John 20:9). The change to a plural third-person pronoun logically includes both Peter and the beloved disciple, although we read nothing about Peter's reaction of belief. We also don't know if Mary even went into the empty tomb.

Three disciples came to the empty tomb after Jesus' resurrection. They did not see any angels or receive any messages. One saw an open tomb and jumped to a wrong conclusion. Two saw the strips of cloth inside the tomb and left without understanding, even though one is said to have believed.

◆ Why does John's Gospel give us the details about a footrace to the empty tomb?

◆ Why does our Gospel reading end at John 20:9 rather than continuing with the passage where the resurrected Jesus appears to Mary Magdalene and calls her by name?

◆ In the liminal space between an empty tomb and the appearance of the resurrected Jesus, what do you see or need to understand?

READING I   *Acts 4:32–35*

The community of believers was of one heart and mind, and no one claimed that any of his possessions was his own, but they had everything in common. With great power the apostles bore witness to the resurrection of the Lord Jesus, and great favor was accorded them all. There was no needy person among them, for those who owned property or houses would sell them, bring the proceeds of the sale, and put them at the feet of the apostles, and they were distributed to each according to need.

RESPONSORIAL PSALM
Psalm 118:2–4, 13–15, 22–24 (1)

R. Give thanks to the Lord, for he is good; his
    love is everlasting.
  or: Alleluia.

Let the house of Israel say,
  "His mercy endures forever."
Let the house of Aaron say,
  "His mercy endures forever."
Let those who fear the LORD say,
  "His mercy endures forever."   R.

I was hard pressed and was falling,
  but the LORD helped me.
My strength and my courage is the LORD,
  and he has been my savior.
The joyful shout of victory
  in the tents of the just.   R.

The stone which the builders rejected
  has become the cornerstone.
By the LORD has this been done;
  it is wonderful in our eyes.
This is the day the LORD has made;
  let us be glad and rejoice in it.   R.

READING II   *1 John 5:1–6*

Beloved: Everyone who believes that Jesus is the Christ is begotten by God, and everyone who loves the Father loves also the one begotten by him. In this way we know that we love the children of God when we love God and obey his commandments.

For the love of God is this, that we keep his commandments. And his commandments are not burdensome, for whoever is begotten by God conquers the world. And the victory that conquers the world is our faith. Who indeed is the victor over the world but the one who believes that Jesus is the Son of God?

This is the one who came through water and blood, Jesus Christ, not by water alone, but by water and blood. The Spirit is the one that testifies, and the Spirit is truth.

GOSPEL   *John 20:19–31*

On the evening of that first day of the week, when the doors were locked, where the disciples were, for fear of the Jews, Jesus came and stood in their midst and said to them, "Peace be with you." When he had said this, he showed them his hands and his side. The disciples rejoiced when they saw the Lord. Jesus said to them again, "Peace be with you. As the Father has sent me, so I send you." And when he had said this, he breathed on them and said to them, "Receive the Holy Spirit. Whose sins you forgive are forgiven them, and whose sins you retain are retained."

Thomas, called Didymus, one of the Twelve, was not with them when Jesus came. So the other disciples said to him, "We have seen the Lord." But he said to them, "Unless I see the mark of the nails in his hands and put my finger into the nailmarks and put my hand into his side, I will not believe."

Now a week later his disciples were again inside and Thomas was with them. Jesus came, although the doors were locked, and stood in their midst and said, "Peace be with you." Then he said to Thomas, "Put your finger here and see my hands, and bring your hand and put it into my side, and do not be unbelieving, but believe." Thomas answered and said to him, "My Lord and my God!" Jesus said to him, "Have you come to believe because you have seen me? Blessed are those who have not seen and have believed."

Now Jesus did many other signs in the presence of his disciples that are not written in this book. But these are written that you may come to believe that Jesus is the Christ, the Son of God, and that through this belief you may have life in his name.

Practice of Charity

"Blessed are those who have not seen and have believed." Do you believe easily, or do you sometimes doubt that God is with you? ◆ Ask for St. Thomas' intercession as you bring your concerns to God. Imagine yourself in the upper room, seeing the risen Jesus and receiving the peace he offers you. ◆ On the Second Sunday of Easter we also celebrate the Sunday of Divine Mercy. What do you know about this day? Read more at www .usccb.org/prolife/divine-mercy-sunday. ◆ Out of devotion to Christ and his Church early converts brought their material wealth to the apostles. Review your monthly household budget. Are you making a suitable financial contribution to your parish?

Download more questions and activities for families, initiation groups, and other adult groups at http://www.ltp.org/ahw.

Scripture Insights

Today's Gospel reading gives us much more to consider besides the question of doubt. Jesus shows his hands and side twice in this Gospel. Before responding to Thomas' request (John 20:24–28), Jesus volunteered to do so a week earlier (John 20:20) for two purposes: (1) to authenticate that he is indeed the crucified Jesus; and (2) to confirm that he is not an apparition.

Surprisingly, the disciples are still hiding behind locked or closed doors when the resurrected Jesus shows up the second time, since the verbs about the doors being locked or closed are the same in John 20:19, 26. Are they afraid that they will suffer what Jesus suffered? Although these two resurrection appearances emphasize the wounds he suffered from the Roman Empire, they simultaneously announce that resurrection faith is about believing in life even when traumatic deaths and losses surround us (John 20:31). The resurrected Jesus visits them and sends them out into the world with the Holy Spirit and his peace to tell the world that there is life amid sin and death (John 20:19, 21–23, 26).

Our other New Testament readings provide beautiful pictures of the post-Easter community. Among themselves, the disciples share their possessions (Acts 4:32, 34–35). Nevertheless, they are not an in-grown community that ignores the rest of the world. They testify to Jesus' resurrection "with great power" (Acts 4:33), because their faith in Jesus and in life is more powerful than all the powers of this world (1 John 5:1–6).

◆ Jesus was crucified by the Romans and John's Gospel is clear that the Romans were the only ones who had the power to kill (John 18:31). Then why are the disciples said to be afraid of "the Jews" (John 20:19)?

◆ Does the reference to the time of the resurrected Jesus' first appearance to the disciples ("on the evening," John 20:19) have any significance, especially in light of the fact that John also has Mary Magdalene going to the empty tomb "while it was still dark" (John 20:1)?

◆ What causes us to want to lock up and lock down in fear today?

READING I *Acts 3:13–15, 17–19*

Peter said to the people: "The God of Abraham, the God of Isaac, and the God of Jacob, the God of our fathers, has glorified his servant Jesus, whom you handed over and denied in Pilate's presence when he had decided to release him. You denied the Holy and Righteous One and asked that a murderer be released to you. The author of life you put to death, but God raised him from the dead; of this we are witnesses. Now I know, brothers, that you acted out of ignorance, just as your leaders did; but God has thus brought to fulfillment what he had announced beforehand through the mouth of all the prophets, that his Christ would suffer. Repent, therefore, and be converted, that your sins may be wiped away."

RESPONSORIAL PSALM
Psalm 4:2, 4, 7–8, 9 (7a)

R. Lord, let your face shine on us.
  or: Alleluia.

When I call, answer me, O my just God,
  you who relieve me when I am in distress;
  have pity on me, and hear my prayer! R.

Know that the LORD does wonders for his
    faithful one;
  the LORD will hear me when I call
    upon him. R.

O LORD, let the light of your countenance shine
    upon us!
  You put gladness into my heart. R.

As soon as I lie down, I fall peacefully asleep,
  for you alone, O LORD,
  bring security to my dwelling. R.

READING II *1 John 2:1–5a*

My children, I am writing this to you so that you may not commit sin. But if anyone does sin, we have an Advocate with the Father, Jesus Christ the righteous one. He is expiation for our sins, and not for our sins only but for those of the whole world. The way we may be sure that we know him is to keep his commandments. Those who say, "I know him," but do not keep his commandments are liars, and the truth is not in them. But whoever keeps his word, the love of God is truly perfected in him.

GOSPEL *Luke 24:35–48*

The two disciples recounted what had taken place on the way, and how Jesus was made known to them in the breaking of bread.

While they were still speaking about this, he stood in their midst and said to them, "Peace be with you." But they were startled and terrified and thought that they were seeing a ghost. Then he said to them, "Why are you troubled? And why do questions arise in your hearts? Look at my hands and my feet, that it is I myself. Touch me and see, because a ghost does not have flesh and bones as you can see I have." And as he said this, he showed them his hands and his feet. While they were still incredulous for joy and were amazed, he asked them, "Have you anything here to eat?" They gave him a piece of baked fish; he took it and ate it in front of them.

He said to them, "These are my words that I spoke to you while I was still with you, that everything written about me in the law of Moses and in the prophets and psalms must be fulfilled." Then he opened their minds to understand the Scriptures. And he said to them, "Thus it is written that the Christ would suffer and rise from the dead on the third day and that repentance, for the forgiveness of sins, would be preached in his name to all the nations, beginning from Jerusalem. You are witnesses of these things."

Practice of Faith

Imagine eating with the risen Jesus. What would you serve him? What would you talk about? Would you laugh or be serious? ◆ Although we're called to be witnesses of the Gospel, many Catholics think of their faith as something private. Read about evangelization in the first part of Go and Make Disciples (available at www.usccb.org /beliefs-and-teachings/how-we-teach/evangelization /go-and-make-disciples/go-and-make-disciples -a-national-plan-and-strategy-for-catholic -evangelization-in-the-united-states). What new insights into evangelization does this text offer you? ◆ When Jesus appeared to his disciples, "he opened their minds to understand" (Luke 24:45). What aspects of our faith tradition do you struggle to understand? ◆ Join or form a discussion group. Invite a lay or ordained minister to offer you their insights or other resources.

Download more questions and activities for families, initiation groups, and other adult groups at http://www.ltp.org/ahw.

Scripture Insights

Luke 24:35 indicates that we should connect today's reading with its preceding passage. In both passages, we find (1) some disciples failing to recognize the resurrected Jesus because they are in doubt and disappointment over Jesus' death (Luke 24:13–24, 36–37); (2) the resurrected Jesus spends time eating with them, and uses Scripture to explain the meaning of his death and resurrection (Luke 24:25–30, 38–49); and (3) their meeting ends with Jesus leaving (Luke 24:31, 50–51).

Both passages, especially with the reference to Jesus eating with them (Luke 24:30, 41–43), underscore the reality of the resurrection. Our passage today doubles down on this emphasis with two appearances of the word *ghost* (Luke 24:37, 39) and details about the resurrected Jesus showing the disciples his hands and feet (Luke 24:39–40).

Emphasis is placed on the resurrected Jesus being "in their midst" (Luke 24:36) and "in front of them" (Luke 24:43). The reference to eating reminds us of Jesus' hospitality. He eats with people, including "tax collectors and sinners" (Luke 5:27–32; 19:1–7). He further self-identifies as a server at meals (Luke 22:27). The practice of hospitality can make our experience of the resurrected Jesus become more real, especially when we welcome people who are feared by society.

There is one more parallel between Luke 24:13–35 and 24:35–48: the disciples go and witness to the life, death, and resurrection of Jesus (Luke 24:33–35, 47–48). Peter does exactly that in Acts 3. We should follow Peter's example: listen to Jesus (1 John 2:1–5a) and serve as his witness through both our words and deeds.

◆ In both appearances of the resurrected Jesus to his disciples, the explanation and then understanding of his death and resurrection are tied to Scriptures. Why might that be significant?

◆ In our passage today, what the disciples should proclaim is specifically given. How should we understand "repentance and forgiveness of sins" (Luke 24:47)?

◆ Could the Church today be frightened, like the disciples are in Luke's Gospel, because of a visit by the resurrected Jesus? If so, why?

READING I *Acts 4:8–12*

Peter, filled with the Holy Spirit, said: "Leaders of the people and elders: If we are being examined today about a good deed done to a cripple, namely, by what means he was saved, then all of you and all the people of Israel should know that it was in the name of Jesus Christ the Nazorean whom you crucified, whom God raised from the dead; in his name this man stands before you healed. He is *the stone rejected by you, the builders, which has become the cornerstone.* There is no salvation through anyone else, nor is there any other name under heaven given to the human race by which we are to be saved."

RESPONSORIAL PSALM *Psalm 118:1, 8–9, 21–23, 26, 28, 29 (22)*

R. The stone rejected by the builders has become
the cornerstone.
or: Alleluia.

Give thanks to the LORD, for he is good,
for his mercy endures forever.
It is better to take refuge in the LORD
than to trust in man.
It is better to take refuge in the LORD
than to trust in princes. R.

I will give thanks to you, for you have
answered me
and have been my savior.
The stone which the builders rejected
has become the cornerstone.
By the LORD has this been done;
it is wonderful in our eyes. R.

Blessed is he who comes in the name of the LORD;
we bless you from the house of the LORD.
I will give thanks to you,
for you have answered me
and have been my savior.
Give thanks to the LORD, for he is good;
for his kindness endures forever. R.

READING II *1 John 3:1–2*

Beloved: See what love the Father has bestowed on us that we may be called the children of God. Yet so we are. The reason the world does not know us is that it did not know him. Beloved, we are God's children now; what we shall be has not yet been revealed. We do know that when it is revealed we shall be like him, for we shall see him as he is.

GOSPEL *John 10:11–18*

Jesus said: "I am the good shepherd. A good shepherd lays down his life for the sheep. A hired man, who is not a shepherd and whose sheep are not his own, sees a wolf coming and leaves the sheep and runs away, and the wolf catches and scatters them. This is because he works for pay and has no concern for the sheep. I am the good shepherd, and I know mine and mine know me, just as the Father knows me and I know the Father; and I will lay down my life for the sheep. I have other sheep that do not belong to this fold. These also I must lead, and they will hear my voice, and there will be one flock, one shepherd. This is why the Father loves me, because I lay down my life in order to take it up again. No one takes it from me, but I lay it down on my own. I have power to lay it down, and power to take it up again. This command I have received from my Father."

Practice of Charity

Every Fourth Sunday of Easter the Gospel passage presents Jesus as the Good Shepherd. ◆ Choose an image in your home or from the internet in which Jesus is portrayed as a shepherd. Spend time reflecting on the image. Conclude with your own prayer to Jesus, our shepherd. ◆ Do you know why we have the readings that we do each Sunday? For a deeper appreciation of the lectionary, read the introduction at the beginning of *At Home with the Word*. ◆ During the Easter season many parishes celebrate first Communion and confirmation, moments that strengthen the younger members of God's flock. Offer to help with one of these events. If the parish is hosting a reception, offer to assist with the setup or cleanup after the event.

Download more questions and activities for families, initiation groups, and other adult groups at http://www.ltp.org/ahw.

Scripture Insights

In contrast to "the hired hand" who only watches out for oneself and does not really care about the sheep (John 10:12–13), John's Jesus is willing to die for the protection and well-being of his sheep (John 10:18). Given the presence of thieves, bandits, and wolves (John 10:1, 7, 10, 12), "the good shepherd" has a dangerous job. There are attempts to stone Jesus both before and after today's passage (John 8:59; 10:31). The phrase "lay down . . . life" appears five times in this passage of eight verses.

Unlike "the hired hand" who seeks to exclude (remember how the religious leaders "drove out" the man born blind whom John's Jesus cures in John 9:34–35), "the good shepherd" seeks to enlarge his sheepfold. After stating that Jesus' sheep know him just as Jesus knows them in ways similar to the mutual knowing between Jesus and his Father (John 10:14–15; see also 10:4), Jesus states that "other sheep" will need to be introduced to and included in his sheepfold, which is characterized by its oneness (John 10:16). We, as sheep in the sheepfold, also do not get to decide who belongs and does not belong. Instead, we need to strive for unity in diversity, keeping in mind the goal of being "one flock" under "one shepherd" that is expressed in John 10:16.

John 10:17–18 identifies another motivation for the good shepherd's willingness to die for the flock: in addition to a genuine care for the safety and welfare of the sheep, Jesus acts out of a loyal and loving relationship with God.

◆ What Scriptures from the Old Testament come to mind when you read about sheep and shepherd in today's Gospel passage?

◆ Read John 10:19–21, which concludes this account. What do you make of the response of the people after hearing Jesus talk about "one flock, one shepherd" (John 10:16)? What is the significance of these last verses?

◆ Who may be "the other sheep" that we need to include in the divine sheepfold today?

READING I *Acts 9:26–31*

When Saul arrived in Jerusalem he tried to join the disciples, but they were all afraid of him, not believing that he was a disciple. Then Barnabas took charge of him and brought him to the apostles, and he reported to them how he had seen the Lord, and that he had spoken to him, and how in Damascus he had spoken out boldly in the name of Jesus. He moved about freely with them in Jerusalem, and spoke out boldly in the name of the Lord. He also spoke and debated with the Hellenists, but they tried to kill him. And when the brothers learned of this, they took him down to Caesarea and sent him on his way to Tarsus.

The church throughout all Judea, Galilee, and Samaria was at peace. It was being built up and walked in the fear of the Lord, and with the consolation of the Holy Spirit it grew in numbers.

RESPONSORIAL PSALM
Psalm 22:26–27, 28, 30, 31–32 (26a)

R. I will praise you, Lord, in the assembly
   of your people.
  or: Alleluia.

I will fulfill my vows before those who fear
   the LORD.
  The lowly shall eat their fill;
they who seek the LORD shall praise him:
  "May your hearts live forever!" R.

All the ends of the earth
   shall remember and turn to the LORD;
all the families of the nations
   shall bow down before him. R.

To him alone shall bow down
   all who sleep in the earth;
before him shall bend
   all who go down into the dust. R.

And to him my soul shall live;
   my descendants shall serve him.
Let the coming generation be told of the LORD
   that they may proclaim to a people yet
     to be born
   the justice he has shown. R.

READING II *1 John 3:18–24*

Children, let us love not in word or speech but in deed and truth.

Now this is how we shall know that we belong to the truth and reassure our hearts before him in whatever our hearts condemn, for God is greater than our hearts and knows everything. Beloved, if our hearts do not condemn us, we have confidence in God and receive from him whatever we ask, because we keep his commandments and do what pleases him. And his commandment is this: we should believe in the name of his Son, Jesus Christ, and love one another just as he commanded us. Those who keep his commandments remain in him, and he in them, and the way we know that he remains in us is from the Spirit he gave us.

GOSPEL *John 15:1–8*

Jesus said to his disciples: "I am the true vine, and my Father is the vine grower. He takes away every branch in me that does not bear fruit, and every one that does he prunes so that it bears more fruit. You are already pruned because of the word that I spoke to you. Remain in me, as I remain in you. Just as a branch cannot bear fruit on its own unless it remains on the vine, so neither can you unless you remain in me. I am the vine, you are the branches. Whoever remains in me and I in him will bear much fruit, because without me you can do nothing. Anyone who does not remain in me will be thrown out like a branch and wither; people will gather them and throw them into a fire and they will be burned. If you remain in me and my words remain in you, ask for whatever you want and it will be done for you. By this is my Father glorified, that you bear much fruit and become my disciples."

Practice of Faith

The Holy Spirit brought peace to the early Church. What parts of the world are especially in need of God's peace today? ◆ Pray the Rosary for those trapped in regions of conflict and for those working to resolve those conflicts peacefully. ◆ When Jesus speaks of himself as the true vine, we are reminded of his presence in the Eucharist. The Catholic Church's theology of the Eucharist is rich and vast. Find the *Catechism of the Catholic Church* online and see what it offers in its discussion of the Eucharist. ◆ Write cards of welcome and support to those in your faith community who became Catholic at the Easter Vigil. Invite friends in your community to sign your cards or to write their own.

Download more questions and activities for families, initiation groups, and other adult groups at http://www.ltp.org/ahw.

Scripture Insights

John 15 is part of a longer discourse by Jesus (John 14—17) to help prepare his disciples for his death.

Today's Gospel reading revolves around three figures: God as the vine grower, Jesus as the vine, and Jesus' followers as the branches. We are invited to "remain" in Jesus, which appears eight times (four times in John 15:4; once in John 15:5 and 15:6; twice in John 15:7), and to "bear fruit," which appears six times (thrice in John 15:2; once in John 15:4, 15:5, and 15:8).

The verb translated as "remain" also appears in John 14, where it is translated as "dwell" when Jesus presents God's house having many "places" for people to remain or "dwell" (John 14:2) and the divine remaining with or dwelling with Jesus (John 14:10). "Remain," then, refers to a relationship in which one feels at home, and it signifies the intimate and mutual love that exists between the Father and Jesus.

Fruitfulness as the result of "remaining" is also emphasized. The passage explains that the vine grower prunes to bring about growth and abundance. Moreover, bearing fruit is identified as a mark of discipleship (John 15:2, 8).

The imperatives in this passage—to "remain" (John 15:4) and to "ask" (John 15:7)—are related. If the result of "remaining" is bearing fruit, then what we are told or invited to "ask" may well be our fruitfulness—or something that has been pruned or cleansed by Jesus' teaching (John 15:2–3; see also 1 John 3:18–24). If we follow the metaphor, the fruits borne by branches of a vine are not for the branches' consumption but for others' use or benefit (see also Psalm 22:26–32).

◆ What may be the significance that the second-person Greek pronoun ("you") in this passage is always in the plural?

◆ How may we understand the specific meaning of bearing fruit in this passage? Does the passage in Acts 9 for today help as we consider this question?

◆ In what ways do you find the passage from Acts meaningful on this Fifth Sunday of Easter?

READING I
Acts 10:25–26, 34–35, 44–48

When Peter entered, Cornelius met him and, falling at his feet, paid him homage. Peter, however, raised him up, saying, "Get up. I myself am also a human being."

Then Peter proceeded to speak and said, "In truth, I see that God shows no partiality. Rather, in every nation whoever fears him and acts uprightly is acceptable to him."

While Peter was still speaking these things, the Holy Spirit fell upon all who were listening to the word. The circumcised believers who had accompanied Peter were astounded that the gift of the Holy Spirit should have been poured out on the Gentiles also, for they could hear them speaking in tongues and glorifying God. Then Peter responded, "Can anyone withhold the water for baptizing these people, who have received the Holy Spirit even as we have?" He ordered them to be baptized in the name of Jesus Christ.

RESPONSORIAL PSALM
Psalm 98:1, 2–3, 3–4 (see 2b)

R. The Lord has revealed to the nations his
   saving power.
 or: Alleluia.

Sing to the LORD a new song,
   for he has done wondrous deeds;
His right hand has won victory for him,
   his holy arm.   R.

The LORD has made his salvation known:
   in the sight of the nations he has revealed
      his justice.
He has remembered his kindness and
      his faithfulness
   toward the house of Israel.   R.

All the ends of the earth have seen
   the salvation by our God.
Sing joyfully to the LORD, all you lands;
   break into song; sing praise.   R.

READING II *1 John 4:7–10*

Beloved, let us love one another, because love is of God; everyone who loves is begotten by God and knows God. Whoever is without love does not know God, for God is love. In this way the love of God was revealed to us: God sent his only Son into the world so that we might have life through him. In this is love: not that we have loved God, but that he loved us and sent his Son as expiation for our sins.

GOSPEL *John 15:9–17*

Jesus said to his disciples: "As the Father loves me, so I also love you. Remain in my love. If you keep my commandments, you will remain in my love, just as I have kept my Father's commandments and remain in his love.

"I have told you this so that my joy may be in you and your joy might be complete. This is my commandment: love one another as I love you. No one has greater love than this, to lay down one's life for one's friends. You are my friends if you do what I command you. I no longer call you slaves, because a slave does not know what his master is doing. I have called you friends, because I have told you everything I have heard from my Father. It was not you who chose me, but I who chose you and appointed you to go and bear fruit that will remain, so that whatever you ask the Father in my name he may give you. This I command you: love one another."

Practice of Charity

Jesus tells us to love one another, but sometimes this commandment is hard. ◆ Each day this week pray for those whom you struggle to love. By loving others, we imitate God, who first loved us, and we invite others to become more loving people, too. ◆ Gather family members or friends. Ask them to share stories in which a loving, compassionate response to an act of wrongdoing changed the outcome of a particular situation. ◆ In the Acts of the Apostles, the Holy Spirit surprises Peter by bestowing his presence upon a Gentile household. God's Spirit is often several steps ahead of us, but we drag our feet. Peter does not resist the Spirit but accepts the Gentiles into the Church. What is the Spirit urging you to do that you've been resisting?

Download more questions and activities for families, initiation groups, and other adult groups at http://www.ltp.org/ahw.

Scripture Insights

Today's Gospel reading contains a sentence that is stated twice: the command that we love one another (see also 1 John 4:7–10). We can divide this passage into two related sections (John 15:9–12, 15:13–17), with this repeated sentence serving as the conclusion of each.

The first section emphasizes that we have a model of abiding love in Jesus. We are loved by him as he is loved by God, and we should obey his commands as he obeys God's commands. With Jesus as an example, we learn that obedience out of an abiding love brings joy (John 15:11). The concluding verse of this section (John 15:12) specifies the objects of our love and turns the plural commands or commandments of John 15:10 into a singular one: "love one another."

The second section explains what this singular love commandment means. Love is a conscious decision to act. It involves the willingness to die for one's friends (John 15:13). What is being asked of us is again based on God's and Jesus' example. This commandment of self-giving love for others may be "new" to us and for us (John 13:34), but it is something that has already been practiced and seen in God's giving of Jesus and in Jesus. The repetition of "as" or "just as" in the first section reminds us of that.

Jesus made us his friends on his own initiative (John 15:15–16). He chooses, appoints, and calls us to be his friends by opening himself up and sharing what he knows with us. Having received this gift of friendship from Jesus, it's now up to us to give this gift of love and friendship by giving of ourselves *without* limiting "friends" to other followers of Jesus.

◆ This passage mentions bearing fruit again, but it also differentiates "fruit that will remain" (John 15:16) and fruit that will not last. How should we understand these two kinds of fruit?

◆ How may the passage from Acts 10 be related to today's Gospel reading?

◆ What makes it hard for you to make friends with strangers or to love strangers?

85

READING I *Acts 1:1–11*

In the first book, Theophilus, I dealt with all that Jesus did and taught until the day he was taken up, after giving instructions through the Holy Spirit to the apostles whom he had chosen. He presented himself alive to them by many proofs after he had suffered, appearing to them during forty days and speaking about the kingdom of God. While meeting with them, he enjoined them not to depart from Jerusalem, but to wait for "the promise of the Father about which you have heard me speak; for John baptized with water, but in a few days you will be baptized with the Holy Spirit."

When they had gathered together they asked him, "Lord, are you at this time going to restore the kingdom to Israel?" He answered them, "It is not for you to know the times or seasons that the Father has established by his own authority. But you will receive power when the Holy Spirit comes upon you, and you will be my witnesses in Jerusalem, throughout Judea and Samaria, and to the ends of the earth." When he had said this, as they were looking on, he was lifted up, and a cloud took him from their sight. While they were looking intently at the sky as he was going, suddenly two men dressed in white garments stood beside them. They said, "Men of Galilee, why are you standing there looking at the sky? This Jesus who has been taken up from you into heaven will return in the same way as you have seen him going into heaven."

RESPONSORIAL PSALM
Psalm 47:2–3, 6–7, 8–9 (6)

R. God mounts his throne to shouts of joy:
   a blare of trumpets for the Lord.
 or: Alleluia.

All you peoples, clap your hands,
   shout to God with cries of gladness.
For the LORD, the Most High, the awesome,
   is the great king over all the earth.   R.

God mounts his throne amid shouts of joy;
   the LORD, amid trumpet blasts.
Sing praise to God, sing praise;
   sing praise to our king, sing praise.   R.

For king of all the earth is God;
   sing hymns of praise.
God reigns over the nations,
   God sits upon his holy throne.   R.

READING II *Ephesians 4:1–13*

Shorter: Ephesians 4:1–7, 11–13
Alternate: Ephesians 1:17–23

Brothers and sisters, I, a prisoner for the Lord, urge you to live in a manner worthy of the call you have received, with all humility and gentleness, with patience, bearing with one another through love, striving to preserve the unity of the spirit through the bond of peace: one body and one Spirit, as you were also called to the one hope of your call; one Lord, one faith, one baptism; one God and Father of all, who is over all and through all and in all.

But grace was given to each of us according to the measure of Christ's gift. Therefore, it says: *He ascended on high and took prisoners captive; he gave gifts to men.* What does "he ascended" mean except that he also descended into the lower regions of the earth? The one who descended is also the one who ascended far above all the heavens, that he might fill all things.

And he gave some as apostles, others as prophets, others as evangelists, others as pastors and teachers, to equip the holy ones for the work of ministry, for building up the body of Christ, until we all attain to the unity of faith and knowledge of the Son of God, to mature manhood, to the extent of the full stature of Christ.

GOSPEL *Mark 16:15–20*

Jesus said to his disciples: "Go into the whole world and proclaim the gospel to every creature. Whoever believes and is baptized will be saved; whoever does not believe will be condemned. These signs will accompany those who believe: in my name they will drive out demons, they will speak new languages. They will pick up serpents with their hands, and if they drink any deadly thing, it will not harm them. They will lay hands on the sick, and they will recover."

So then the Lord Jesus, after he spoke to them, was taken up into heaven and took his seat at the right hand of God. But they went forth and preached everywhere, while the Lord worked with them and confirmed the word through accompanying signs.

Practice of Hope

Each day this week, in anticipation of Pentecost, pray for the Holy Spirit:

Come Holy Spirit, fill the hearts of your faithful.
And kindle in them the fire of your love.
Send forth your Spirit, and they shall be created.
And you will renew the face of the earth.
O, God,
who by the light of the Holy Spirit,
did instruct the hearts of the faithful,
grant that by the same Holy Spirit we may be
    truly wise
and ever enjoy his consolations.
We ask this through Christ our Lord.
Amen.

◆ How can you be a sign of God's saving presence? Is there a weekly service you can undertake for the summer? ◆ Our second reading reminds us of the call to holiness and our role as members of Christ's body. Read chapter five of Vatican II's *Dogmatic Constitution on the Church* (*Lumen gentium*), which echoes this call.

Download more questions and activities for families, initiation groups, and other adult groups at http://www.ltp.org/ahw.

Scripture Insights

The two mysterious figures in the empty tomb scene in Luke's Gospel and in the ascension narrative in Acts begin their question in similar ways: "Why do you seek?" (Luke 24:5) and "Why are you standing there looking?" (Acts 1:11). For Luke, the meaning of Jesus' resurrection must be understood alongside his ascension because the empty tomb means both God's validation of Jesus and God's exaltation of Jesus as Lord (Acts 2:23–28).

After his resurrection and ascension, Jesus' presence will be mediated through the Holy Spirit (see also Luke 3:16; Acts 1:4–5). Just as the Holy Spirit is present in Jesus' birth and ministry (Luke 1:35; 3:21–22), it will accompany and empower the disciples after Jesus' resurrection and ascension.

We don't know if the disciples equate Israel's kingdom with God's kingdom, but they want to know if Jesus will restore Israel's kingdom without further delay (Acts 1:6). In response to their impatience or presumption (or both), Luke's resurrected Jesus tells them that God's kingdom is not only of a different schedule, makeup, and scale, it is in need of their active involvement (Acts 1:7–8). With the power of the Holy Spirit, the disciples will be sent out to witness for Jesus. Mesmerized by Jesus' ascension or disappointed by Jesus' disappearance, they are redirected to focus away from heaven because Jesus will return to earth (Acts 1:9–11).

◆ Linking Jesus' ascension with his supremacy, Ephesians 4:8a–b states that "he took prisoners captive." Besides the power of death, what other earthly powers might make human beings captive in the first-century context of the New Testament writers?

◆ What is the evidence that Ephesians 4:9 is referring to Jesus' incarnation instead of to his second coming?

◆ How might we be like the disciples, who seem to not only presume that they know God's schedule or plan but also need to be reminded to redirect their focus from heaven?

READING I *Acts 1:15–17, 20a, 20c–26*

Peter stood up in the midst of the brothers—there was a group of about one hundred and twenty persons in the one place—. He said, "My brothers, the Scripture had to be fulfilled which the Holy Spirit spoke beforehand through the mouth of David, concerning Judas, who was the guide for those who arrested Jesus. He was numbered among us and was allotted a share in this ministry.

"For it is written in the Book of Psalms: *May another take his office.*

"Therefore, it is necessary that one of the men who accompanied us the whole time the Lord Jesus came and went among us, beginning from the baptism of John until the day on which he was taken up from us, become with us a witness to his resurrection." So they proposed two, Judas called Barsabbas, who was also known as Justus, and Matthias. Then they prayed, "You, Lord, who know the hearts of all, show which one of these two you have chosen to take the place in this apostolic ministry from which Judas turned away to go to his own place." Then they gave lots to them, and the lot fell upon Matthias, and he was counted with the eleven apostles.

RESPONSORIAL PSALM
Psalm 103:1–2, 11–12, 19–20 (19a)

R. The Lord has set his throne in heaven.
   or: Alleluia.

Bless the LORD, O my soul;
   and all my being, bless his holy name.
Bless the LORD, O my soul,
   and forget not all his benefits.   R.

For as the heavens are high above the earth,
   so surpassing is his kindness toward those
      who fear him.
As far as the east is from the west,
   so far has he put our transgressions
      from us.   R.

The LORD has established his throne in heaven,
   and his kingdom rules over all.
Bless the LORD, all you his angels,
   you mighty in strength,
      who do his bidding.   R.

READING II *1 John 4:11–16*

Beloved, if God so loved us, we also must love one another. No one has ever seen God. Yet, if we love one another, God remains in us, and his love is brought to perfection in us.

This is how we know that we remain in him and he in us, that he has given us of his Spirit. Moreover, we have seen and testify that the Father sent his Son as savior of the world. Whoever acknowledges that Jesus is the Son of God, God remains in him and he in God. We have come to know and to believe in the love God has for us.

God is love, and whoever remains in love remains in God and God in him.

GOSPEL *John 17:11b–19*

Lifting up his eyes to heaven, Jesus prayed, saying: "Holy Father, keep them in your name that you have given me, so that they may be one just as we are one. When I was with them I protected them in your name that you gave me, and I guarded them, and none of them was lost except the son of destruction, in order that the Scripture might be fulfilled. But now I am coming to you. I speak this in the world so that they may share my joy completely. I gave them your word, and the world hated them, because they do not belong to the world any more than I belong to the world. I do not ask that you take them out of the world but that you keep them from the evil one. They do not belong to the world any more than I belong to the world. Consecrate them in the truth. Your word is truth. As you sent me into the world, so I sent them into the world. And I consecrate myself for them, so that they also may be consecrated in truth."

Practice of Faith

In John 17 Jesus offers a long prayer in the presence of his disciples. ◆ Which parts of the prayer that we hear this Sunday most resonate with you? Incorporate these parts of Jesus' prayer into your own prayer to the Father. ◆ Pray for all those who seek the truth and oppose evil. ◆ How familiar are you with the ordination process? Invite your local priest or deacon to share why he became ordained and what that process was like. ◆ Is there someone in your local faith community who is in seminary or entering religious life? Send that person a note of support. If possible, host a meal for the individual as a sign of the community's love and care.

Download more questions and activities for families, initiation groups, and other adult groups at http://www.ltp.org/ahw.

Scripture Insights

Our Gospel passage is part of the farewell discourse of Jesus (John 13–17), as he prepares his disciples for his crucifixion and departure. More specifically, it is part of a prayer in which Jesus prays for his disciples, who will be left in the world without his physical presence.

The intercessory prayer of Jesus in John 17:11b–19 is a prayer for the disciples' protection, but it involves several specific elements. First, there is a specific concern for the disciples' unity (John 17:11b).

Second, the prayer specifies two reasons why protection is needed for the disciples: (1) "the evil one" and the presence of hate rob the disciples of a sense of belonging in this world (John 17:14–16); and (2) the disciples are sent into this world just as Jesus has been sent because the world is the object of God's ongoing love and mission (John 17:18).

Third, there is a specific request for God to set the disciples apart: namely, their sanctification in truth, which is equated with God's Word (John 17:17, 19). Earlier in the prayer, Jesus has stated that he has already given to his disciples the word that he has received from God (John 17:8), so we know that the truth is none other than Jesus' word and, according to John 14:6, Jesus himself. After all, the Word has become flesh in Jesus (John 1:14), and this Word has "the words of eternal life" (John 6:69). Since the two references to sanctification enclose the sending of the disciples in God's mission of love (John 17:18), their sanctification does not mean their isolation or quarantine from the world, but rather, their loyalty to Jesus and to God.

◆ What is the significance of this connection that is being repeatedly emphasized among Jesus, the Father, and the disciples?

◆ It makes sense that love, mission, and protection appear in this passage, but what can we say about the somewhat sudden reference to joy in John 17:13?

◆ How can we be a part of the world and yet be set apart from the world?

May 19, 2024 PENTECOST SUNDAY

READING I *Acts 2:1–11*

When the time for Pentecost was fulfilled, they were all in one place together. And suddenly there came from the sky a noise like a strong driving wind, and it filled the entire house in which they were. Then there appeared to them tongues as of fire, which parted and came to rest on each one of them. And they were all filled with the Holy Spirit and began to speak in different tongues, as the Spirit enabled them to proclaim.

Now there were devout Jews from every nation under heaven staying in Jerusalem. At this sound, they gathered in a large crowd, but they were confused because each one heard them speaking in his own language. They were astounded, and in amazement they asked, "Are not all these people who are speaking Galileans? Then how does each of us hear them in his native language? We are Parthians, Medes, and Elamites, inhabitants of Mesopotamia, Judea and Cappadocia, Pontus and Asia, Phrygia and Pamphylia, Egypt and the districts of Libya near Cyrene, as well as travelers from Rome, both Jews and converts to Judaism, Cretans and Arabs, yet we hear them speaking in our own tongues of the mighty acts of God."

RESPONSORIAL PSALM *Psalm 104:1, 24, 29–30, 31, 34 (see 30)*

R. Lord, send out your Spirit, and renew the
   face of the earth.
  or: Alleluia.

Bless the LORD, O my soul!
  O LORD, my God, you are great indeed!
How manifold are your works, O LORD!
  The earth is full of your creatures.   R.

If you take away their breath, they perish
  and return to their dust.
When you send forth your spirit, they are created,
  and you renew the face of the earth.   R.

May the glory of the LORD endure forever;
  may the LORD be glad in his works!
Pleasing to him be my theme;
  I will be glad in the LORD.   R.

READING II *Galatians 5:16–25*

Alternate: 1 Corinthians 12:3b–7, 12–13

Brothers and sisters, live by the Spirit and you will certainly not gratify the desire of the flesh. For the flesh has desires against the Spirit, and the Spirit against the flesh; these are opposed to each other, so that you may not do what you want. But if you are guided by the Spirit, you are not under the law. Now the works of the flesh are obvious: immorality, impurity, lust, idolatry, sorcery, hatreds, rivalry, jealousy, outbursts of fury, acts of selfishness, dissensions, factions, occasions of envy, drinking bouts, orgies, and the like. I warn you, as I warned you before, that those who do such things will not inherit the kingdom of God. In contrast, the fruit of the Spirit is love, joy, peace, patience, kindness, generosity, faithfulness, gentleness, self-control. Against such there is no law. Now those who belong to Christ Jesus have crucified their flesh with its passions and desires. If we live in the Spirit, let us also follow the Spirit.

GOSPEL *John 15:26–27; 16:12–15*

Alternate: John 20:19–23

Jesus said to his disciples: "When the Advocate comes whom I will send you from the Father, the Spirit of truth that proceeds from the Father, he will testify to me. And you also testify, because you have been with me from the beginning.

"I have much more to tell you, but you cannot bear it now. But when he comes, the Spirit of truth, he will guide you to all truth. He will not speak on his own, but he will speak what he hears, and will declare to you the things that are coming. He will glorify me, because he will take from what is mine and declare it to you. Everything that the Father has is mine; for this reason I told you that he will take from what is mine and declare it to you."

Practice of Faith

Come, Holy Spirit, come! Today we hear about the movements of the Holy Spirit in Jesus' community. In Acts, Luke paints a picture of an intense gathering. Jesus' followers are gathered in one place, likely still working to understand the death and resurrection of their dear friend and teacher. Despite their confusion, they understand what is told of God's mighty acts. As we imagine ourselves among them, we are called to be amazed and transformed by the movements of the Holy Spirit in our everyday lives. ◆ What "works of the flesh" (Galatians 5:19) are keeping you from following the Spirit, from proclaiming the mighty acts of God? ◆ Read the responsorial psalm a few times. What stands out to you? Carry that with you throughout the day to call the Spirit to mind. ◆ At the end of your day, reflect on how recalling that word or phrase helped you "live in the Spirit" (Galatians 5:25).

Download more questions and activities for families, initiation groups, and other adult groups at http://www.ltp.org/ahw.

Scripture Insights

The Pentecost readings orient us to the Holy Spirit's role in the lives of God's people. Indeed, Paul counsels to both "live in" and "follow the Spirit" (Galatians 5:25). But what might this mean?

The biblical narration of primeval history culminates with the people's attempt to build the tower of Babel to make a name for themselves (Genesis 11:1–9). God's response is to "scatter" the people over the face of the earth and "confuse" their language. The resulting disorder represents a radical break in the covenantal relationship between God and humankind presented in the perfectly ordered creation narrative (Genesis 1). Hereafter, God chooses one person, Abraham, and his descendants, with whom to have covenant relationship, restricting humankind's ability to dwell in right relationship with God. Thus, the psalmist cries to God to "send forth your spirit . . . and renew the face of the earth" (Psalm 104:30).

In John 15—16, Jesus teaches that the Holy Spirit will be our advocate, our gift of a mediator to guide us in all truth and actualize our faith in God through Christ in relationship with one another. Acts 2 narrates God's fulfillment of that promise at Pentecost, a pilgrimage feast that brought God's scattered people of all kinds to Jerusalem to celebrate the revelation of the glory of God in the covenantal gift at Sinai (Exodus 19—20). Here, filled with the Holy Spirit, God's glory is revealed anew, reversing Babel, and reuniting all humankind as people of God in communion through relationship and communication in languages that all understand.

◆ How might connecting the events in Genesis 11 and Exodus 19–20 with Acts 2 deepen your understanding of Scripture?

◆ Christians celebrate Pentecost as the birth of the Church as the Body of Christ. How do you understand this body given God's desire to be in covenant with all humankind?

◆ How does Paul's ethical summons to eschew some actions and fortify other dispositions facilitate living in and following the Spirit?

Ordinary Time, Summer

Prayer before Reading the Word

God, sower of the seed,
we marvel at how your Word accomplishes
the purpose for which you sent it forth:
how few of the seeds you sow take root,
yet how spectacular their abundant yield.
Make us good soil, ready to receive what you sow,
that we may hear the Word and understand it,
bear fruit and yield a hundredfold.
We ask this through our Lord Jesus Christ,
    your Son,
who lives and reigns with you
in the unity of the Holy Spirit,
God, for ever and ever. Amen.

Prayer after Reading the Word

To us, sinners and yet disciples,
O Lord of the harvest,
you entrust a share in the mission of Jesus,
who sent the Twelve to proclaim the Good News
and to bear witness without fear.
With your love forever sheltering and
    surrounding us,
may we proclaim from the housetops
the Gospel we have heard
and acknowledge openly before all
the one whom we confess as Lord,
Jesus Christ, your Son, who lives and reigns
    with you
in the unity of the Holy Spirit,
God, for ever and ever. Amen.

May 20: *Genesis 3:9–15, 20 or Acts 1:12–14; John 19:25–34*
May 21: *James 4:1–10; Mark 9:30–37*
May 22: *James 4:13–17; Mark 9:38–40*
May 23: *James 5:1–6; Mark 9:41–50*
May 24: *James 5:9–12; Mark 10:1–12*
May 25: *James 5:13–20; Mark 10:13–16*

May 27: *1 Peter 1:3–9; Mark 10:17–27*
May 28: *1 Peter 1:10–16; Mark 10:28–31*
May 29: *1 Peter 1:18–25; Mark 10:32–45*
May 30: *1 Peter 2:2–5, 9–12; Mark 10:46–52*
May 31: Feast of the Visitation of the Blessed Virgin Mary
Zephaniah 3:14–18a or Romans 12:9–16; Luke 1:39–56
June 1: *Jude 17, 20b–25; Mark 11:27–33*

June 3: *2 Peter 1:2–7; Mark 12:1–12*
June 4: *2 Peter 3:12–15a, 17–18; Mark 12:13–17*
June 5: *2 Timothy 1:1–3, 6–12; Mark 12:18–27*
June 6: *2 Timothy 2:8–15; Mark 12:28–34*
June 7: Solemnity of the Most Sacred Heart of Jesus
Hosea 11:1, 3–4, 8c–9; Ephesians 3:8–12, 14–19; John 19:31–37
June 8: *2 Timothy 4:1–8; Luke 2:41–51*

June 10: *1 Kings 17:1–6; Matthew 5:1–12*
June 11: *Acts 11:21b–26; 13:1–3; Matthew 5:13–16*
June 12: *1 Kings 18:20–39; Matthew 5:17–19*
June 13: *1 Kings 18:41–46; Matthew 5:20–26*
June 14: *1 Kings 19:9a, 11–16; Matthew 5:27–32*
June 15: *1 Kings 19:19–21; Matthew 5:33–37*

June 17: *1 Kings 21:1–16; Matthew 5:38–42*
June 18: *1 Kings 21:17–29; Matthew 5:43–48*
June 19: *2 Kings 2:1, 6–14; Matthew 6:1–6, 16–18*
June 20: *Sirach 48:1–14; Matthew 6:7–15*
June 21: *2 Kings 11:1–4, 9–18, 20; Matthew 6:19–23*
June 22: *2 Chronicles 24:17–25; Matthew 6:24–34*

June 24: Solemnity of the Nativity of St. John the Baptist
Isaiah 49:1–6; Acts 13:22–26; Luke 1:57–66, 80
June 25: *2 Kings 19:9b–11, 14–21, 31–35a, 36; Matthew 7:6, 12–14*
June 26: *2 Kings 22:8–13; 23:1–3; Matthew 7:15–20*
June 27: *2 Kings 24:8–17; Matthew 7:21–29*
June 28: *2 Kings 25:1–12; Matthew 8:1–4*
June 29: Solemnity of Sts. Peter and Paul, Apostles
Day: Acts 12:1–11; 2 Timothy 4:6–8, 17–18; Matthew 16:13–19

July 1: *Amos 2:6–10, 13–16; Matthew 8:18–22*
July 2: *Amos 3:1–8; 4:11–12; Matthew 8:23–27*
July 3: Feast of St. Thomas, Apostle
Ephesians 2:19–22; John 20:24–29
July 4: *Amos 7:10–17; Matthew 9:1–8*
July 5: *Amos 8:4–6, 9–12; Matthew 9:9–13*
July 6: *Amos 9:11–15; Matthew 9:14–17*

July 8: *Hosea 2:16, 17c–18, 21–22; Matthew 9:18–26*
July 9: *Hosea 8:4–7, 11–13; Matthew 9:32–38*
July 10: *Hosea 10:1–3, 7–8, 12; Matthew 10:1–7*
July 11: *Hosea 11:1–4, 8e–9; Matthew 10:7–15*
July 12: *Hosea 14:2–10; Matthew 10:16–23*

July 13: *Isaiah 6:1–8; Matthew 10:24–33*

July 15: *Isaiah 1:10–17; Matthew 10:34—11:1*
July 16: *Isaiah 7:1–9; Matthew 11:20–24*
July 17: *Isaiah 10:5–7, 13b–16; Matthew 11:25–27*
July 18: *Isaiah 26:7–9, 12, 16–19; Matthew 11:28–30*
July 19: *Isaiah 38:1–6, 21–22, 7–8; Matthew 12:1–8*
July 20: *Micah 2:1–5; Matthew 12:14–21*

July 22: Feast of St. Mary Magdalene
Song of Songs 3:1–4b or 2 Corinthians 5:14–17;
**   John 20:1–2, 11–18**
July 23: *Micah 7:14–15, 18–20; Matthew 12:46–50*
July 24: *Jeremiah 1:1, 4–10; Matthew 13:1–9*
July 25: Feast of St. James, Apostle
2 Corinthians 4:7–15; Matthew 20:20–28
July 26: *Jeremiah 3:14–17; Matthew 13:18–23*
July 27: *Jeremiah 7:1–11; Matthew 13:24–30*

July 29: *Jeremiah 13:1–11; John 11:19–27 or Luke 10:38–42*
July 30: *Jeremiah 14:17–22; Matthew 13:36–43*
July 31: *Jeremiah 15:10, 16–21; Matthew 13:44–46*
August 1: *Jeremiah 18:1–6; Matthew 13:47–53*
August 2: *Jeremiah 26:1–9; Matthew 13:54–58*
August 3: *Jeremiah 26:11–16, 24; Matthew 14:1–12*

August 5: *Jeremiah 28:1–17; Matthew 14:13–21*
August 6: Feast of the Transfiguration of the Lord
Daniel 7:9–10, 13–14; 2 Peter 1:16–19; Mark 9:2–10
August 7: *Jeremiah 31:1–7; Matthew 15:21–28*
August 8: *Jeremiah 31:31–34; Matthew 16:13–23*
August 9: *Nahum 2:1, 3; 3:1–3, 6–7; Matthew 16:24–28*
August 10: Feast of St. Lawrence, Deacon and Martyr
2 Corinthians 9:6–10; John 12:24–26

August 12: *Ezekiel 1:2–5, 24–28c; Matthew 17:22–27*
August 13: *Ezekiel 2:8—3:4; Matthew 18:1–5, 10, 12–14*
August 14: *Ezekiel 9:1–7; 10:18–22; Matthew 18:15–20*
August 15: Solemnity of the Assumption of the Blessed
**   Virgin Mary**
Day: Revelation 11:19a; 12:1–6a, 10ab; 1 Corinthians
**   15:20–27; Luke 1:39–56**
August 16: *Ezekiel 16:1–15, 60, 63 or 16:59–63; Matthew 19:3–12*
August 17: *Ezekiel 18:1–10, 13b, 30–32; Matthew 19:13–15*

August 19: *Ezekiel 24:15–23; Matthew 19:16–22*
August 20: *Ezekiel 28:1–10; Matthew 19:23–30*
August 21: *Ezekiel 34:1–11; Matthew 20:1–16*
August 22: *Ezekiel 36:23–28; Matthew 22:1–14*
August 23: *Ezekiel 37:1–14; Matthew 22:34–40*
August 24: Feast of St. Bartholomew, Apostle
Revelation 21:9b–14; John 1:45–51

August 26: *2 Thessalonians 1:1–5, 11–12; Matthew 23:13–22*
August 27: *2 Thessalonians 2:1–3a, 14–17; Matthew 23:23–26*
August 28: *2 Thessalonians 3:6–10, 16–18; Matthew 23:27–32*
August 29: *1 Corinthians 1:1–9; Mark 6:17–29*
August 30: *1 Corinthians 1:17–25; Matthew 25:1–13*
August 31: *1 Corinthians 1:26–31; Matthew 25:14–30*

READING I
Deuteronomy 4:32–34, 39–40

Moses said to the people: "Ask now of the days of old, before your time, ever since God created man upon the earth; ask from one end of the sky to the other: Did anything so great ever happen before? Was it ever heard of? Did a people ever hear the voice of God speaking from the midst of fire, as you did, and live? Or did any god venture to go and take a nation for himself from the midst of another nation, by testings, by signs and wonders, by war, with strong hand and outstretched arm, and by great terrors, all of which the LORD, your God, did for you in Egypt before your very eyes? This is why you must now know, and fix in your heart, that the LORD is God in the heavens above and on earth below, and that there is no other. You must keep his statutes and commandments that I enjoin on you today, that you and your children after you may prosper, and that you may have long life on the land which the LORD, your God, is giving you forever."

RESPONSORIAL PSALM *Psalm 33:4–5, 6, 9, 18–19, 20, 22 (12b)*

R. Blessed the people the Lord has chosen to be
   his own.

Upright is the word of the LORD,
   and all his works are trustworthy.
He loves justice and right;
   of the kindness of the LORD the earth
      is full. R.

By the word of the LORD the heavens were made;
   by the breath of his mouth all their host.
For he spoke, and it was made;
   he commanded, and it stood forth. R.

See, the eyes of the LORD are upon those who
      fear him,
   upon those who hope for his kindness,
to deliver them from death
   and preserve them in spite of famine. R.

Our soul waits for the LORD,
   who is our help and our shield.
May your kindness, O LORD, be upon us
   who have put our hope in you. R.

READING II *Romans 8:14–17*

Brothers and sisters: Those who are led by the Spirit of God are sons of God. For you did not receive a spirit of slavery to fall back into fear, but you received a Spirit of adoption, through whom we cry, "Abba, Father!" The Spirit himself bears witness with our spirit that we are children of God, and if children, then heirs, heirs of God and joint heirs with Christ, if only we suffer with him so that we may also be glorified with him.

GOSPEL *Matthew 28:16–20*

The eleven disciples went to Galilee, to the mountain to which Jesus had ordered them. When they all saw him, they worshiped, but they doubted. Then Jesus approached and said to them, "All power in heaven and on earth has been given to me. Go, therefore, and make disciples of all nations, baptizing them in the name of the Father, and of the Son, and of the Holy Spirit, teaching them to observe all that I have commanded you. And behold, I am with you always, until the end of the age."

Practice of Charity

Human beings are made in the image and likeness of a God who is relationship—Father, Son, and Holy Spirit. Though the word Trinity never appears in the Bible, we know it intimately through the example of the Father, Son, and Spirit. Today we celebrate this unity, which models for us how to create a community that reflects the love of God. ◆ As a Church, we pray the Nicene Creed. Look at it today and explore the Trinitarian language. ◆ Say a prayer of gratitude for someone who has embodied the call to "make disciples of all nations" (Matthew 28:19). How has this person shown you what it means to create, with God, a community that reflects the love of the Trinity? ◆ Today's reading from Paul's Letter to the Romans tells us that "we suffer with him [Christ] so that we may also be glorified with him" (Romans 8:17). Who is suffering in your community? How can you accompany them? Perhaps you will have an opportunity to share something with someone in need.

Download more questions and activities for families, initiation groups, and other adult groups at http://www.ltp.org/ahw.

Scripture Insights

On this Trinity Sunday, we read Matthew's "great commission" that narrates with breathtaking beauty and brevity the disciples' encounter with the risen Christ on a mountain in Galilee. So much happens in these five verses—the most beautiful of which is the expression of human hope and frailty in the reality that "they worshiped, but they doubted." How could they not? They had tried so hard, and had loved, lost, and experienced so much, as we do every day.

This encounter affirms that it is acceptable for faith to seek understanding. Such seeking does not deter the risen Christ whatsoever. He nonetheless declares his power and gives the disciples their mission to go, make, baptize, and teach. We are the imperfect disciples of Christ, who are doing the best that we can. Fortunately, more of the Good News is that he will be with us always, guiding us through the Holy Spirit to relationship with God as Father, Creator, and Lord of all.

The remainder of the Good News in this proclamation is that "all nations" can now be in covenant relationship with God as a parent, through the gift of the life, death, and resurrection of the Son, and now actualized by the Holy Spirit in our lives. Matthew's great commission seeds the development of the doctrine of the Trinity. More individually, it calls each of us to intimate participation in this relationship that continues to create the world in which we live. The psalmist proclaims that God is just and right, and Paul declares that we are joint heirs in the Trinitarian relationship. The Trinity is our foundation of support and our summons to active living.

◆ The reading from Deuteronomy presents a poetic image of God's creative sovereignty. How does this image resonate in your life?

◆ Paul challenges us to be led by the Spirit in our lives. What does this mean for you?

◆ These readings together harken the dignity of all humankind in relationship with the Trinitarian God. How might you work toward this end in your life?

READING I *Exodus 24:3–8*

When Moses came to the people and related all the words and ordinances of the LORD, they all answered with one voice, "We will do everything that the LORD has told us." Moses then wrote down all the words of the LORD and, rising early the next day, he erected at the foot of the mountain an altar and twelve pillars for the twelve tribes of Israel. Then, having sent certain young men of the Israelites to offer holocausts and sacrifice young bulls as peace offerings to the LORD, Moses took half of the blood and put it in large bowls; the other half he splashed on the altar. Taking the book of the covenant, he read it aloud to the people, who answered, "All that the LORD has said, we will heed and do." Then he took the blood and sprinkled it on the people, saying, "This is the blood of the covenant that the LORD has made with you in accordance with all these words of his."

RESPONSORIAL PSALM
Psalm 116:12–13, 15–16, 17–18 (13)

R. I will take the cup of salvation, and call on
   the name of the Lord.
   or: Alleluia.

How shall I make a return to the LORD
   for all the good he has done for me?
The cup of salvation I will take up,
   and I will call upon the name of the LORD. R.

Precious in the eyes of the LORD
   is the death of his faithful ones.
I am your servant, the son of your handmaid;
   you have loosed my bonds. R.

To you will I offer sacrifice of thanksgiving,
   and I will call upon the name of the LORD.
My vows to the LORD I will pay
   in the presence of all his people. R.

READING II *Hebrews 9:11–15*

Brothers and sisters: When Christ came as high priest of the good things that have come to be, passing through the greater and more perfect tabernacle not made by hands, that is, not belonging to this creation, he entered once for all into the sanctuary, not with the blood of goats and calves but with his own blood, thus obtaining eternal redemption. For if the blood of goats and bulls and the sprinkling of a heifer's ashes can sanctify those who are defiled so that their flesh is cleansed, how much more will the blood of Christ, who through the eternal Spirit offered himself unblemished to God, cleanse our consciences from dead works to worship the living God.

For this reason he is mediator of a new covenant: since a death has taken place for deliverance from transgressions under the first covenant, those who are called may receive the promised eternal inheritance.

GOSPEL *Mark 14:12–16, 22–26*

On the first day of the Feast of Unleavened Bread, when they sacrificed the Passover lamb, Jesus' disciples said to him, "Where do you want us to go and prepare for you to eat the Passover?" He sent two of his disciples and said to them, "Go into the city and a man will meet you, carrying a jar of water. Follow him. Wherever he enters, say to the master of the house, 'The Teacher says, "Where is my guest room where I may eat the Passover with my disciples?"' Then he will show you a large upper room furnished and ready. Make the preparations for us there." The disciples then went off, entered the city, and found it just as he had told them; and they prepared the Passover.

While they were eating, he took bread, said the blessing, broke it, gave it to them, and said, "Take it; this is my body." Then he took a cup, gave thanks, and gave it to them, and they all drank from it. He said to them, "This is my blood of the covenant, which will be shed for many. Amen, I say to you, I shall not drink again the fruit of the vine until the day when I drink it new in the kingdom of God." Then, after singing a hymn, they went out to the Mount of Olives.

Practice of Charity

Today's Solemnity of the Most Holy Body and Blood of Christ gives us an opportunity to meditate on Christ's real presence in the Eucharist. The Gospel of Mark tells us that while the disciples were eating the Passover meal, Jesus "took bread, said the blessing, broke it, gave it to them, and said, 'Take it; this is my body'" (Mark 14:22). He offers the same sacrifice with the cup. The Liturgy of the Eucharist follows this example. ♦ The word Eucharist comes from the Greek word *eucharistia*, which means thanksgiving. Take some time to learn about the main elements of the Eucharistic Prayer and consider how they express thanksgiving. ♦ The next time you go to Mass, reflect on the example Jesus gives us to take, bless, break, and give. ♦ How does Christ's real presence in the Eucharist transform you? How does receiving his Body and Blood inspire you to give to your community?

Download more questions and activities for families, initiation groups, and other adult groups at http://www.ltp.org/ahw.

Scripture Insights

Exodus 11—12 tells of the final plague that God sends upon Egypt. The Israelites must prepare for the angel of death to "pass over" and commemorate this event that precipitates their liberation from Egypt and the start of their journey to become God's chosen people. Moses then leads the people out of Egypt into the Sinai wilderness where they commence a new relational stage with God through the revelation of God's glory and the gift of the Ten Commandments (Exodus 19–20). There they gave their initial response to God's offer to be his treasured people, a holy nation (Exodus 19:8).

Today's readings culminate that covenant-making event. They twice repeat their dedication to do all that the Lord has spoken (Exodus 24:3, 7). As is often the case in the Hebrew Scriptures, the third time is the charm. God, through Moses, completes the covenant with the Israelites here at the foot of Mount Sinai. According to the torah presented as the fullness of the Sinai covenant, the Israelites offer sacrifice to atone for sin.

In Mark 14, Jesus celebrates that same Passover tradition, while also preparing his disciples for God's new act of covenant in and through him. As they gather for the Passover supper, Jesus blesses the bread and wine in thanksgiving (*eucharisteo*) for all God's gifts. He then indicates that it is his body and blood that will be the sacrifice that atones for the sins of all. His body and blood of the covenant will fulfill the obligations of the prior covenants and put in place a new one, now open to all who choose to participate in the kingdom of God.

♦ The Israelites thrice proclaim, "all that the Lord says, we will do" (Exodus 24:7). Are you able to rise to that challenge?

♦ The Letter to the Hebrews declares that Christ is the mediator of the new covenant available to everyone. How do you respond to this offer and call to full community?

♦ Although we cannot rise to Jesus' level of sacrifice, what can we give to bring about the kingdom of God? What does this look like in the twenty-first century?

Reading I *Genesis 3:9–15*

After the man, Adam, had eaten of the tree, the LORD God called to the man and asked him, "Where are you?" He answered, "I heard you in the garden; but I was afraid, because I was naked, so I hid myself." Then he asked, "Who told you that you were naked? You have eaten, then, from the tree of which I had forbidden you to eat!" The man replied, "The woman whom you put here with me—she gave me fruit from the tree, and so I ate it." The LORD God then asked the woman, "Why did you do such a thing?" The woman answered, "The serpent tricked me into it, so I ate it."

Then the LORD God said to the serpent:
"Because you have done this,
    you shall be banned
        from all the animals and from all
            the wild creatures;
on your belly shall you crawl,
    and dirt shall you eat
        all the days of your life.
I will put enmity between you and the woman,
    and between your offspring and hers;
he will strike at your head,
    while you strike at his heel."

Responsorial Psalm
Psalm 130:1–2, 3–4, 5–6, 7–8 (7bc)

R. With the Lord there is mercy, and fullness
    of redemption.

Out of the depths I cry to you, O LORD;
    LORD, hear my voice!
Let your ears be attentive
    to my voice in supplication. R.

If you, O LORD, mark iniquities,
    LORD, who can stand?
But with you is forgiveness,
    that you may be revered. R.

I trust in the LORD;
    my soul trusts in his word.
More than sentinels wait for the dawn,
    let Israel wait for the LORD. R.

For with the LORD is kindness
    and with him is plenteous redemption;
and he will redeem Israel
    from all their iniquities. R.

Reading II *2 Corinthians 4:13—5:1*

Brothers and sisters:
Since we have the same spirit of faith, according to what is written, *I believed, therefore I spoke*, we too believe and therefore we speak, knowing that the one who raised the Lord Jesus will raise us also with Jesus and place us with you in his presence. Everything indeed is for you, so that the grace bestowed in abundance on more and more people may cause the thanksgiving to overflow for the glory of God. Therefore, we are not discouraged; rather, although our outer self is wasting away, our inner self is being renewed day by day. For this momentary light affliction is producing for us an eternal weight of glory beyond all comparison, as we look not to what is seen but to what is unseen; for what is seen is transitory, but what is unseen is eternal. For we know that if our earthly dwelling, a tent, should be destroyed, we have a building from God, a dwelling not made with hands, eternal in heaven.

Gospel *Mark 3:20–35*

Jesus came home with his disciples. Again the crowd gathered, making it impossible for them even to eat. When his relatives heard of this they set out to seize him, for they said, "He is out of his mind." The scribes who had come from Jerusalem said, "He is possessed by Beelzebul," and "By the prince of demons he drives out demons."

Summoning them, he began to speak to them in parables, "How can Satan drive out Satan? If a kingdom is divided against itself, that kingdom cannot stand. And if a house is divided against itself, that house will not be able to stand. And if Satan has risen up against himself and is divided, he cannot stand; that is the end of him. But no one can enter a strong man's house to plunder his property unless he first ties up the strong man. Then he can plunder the house. Amen, I say to you, all sins and all blasphemies that people utter will be forgiven them. But whoever blasphemes against the Holy Spirit will never have forgiveness, but is guilty of an everlasting sin." For they had said, "He has an unclean spirit."

His mother and his brothers arrived. Standing outside they sent word to him and called him. A crowd seated around him told him, "Your mother and your brothers and your sisters are outside asking for you." But he said to them in reply, "Who are my mother and my brothers?" And looking around at those seated in the circle he said, "Here are my mother and my brothers. For whoever does the will of God is my brother and sister and mother."

Practice of Hope

When have you found yourself afraid and hiding, like Adam in today's excerpt from Genesis? When have you found yourself crying out of the depths to the Lord? ◆ The story we hear in today's Old Testament passage can spark fear of a God who bans us, who puts enmity between us. It is easy to hear these words and stop there, only knowing of a God who condemns us. But let us believe and therefore speak! As we proclaim in the psalm: there is mercy and fullness of redemption with the Lord. ◆ Read the psalm several times, aloud and in silence. Let the words wash over you and sit with the Lord's mercy. ◆ Learn about the seven spiritual works of mercy: go to usccb.org and search for "spiritual works of mercy." Pick one of the spiritual works of mercy to focus on. How can you live it out today?

Download more questions and activities for families, initiation groups, and other adult groups at http://www.ltp.org/ahw.

Scripture Insights

Today's Genesis narrative recounts the consequences of humankind's disobedience to God. God presented his covenantal promises through Adam: he may dwell in and nurture Eden, but he must obey the one prohibition of eating from the tree of knowledge of good and evil. God then creates Adam's partner. The woman was led to forsake the covenant by the cunning serpent and Adam followed suit. When God was strolling amid creation during the breezy time of day, he found humankind in shame and hiding due to their new knowledge.

As all-knowing Creator, God's questions about what happened must be understood as a way to allow Adam to take responsibility for his actions. Adam fails; he blames both the woman and God! The woman likewise fails and blames the serpent. It is with these actions and consequences that the snake came to embody evil for the nomadic household. As the consequences continue, we learn of the world we inhabit. Relationships with one another and with creation have been disordered by these early choices.

In the Gospel of Mark, Jesus' early ministry conflicts with those who think they know him. He teaches by telling stories through metaphor to get his listeners to think beyond what they believe they know. Jesus is then forced to look beyond his biological family for advocates and understanding. It is living and doing the will of God that now creates family and facilitates the kingdom of God.

◆ How does the Genesis account of the failure to take responsibility for our decisions impact you? Have you done this? How might God summon you to do better?

◆ Jesus makes a controversial declaration about what it means to be part of his family. Have you experienced this? How might we resolve such conflicts with love and solidarity?

◆ Sometimes our expectations about our lives in this disordered world are so ingrained that only by force do our eyes open anew to the kingdom of God. Has this happened to you? If not, should it?

READING I   *Ezekiel 17:22–24*

Thus says the Lord GOD:
I, too, will take from the crest of the cedar,
from its topmost branches tear off
a tender shoot,
and plant it on a high and lofty mountain;
on the mountain heights of Israel I will
plant it.
It shall put forth branches and bear fruit,
and become a majestic cedar.
Birds of every kind shall dwell beneath it,
every winged thing in the shade of its boughs.
And all the trees of the field shall know
that I, the LORD,
bring low the high tree,
lift high the lowly tree,
wither up the green tree,
and make the withered tree bloom.
As I, the LORD, have spoken, so will I do.

RESPONSORIAL PSALM
Psalm 92:2–3, 13–14, 15–16 (see 2a)

R Lord, it is good to give thanks to you.

It is good to give thanks to the LORD,
to sing praise to your name, Most High,
To proclaim your kindness at dawn
and your faithfulness throughout
the night. R.

The just one shall flourish like the palm tree,
like a cedar of Lebanon shall he grow.
They that are planted in the house of the LORD
shall flourish in the courts of our God. R.

They shall bear fruit even in old age;
vigorous and sturdy shall they be,
declaring how just is the LORD,
my rock, in whom there is no wrong. R.

READING II   *2 Corinthians 5:6–10*

Brothers and sisters: We are always courageous, although we know that while we are at home in the body we are away from the Lord, for we walk by faith, not by sight. Yet we are courageous, and we would rather leave the body and go home to the Lord. Therefore, we aspire to please him, whether we are at home or away. For we must all appear before the judgment seat of Christ, so that each may receive recompense, according to what he did in the body, whether good or evil.

GOSPEL   *Mark 4:26–34*

Jesus said to the crowds: "This is how it is with the kingdom of God; it is as if a man were to scatter seed on the land and would sleep and rise night and day and through it all the seed would sprout and grow, he knows not how. Of its own accord the land yields fruit, first the blade, then the ear, then the full grain in the ear. And when the grain is ripe, he wields the sickle at once, for the harvest has come."

He said, "To what shall we compare the kingdom of God, or what parable can we use for it? It is like a mustard seed that, when it is sown in the ground, is the smallest of all the seeds on the earth. But once it is sown, it springs up and becomes the largest of plants and puts forth large branches, so that the birds of the sky can dwell in its shade." With many such parables he spoke the word to them as they were able to understand it. Without parables he did not speak to them, but to his own disciples he explained everything in private.

Practice of Faith

Sts. Thomas Aquinas and Ignatius of Loyola and other saints teach us that ingratitude is the root of sinfulness. Today's readings provide a beautiful visual of what happens when we give thanks to God. As we pray in the responsorial psalm, it is good to give thanks to the Lord! We are called to walk by faith, which is fueled by the practice of gratitude. We sow the mustard seed of our faith and we spring up, by giving thanks to the Lord.
◆ Spend some time learning about what Sts. Thomas and Ignatius say about gratitude. ◆ The next time you pray, visualize planting a seed. How can you foster its growth? How is your faith like the seed? How can you help your faith spring up like the seed? ◆ For the next several days, write down three things for which you are grateful. Share the list with loved ones and invite them to do the same with you.

Download more questions and activities for families, initiation groups, and other adult groups at http://www.ltp.org/ahw.

Scripture Insights

Mark's Gospel tells us that Jesus taught in parables. This term *parable* comes from Greek and means "to go around." The stories that Jesus shares go around the intended message in such a way as to affect the hearer or reader profoundly. People often asked Jesus for significant or complex information. He could have answered directly, but that might have been difficult to do and may have failed to make the desired impression. Instead, Jesus told stories to make his point. Stories often have a weightier impact than the plain message because they draw people in by inviting further reflection and sparking hope.

Though their meaning at first could appear unclear, Jesus' parables caused listeners to think more deeply, reflecting upon their presuppositions or what they thought they knew. An example of this is his proclamation that the kingdom of God should be compared to a mustard seed. Mustard seeds may be the smallest of all but they are hardy and can grow rampantly. Farmers even find their fields overrun by mustard plants and try to limit their intrusion into more established crops. How then, is the mustard seed an appropriate image for God's kingdom?

If Jesus only used the established religious and cultural symbols for his teaching, we might yawn and miss his point. That he uses these provocative images for his teaching of the coming kingdom of God should make us think. The hope is that we eventually realize the power and beauty of something so small as to be dismissed that becomes pervasive and life-giving.

◆ In 2 Corinthians, Paul discusses courage in terms of those who walk by faith and are judged accordingly. How might this look in your life?

◆ Ezekiel teaches that God's omnipotence plans for the rising of those who are just. How do you fit in this plan?

◆ God still speaks to us in parables through issues of justice and human dignity. How do you respond?

READING I *Job 38:1, 8–11*

The Lord addressed Job out of the storm and said:
Who shut within doors the sea,
when it burst forth from the womb;
when I made the clouds its garment
and thick darkness its swaddling bands?
When I set limits for it
and fastened the bar of its door,
and said: Thus far shall you come but
no farther,
and here shall your proud waves be stilled!

RESPONSORIAL PSALM *Psalm 107:23–24, 25–26, 28–29, 30–31 (1b)*

R. Give thanks to the Lord, his love is everlasting.
or: Alleluia.

They who sailed the sea in ships,
trading on the deep waters,
these saw the works of the LORD
and his wonders in the abyss.   R.

His command raised up a storm wind
which tossed its waves on high.
They mounted up to heaven;
they sank to the depths;
their hearts melted away in their plight.   R.

They cried to the LORD in their distress;
from their straits he rescued them.
He hushed the storm to a gentle breeze,
and the billows of the sea were stilled.   R.

They rejoiced that they were calmed,
and he brought them to their desired haven.
Let them give thanks to the LORD for his kindness
and his wondrous deeds
to the children of men.   R.

READING II *2 Corinthians 5:14–17*

Brothers and sisters: The love of Christ impels us, once we have come to the conviction that one died for all; therefore, all have died. He indeed died for all, so that those who live might no longer live for themselves but for him who for their sake died and was raised.

Consequently, from now on we regard no one according to the flesh; even if we once knew Christ according to the flesh, yet now we know him so no longer. So whoever is in Christ is a new creation: the old things have passed away; behold, new things have come.

GOSPEL *Mark 4:35–41*

On that day, as evening drew on, Jesus said to his disciples: "Let us cross to the other side." Leaving the crowd, they took Jesus with them in the boat just as he was. And other boats were with him. A violent squall came up and waves were breaking over the boat, so that it was already filling up. Jesus was in the stern, asleep on a cushion. They woke him and said to him, "Teacher, do you not care that we are perishing?" He woke up, rebuked the wind, and said to the sea, "Quiet! Be still!" The wind ceased and there was great calm. Then he asked them, "Why are you terrified? Do you not yet have faith?" They were filled with great awe and said to one another, "Who then is this whom even wind and sea obey?"

Practice of Charity

The difficulties and hardships we experience can leave us feeling like we are hit with a violent squall. Today's readings invite us to do hard work: to choose to see God's wonders amid the tempest. ◆ Take a moment to reflect on a time when you asked Jesus, as the disciples did in today's Gospel passage, if he even cares that you are perishing. Instead of being terrified as your boat fills up, how can you work with the Lord to still the waves and cultivate quiet and stillness? ◆ Choose an issue of justice with which you are unfamiliar and spend time learning about it. Resources are available under "Issues and Action" at the United States Conference of Catholic Bishops' website, usccb.org. ◆ Consider how, as a member of a larger community, you can calm unjust seas with the Lord by advocating for justice.

Download more questions and activities for families, initiation groups, and other adult groups at http://www.ltp.org/ahw.

Scripture Insights

Mark's brief narrative of Jesus controlling the waters is replete with scriptural symbolism and interpretive force. In the Old Testament Scriptures, this creative force reveals both the power and presence of God. The manifestation of God in the lives of people, from creation throughout history, is called *theophany.*

At creation, God formed and separated the waters to create the seas, the skies, and the land, then populated them with all manner of fauna to roam the earth and sky. This powerful creative imagery flows seamlessly into God's controlling of the waters in the Exodus and returns throughout the Scriptures to show God's power and care over creation. Job indicates that God alone "shut within doors the sea, / when it burst forth from the womb / . . . / and said: Thus far shall you come but no farther, / and here shall your proud waves be stilled" (Job 38:8, 11). The psalmist confirms God's ability to raise and still the stormy seas. When the people cry out in distress, the Lord rescued them, "he hushed the storm to a gentle breeze, / and the billows of the sea were stilled" (Psalm 107:29).

In Mark's Gospel, Jesus does, through his power over the waters, what only God can do. Leaving the crowds for time with his disciples, Jesus suggests that they cross the sea of Galilee. He then sleeps through a violent squall that threatens to capsize their boat. Upon awakening, Jesus commands quiet and stillness. As calm overtakes the waters, he challenges his disciples' faith, and they recognize the theophany.

◆ In the face of the storm and terrified disciples, Jesus commands quiet and stillness. To whom is he speaking? Just the wind and sea? Or the disciples as well?

◆ How might quiet and stillness calm our stormy minds and open us to the power and presence of God in our lives even in chaotic times?

◆ Paul challenges us to live in Christ as in a new creation. How might this look in your life?

READING I *Wisdom 1:13–15; 2:23–24*

God did not make death,
    nor does he rejoice in the destruction of
        the living.
For he fashioned all things that they might
    have being;
    and the creatures of the world
        are wholesome,
and there is not a destructive drug among them
    nor any domain of the netherworld on earth,
    for justice is undying.
For God formed man to be imperishable;
    the image of his own nature he made him.
But by the envy of the devil, death entered
    the world,
    and they who belong to his company
        experience it.

RESPONSORIAL PSALM
Psalm 30:2, 4, 5–6, 11, 12, 13 (2a)

R. I will praise you, Lord, for you have
    rescued me.

I will extol you, O LORD, for you drew me clear
    and did not let my enemies rejoice over me.
O LORD, you brought me up
    from the netherworld;
    you preserved me from among those going
        down into the pit. R.

Sing praise to the LORD, you his faithful ones,
    and give thanks to his holy name.
For his anger lasts but a moment;
    a lifetime, his good will.
At nightfall, weeping enters in,
    but with the dawn, rejoicing. R.

Hear, O LORD, and have pity on me;
    O LORD, be my helper.
You changed my mourning into dancing;
    O LORD, my God, forever will I give
        you thanks. R.

READING II *2 Corinthians 8:7, 9, 13–15*

Brothers and sisters: As you excel in every respect,
in faith, discourse, knowledge, all earnestness, and
in the love we have for you, may you excel in this
gracious act also.

For you know the gracious act of our Lord
Jesus Christ, that though he was rich, for your sake
he became poor, so that by his poverty you might
become rich. Not that others should have relief
while you are burdened, but that as a matter of
equality your abundance at the present time should
supply their needs, so that their abundance may
also supply your needs, that there may be equality.
As it is written: / *Whoever had much did not have
more, / and whoever had little did not have less.*

GOSPEL *Mark 5:21–43*

Shorter: Mark 5:21–24, 35b–43

When Jesus had crossed again in the boat to the
other side, a large crowd gathered around him, and
he stayed close to the sea. One of the synagogue
officials, named Jairus, came forward. Seeing
him he fell at his feet and pleaded earnestly with
him, saying, "My daughter is at the point of death.
Please, come lay your hands on her that she may
get well and live." He went off with him, and a
large crowd followed him and pressed upon him.

There was a woman afflicted with hemor-
rhages for twelve years. She had suffered greatly at
the hands of many doctors and had spent all that
she had. Yet she was not helped but only grew
worse. She had heard about Jesus and came up
behind him in the crowd and touched his cloak.
She said, "If I but touch his clothes, I shall be
cured." Immediately her flow of blood dried up.
She felt in her body that she was healed of her
affliction. Jesus, aware at once that power had gone
out from him, turned around in the crowd and
asked, "Who has touched my clothes?" But his
disciples said to Jesus, "You see how the crowd is
pressing upon you, and yet you ask, 'Who touched
me?'" And he looked around to see who had done
it. The woman, realizing what had happened to
her, approached in fear and trembling. She fell
down before Jesus and told him the whole truth.
He said to her, "Daughter, your faith has saved
you. Go in peace and be cured of your affliction."

While he was still speaking, people from the synagogue official's house arrived and said, "Your daughter has died; why trouble the teacher any longer?" Disregarding the message that was reported, Jesus said to the synagogue official, "Do not be afraid; just have faith." He did not allow anyone to accompany him inside except Peter, James, and John, the brother of James. When they arrived at the house of the synagogue official, he caught sight of a commotion, people weeping and wailing loudly. So he went in and said to them, "Why this commotion and weeping? The child is not dead but asleep." And they ridiculed him. Then he put them all out. He took along the child's father and mother and those who were with him and entered the room where the child was. He took the child by the hand and said to her, "*Talitha koum*," which means, "Little girl, I say to you, arise!" The girl, a child of twelve, arose immediately and walked around. At that they were utterly astounded. He gave strict orders that no one should know this and said that she should be given something to eat.

Practice of Faith

Jesus gives Jairus, and us, some seemingly simple advice in today's Gospel: "Do not be afraid; just have faith" (Mark 5:36). ◆ Though we are made in the image of God's nature, death entered the world, and we experience it in our sinfulness. When we are afflicted, it can be easy to be like those weeping and mourning the death of Jairus' daughter and ridicule Jesus as he calls us to not be afraid. However, we must cultivate a prayer life that strengthens us to believe that Christ will meet us as we experience hardships and afflictions. ◆ Read today's Gospel several times and place yourself in Jairus' home. Where do you find yourself? What happens to you when you hear Jesus say "Talitha koum"? After seeing the little girl rise and walk around, what do you do? ◆ How can you accompany someone who is suffering to rise from their hardships?

Download more questions and activities for families, initiation groups, and other adult groups at http://www.ltp.org/ahw.

Scripture Insights

Today, Mark presents one of his characteristic "intercalations." This literary term is colloquially described as a "sandwich story," where a complete event (B) is sandwiched inside another episode (A). In today's passage, story A is that of Jairus and his daughter, while story B revolves around the woman with the bleeding disorder. The interpretive force of these intercalated encounters is felt when we reflect upon them together.

Jesus' ministry crisscrosses the Galilean region as he gains renown. Jairus, a synagogue official, and thus a man of repute and community standing, approaches Jesus in (somewhat surprising) supplication. We learn why: his daughter is on her deathbed and Jesus is her only hope. Jesus, as do we, follows Jairus, enrapt in this story.

Our attention abruptly turns to a woman, devastated by twelve years of menstrual hemorrhaging. This condition has rendered her penniless after visiting doctors who were incapable of curing her, as well as "unclean" and thereby outcast from the sustenance of societal interrelationships. She risks everything to touch even the hem of Jesus' cloak in a last-ditch effort for healing. Public presence in her condition could get her killed, but she has nothing left to lose. Jesus, disregarding religious restrictions, senses both his power and her faith and confirms her new lease on life: "go in peace."

We may have all but forgotten about Jairus' daughter until messengers arrive to announce her death. Jesus commands all to banish fear and nurture faith. Once again disregarding both ridicule and religious restrictions, Jesus takes the hand of the girl of twelve and commands her to arise. She obeys, and he confirms her new lease on life by directing that she have something to eat.

◆ In Mark's narration, how do these events in Jesus' ministry interact with one another?

◆ Jesus shows no partiality to class or religious restrictions in his desire to heal and serve. Are you able to do the same?

◆ Paul likewise counsels us to excel in graciousness, eschewing surplus and endeavoring for equality. How might you actualize this summons in your life?

READING I   *Ezekiel 2:2–5*

As the LORD spoke to me, the spirit entered into me and set me on my feet, and I heard the one who was speaking say to me: Son of man, I am sending you to the Israelites, rebels who have rebelled against me; they and their ancestors have revolted against me to this very day. Hard of face and obstinate of heart are they to whom I am sending you. But you shall say to them: Thus says the Lord GOD! And whether they heed or resist—for they are a rebellious house—they shall know that a prophet has been among them.

RESPONSORIAL PSALM
Psalm 123:1–2, 2, 3–4 (2cd)

R. Our eyes are fixed on the Lord, pleading for his mercy.

To you I lift up my eyes
  who are enthroned in heaven —
as the eyes of servants
  are on the hands of their masters.   R.

As the eyes of a maid
  are on the hands of her mistress,
so are our eyes on the LORD, our God,
  till he have pity on us.   R.

Have pity on us, O LORD, have pity on us,
  for we are more than sated with contempt;
our souls are more than sated
  with the mockery of the arrogant,
  with the contempt of the proud.   R.

READING II   *2 Corinthians 12:7–10*

Brothers and sisters: That I, Paul, might not become too elated, because of the abundance of the revelations, a thorn in the flesh was given to me, an angel of Satan, to beat me, to keep me from being too elated. Three times I begged the Lord about this, that it might leave me, but he said to me, "My grace is sufficient for you, for power is made perfect in weakness." I will rather boast most gladly of my weaknesses, in order that the power of Christ may dwell with me. Therefore, I am content with weaknesses, insults, hardships, persecutions, and constraints, for the sake of Christ; for when I am weak, then I am strong.

GOSPEL   *Mark 6:1–6*

Jesus departed from there and came to his native place, accompanied by his disciples. When the sabbath came he began to teach in the synagogue, and many who heard him were astonished. They said, "Where did this man get all this? What kind of wisdom has been given him? What mighty deeds are wrought by his hands! Is he not the carpenter, the son of Mary, and the brother of James and Joses and Judas and Simon? And are not his sisters here with us?" And they took offense at him. Jesus said to them, "A prophet is not without honor except in his native place and among his own kin and in his own house." So he was not able to perform any mighty deed there, apart from curing a few sick people by laying his hands on them. He was amazed at their lack of faith.

Practice of Hope

Today we hear about the challenges that come with the call to be prophetic, the call to live a Christian life. ◆ The prophet Ezekiel is told that he will be sent to the Israelites, who are "hard of face and obstinate of heart" (Ezekiel 2:4). The Lord tells Ezekiel that he is to proclaim the Lord's words to them regardless of their resistance. Jesus is also faced with this skepticism: the people of his hometown struggle to believe how he, one of their own impoverished and marginalized neighbors, can be a wise teacher. But St. Paul reminds us that God's grace is sufficient to help us proclaim God's truth: the power of Christ dwells in our weakness. ◆ Put yourself in the shoes of the Nazarenes. Say a prayer for someone who has been a prophetic voice for you. ◆ Is there anyone to whom you have shown resistance, similar to the way the Nazarenes resisted Jesus? What is an action you can take to reconcile your differences so that you might understand them?

Download more questions and activities for families, initiation groups, and other adult groups at http://www.ltp.org/ahw.

Scripture Insights

Today's Scripture excerpts the call of Ezekiel. God determines to send him to a rebellious people to speak God's Word. They will likely resist, says God, but they will know that a prophet has been among them. Beyond today's reading, Ezekiel agrees wholeheartedly. Standing strong and speaking boldly the Word of God in the face of extreme resistance becomes the hallmark of his ministry.

Mark likewise recounts Jesus' endeavor to fulfill God's call through his ministry in his hometown. Although he has succeeded across the region, turning hearts and minds toward authentic relationship with God, homecoming is always fraught with story, history, and expectations. Jesus' teaching in the synagogue, the community's traditional gathering place, astonishes, even inspires his audience, but many are caught by their preconceived notions. They know his earthly family, his upbringing, and they are skeptical. How could God be speaking through one such as he? Unfortunately, their openness and amazement at his teaching is overtaken by cynicism about how God could speak through one just like themselves.

Ultimately, their objection to Jesus comes down to insecurity. Their lack of faith in Jesus is a lack of faith in themselves and, finally, a lack of faith at what God can do in and through any person. Jesus acknowledges this deficit in human nature with dismay and disappointment. They could be and do so much more. Then he could be and do so much more for them. Nonetheless, they know that a prophet has been among them.

◆ Have you been challenged by unmalleable family roles in your own life? How have you handled them?

◆ How might God's proclamation that "they shall know that a prophet has been among them" (Ezekiel 2:5) inspire you to speak God's Word even in the most daunting situations?

◆ Paul reminds us that God's grace is sufficient, but more so that Christ dwells within us, in all our strengths and weaknesses. How does this bolster both your faith and your drive to take on new challenges in your vocation?

July 14, 2024 FIFTEENTH SUNDAY IN ORDINARY TIME

READING I *Amos 7:12–15*

Amaziah, priest of Bethel, said to Amos, "Off with you, visionary, flee to the land of Judah! There earn your bread by prophesying, but never again prophesy in Bethel; for it is the king's sanctuary and a royal temple." Amos answered Amaziah, "I was no prophet, nor have I belonged to a company of prophets; I was a shepherd and a dresser of sycamores. The LORD took me from following the flock, and said to me, Go, prophesy to my people Israel."

RESPONSORIAL PSALM
Psalm 85:9–10, 11–12, 13–14 (8)

R. Lord, let us see your kindness, and grant us
   your salvation.

I will hear what God proclaims;
   the LORD—for he proclaims peace.
Near indeed is his salvation to those who fear him,
   glory dwelling in our land. R.

Kindness and truth shall meet;
   justice and peace shall kiss.
Truth shall spring out of the earth,
   and justice shall look down from heaven. R.

The LORD himself will give his benefits;
   our land shall yield its increase.
Justice shall walk before him,
   and prepare the way of his steps. R.

READING II *Ephesians 1:3–14*

Shorter: Ephesians 1:3–10

Blessed be the God and Father of our Lord Jesus Christ, who has blessed us in Christ with every spiritual blessing in the heavens, as he chose us in him, before the foundation of the world, to be holy and without blemish before him. In love he destined us for adoption to himself through Jesus Christ, in accord with the favor of his will, for the praise of the glory of his grace that he granted us in the beloved. In him we have redemption by his blood, the forgiveness of transgressions, in accord with the riches of his grace that he lavished upon us. In all wisdom and insight, he has made known to us the mystery of his will in accord with his favor that he set forth in him as a plan for the fullness of times, to sum up all things in Christ, in heaven and on earth.

In him we were also chosen, destined in accord with the purpose of the One who accomplishes all things according to the intention of his will, so that we might exist for the praise of his glory, we who first hoped in Christ. In him you also, who have heard the word of truth, the gospel of your salvation, and have believed in him, were sealed with the promised Holy Spirit, which is the first installment of our inheritance toward redemption as God's possession, to the praise of his glory.

GOSPEL *Mark 6:7–13*

Jesus summoned the Twelve and began to send them out two by two and gave them authority over unclean spirits. He instructed them to take nothing for the journey but a walking stick—no food, no sack, no money in their belts. They were, however, to wear sandals but not a second tunic. He said to them, "Wherever you enter a house, stay there until you leave. Whatever place does not welcome you or listen to you, leave there and shake the dust off your feet in testimony against them." So they went off and preached repentance. The Twelve drove out many demons, and they anointed with oil many who were sick and cured them.

Practice of Charity

Jesus sends the twelve out two by two to proclaim the Good News: the apostles have a companion with whom to share their journey. ◆ Who has served as your companion on your faith journey? Say a prayer of gratitude for them today. ◆ As Jesus sends the apostles, he instructs the pairs to "take nothing for the journey but a walking stick—no food, no sack, no money" (Mark 6:8). In doing so, he makes a comment about overconsumption, about what is really needed to live a holy life. Take time this week to do a closet audit: What material things do you own in excess (clothing, shoes, appliances, books, etc.)? What do you need to live a holy life? How does a culture of overconsumption prohibit you from fully living the Gospel? ◆ After your closet audit, consider giving glory to God by sharing your wealth: gift or donate your excess material things in good condition to others.

Download more questions and activities for families, initiation groups, and other adult groups at http://www.ltp.org/ahw.

Scripture Insights

The passage from Paul's Letter to the Ephesians is typically called his "thanksgiving." In the verses that immediately follow the address and precede the body of his letters, Paul often gives thanks for the progress in the good news that his recipients have made. He also subtly indicates how they could do better and what he will address with them. Although the authorship of Ephesians is disputed, this role of the thanksgiving remains consistent.

In Ephesians, Paul's thanksgiving is general and amounts to a mini-gospel as he relates the Good News of the redemption of every person who chooses to believe and participates in covenant relationship with God. He focuses on love and God's cosmic choice of each and every believer through the visceral sacrifice of Jesus who is Christ and Lord. This salvific truth, promised by the Holy Spirit, is available to all who have the courage to open themselves to the blessing bestowed by God through Christ.

Such courage in openness to God's call is far earlier embodied by Amos, a shepherd from Tekoa who was rejected by the "professional" prophets of the day. Regardless of societal expectations or even censure by the priest Amaziah, Amos both knows what he is, in all its humility, and confirms his call to speak God's word despite class limitations and societal expectations.

God's work in and through those open to him, however unexpected by societal conventions, is confirmed in today's Gospel. Jesus summons the twelve to share the Good News, and they go without reservation. Their success is not on their own account but rather due to God and how God acts in the world through even the most unexpected means.

◆ The psalmist recommends listening for God, confident that it grants both peace and salvation. How do you make room for this listening in your busy life?

◆ Jesus sends out his disciples with little training or backup as models for all disciples. Do you find this scary or emboldening? Why?

◆ How might you activate the vocation of faith-seeking-guidance advocated in today's readings?

READING I *Jeremiah 23:1–6*

Woe to the shepherds who mislead and scatter the flock of my pasture, says the LORD. Therefore, thus says the LORD, the God of Israel, against the shepherds who shepherd my people: You have scattered my sheep and driven them away. You have not cared for them, but I will take care to punish your evil deeds. I myself will gather the remnant of my flock from all the lands to which I have driven them and bring them back to their meadow; there they shall increase and multiply. I will appoint shepherds for them who will shepherd them so that they need no longer fear and tremble; and none shall be missing, says the LORD.

Behold, the days are coming, says the LORD,
    when I will raise up a righteous shoot
        to David;
as king he shall reign and govern wisely,
    he shall do what is just and right in the land.
In his days Judah shall be saved,
    Israel shall dwell in security.
This is the name they give him:
    "The LORD our justice."

RESPONSORIAL PSALM
Psalm 23:1–3, 3–4, 5, 6 (1)

R. The Lord is my shepherd;
    there is nothing I shall want.

The LORD is my shepherd; I shall not want.
    In verdant pastures he gives me repose;
beside restful waters he leads me;
    he refreshes my soul. R.

He guides me in right paths
    for his name's sake.
Even though I walk in the dark valley
    I fear no evil; for you are at my side
with your rod and your staff
    that give me courage. R.

You spread the table before me
    in the sight of my foes;
you anoint my head with oil;
    my cup overflows. R.

Only goodness and kindness follow me
    all the days of my life;
and I shall dwell in the house of the LORD
    for years to come. R.

READING II *Ephesians 2:13–18*

Brothers and sisters: In Christ Jesus you who once were far off have become near by the blood of Christ.

For he is our peace, he who made both one and broke down the dividing wall of enmity, through his flesh, abolishing the law with its commandments and legal claims, that he might create in himself one new person in place of the two, thus establishing peace, and might reconcile both with God, in one body, through the cross, putting that enmity to death by it. He came and preached peace to you who were far off and peace to those who were near, for through him we both have access in one Spirit to the Father.

GOSPEL *Mark 6:30–34*

The apostles gathered together with Jesus and reported all they had done and taught. He said to them, "Come away by yourselves to a deserted place and rest a while." People were coming and going in great numbers, and they had no opportunity even to eat. So they went off in the boat by themselves to a deserted place. People saw them leaving and many came to know about it. They hastened there on foot from all the towns and arrived at the place before them.

When he disembarked and saw the vast crowd, his heart was moved with pity for them, for they were like sheep without a shepherd; and he began to teach them many things.

Practice of Faith

In today's Gospel, the apostles and Jesus gather as a community and share their ministry with each other. After hearing about their work, Jesus encourages them to retreat: "He said to them, 'Come away by yourselves to a deserted place and rest a while'" (Mark 6:31). ◆ Consider how, much like the disciples, it can be easy to become absorbed by the business of our lives, even if that business is characterized by good and holy work. Jesus reminds us that we must prioritize spending intentional time with God. This is critical as it helps us to see the Lord at our side, guiding us even when we "walk in the dark valley" (Psalm 23:4). ◆ This week, learn about a new way you can retreat. Explore Ignatian contemplation, lectio divina, visio divina, walking meditations, mindful eating, or Eucharistic adoration. ◆ Chose one new practice and devote some time to retreat each day. Remember to limit your distractions.

Download more questions and activities for families, initiation groups, and other adult groups at http://www.ltp.org/ahw.

Scripture Insights

In Mark 6, Jesus designates his inner circle of twelve disciples as apostles who are sent on a mission to share the Good News. In the interim, Mark narrates the martyrdom of John the Baptist. By 6:30–34, we read how the apostles regather. When they focus too much on their success and not those they have served, Jesus takes them into the wilderness for rest, regrouping, and further formation, not unlike earlier wilderness expeditions for Israelites throughout their history. The crowds, needing help and hungry for learning, eventually find them. Jesus, as always, is focused solely on service and the needs of the people. Moved by their openness, he begins to teach them "many things."

Mark thus focuses on discipleship and service. Jesus models the leadership of a shepherd. What might this mean for the lives of those who would follow in his footsteps? What does it mean to be disciples of Christ when other directions might bring more status? Paul's Letter to the Ephesians continues this teaching in terms of peace, and the access to peace that disciples seeking relationship to God the Father manifest through interactive, conciliatory relationship with one another.

The Gospel passage from Mark encapsulates the teaching of both the prophet Jeremiah and the psalmist. God sees the needs of the people and promises to send a righteous branch of David to shepherd the lost sheep, bringing them into justice and right relationship with God. Further, we are encouraged to relate to God in this same manner: the Shepherd who will see to our security through all of life's challenges, even unto death.

◆ According to Mark's Gospel, how might time in the wilderness with Jesus facilitate shaping apostles into leaders?

◆ Psalm 23 is special to many Christians. How does reflecting upon it in the context of Mark's Gospel reading allow us to interpret it for the current age?

◆ How might God be calling you to respond to him as your shepherd? Further, how might God be calling you to serve others in this shepherding role?

READING I   *2 Kings 4:42–44*

A man came from Baal-shalishah bringing to Elisha, the man of God, twenty barley loaves made from the firstfruits, and fresh grain in the ear. Elisha said, "Give it to the people to eat." But his servant objected, "How can I set this before a hundred people?" Elisha insisted, "Give it to the people to eat. For thus says the LORD, 'They shall eat and there shall be some left over.'" And when they had eaten, there was some left over, as the LORD had said.

RESPONSORIAL PSALM   *Psalm 145:10–11, 15–16, 17–18 (see 16)*

R. The hand of the Lord feeds us;
    he answers all our needs.

Let all your works give you thanks, O LORD,
    and let your faithful ones bless you.
Let them discourse of the glory of your kingdom
    and speak of your might.   R.

The eyes of all look hopefully to you,
    and you give them their food in due season;
you open your hand
    and satisfy the desire of every living thing.   R.

The LORD is just in all his ways
    and holy in all his works.
The LORD is near to all who call upon him,
    to all who call upon him in truth.   R.

READING II   *Ephesians 4:1–6*

Brothers and sisters: I, a prisoner for the Lord, urge you to live in a manner worthy of the call you have received, with all humility and gentleness, with patience, bearing with one another through love, striving to preserve the unity of the spirit through the bond of peace: one body and one Spirit, as you were also called to the one hope of your call; one Lord, one faith, one baptism; one God and Father of all, who is over all and through all and in all.

GOSPEL   *John 6:1–15*

Jesus went across the Sea of Galilee. A large crowd followed him, because they saw the signs he was performing on the sick. Jesus went up on the mountain, and there he sat down with his disciples. The Jewish feast of Passover was near. When Jesus raised his eyes and saw that a large crowd was coming to him, he said to Philip, "Where can we buy enough food for them to eat?" He said this to test him, because he himself knew what he was going to do. Philip answered him, "Two hundred days' wages worth of food would not be enough for each of them to have a little." One of his disciples, Andrew, the brother of Simon Peter, said to him, "There is a boy here who has five barley loaves and two fish; but what good are these for so many?" Jesus said, "Have the people recline." Now there was a great deal of grass in that place. So the men reclined, about five thousand in number. Then Jesus took the loaves, gave thanks, and distributed them to those who were reclining, and also as much of the fish as they wanted. When they had had their fill, he said to his disciples, "Gather the fragments left over, so that nothing will be wasted." So they collected them, and filled twelve wicker baskets with fragments from the five barley loaves that had been more than they could eat. When the people saw the sign he had done, they said, "This is truly the Prophet, the one who is to come into the world." Since Jesus knew that they were going to come and carry him off to make him king, he withdrew again to the mountain alone.

Practice of Charity

In the Second Book of Kings, Elisha feeds a hundred people with just twenty barley loaves; in the Gospel, Jesus feeds five thousand with five barley loaves and two fish. Both stories tell us that there are leftovers from the abundance of food. This physical nourishment is paired with need for spiritual nourishment: Elisha's servant and Philip and Andrew all doubt that the Lord will provide and answer all their needs. ◆ In your prayer today, reflect on when you have doubted how the Lord "[satisfies] the desire of every living thing" (Psalm 145:16). Ask the Lord to help you see how God has provided in abundance. ◆ Learn about the seven corporal works of mercy: go to the US Conference of Catholic Bishops' website, usccb.org, and search for "corporal works of mercy." ◆ Focus on one corporal work of mercy. How can you give of yourself and work with God to feed others?

Download more questions and activities for families, initiation groups, and other adult groups at http://www.ltp.org/ahw.

Scripture Insights

John 6 opens with the Passover festival approaching. This annual spring festival contextualizes the events at hand. Jesus, his disciples, and crowds impressed by Jesus' powerful signs congregate by the Sea of Galilee. Jesus miraculously feeds five thousand people with a boy's provision of five barley loaves and two fish, with leftovers gathered such that nothing is wasted. The language of thanksgiving, or Eucharist, pervades as Jesus blesses and distributes the meal. Given the abundance Jesus provides and his presentation as a prophet like Moses who perfects God's promises, the crowds clamor forcefully to make Jesus their king. Realizing the limits to the crowd's understanding of how he is the messiah-king, Jesus withdraws alone to the mountain.

Interpreters suggest that the symbolism of Passover contributes more to John's Gospel than anything else (see John 2:13, 6:4, and 11:55, contextualizing John:12–20). In Judaism's Second Temple period (ca. 515 BC–AD 70), Passover was a pilgrimage festival that bore both God's presence in the Exodus event and the nation's messianic hopes. Celebrating winter's passage to spring and creation's rebirth also symbolizes God's liberation of the people from all slavery. Jerusalem's population would swell as diaspora pilgrims traveled great distances to celebrate, ensuring that the memorial continually made present God's saving liberation.

John's rich Passover imagery recalling the gift of manna situates Jesus in the tradition of Moses and affirms God's gift of freedom. The abundance evokes liberative banquet images of the messianic age. Jesus communicates how he embodies God's power and presence, inviting everyone to this new relationship.

◆ Jesus' action reflects Elisha's prophetic activity. Why might John present Jesus in line with God's prophets?

◆ Both Elisha and Jesus wield God's power for service. How might this manifest in your call?

◆ Paul's Letter to the Ephesians summons them to solidarity in community ahead of individual ambition. How is this call heard in our lives today?

READING I *Exodus 16:2–4, 12–15*

The whole Israelite community grumbled against Moses and Aaron. The Israelites said to them, "Would that we had died at the LORD's hand in the land of Egypt, as we sat by our fleshpots and ate our fill of bread! But you had to lead us into this desert to make the whole community die of famine!"

Then the LORD said to Moses, "I will now rain down bread from heaven for you. Each day the people are to go out and gather their daily portion; thus will I test them, to see whether they follow my instructions or not.

"I have heard the grumbling of the Israelites. Tell them: In the evening twilight you shall eat flesh, and in the morning you shall have your fill of bread, so that you may know that I, the LORD, am your God."

In the evening quail came up and covered the camp. In the morning a dew lay all about the camp, and when the dew evaporated, there on the surface of the desert were fine flakes like hoarfrost on the ground. On seeing it, the Israelites asked one another, "What is this?" for they did not know what it was. But Moses told them, "This is the bread that the LORD has given you to eat."

RESPONSORIAL PSALM
Psalm 78:3–4, 23–24, 25, 54 (24b)

R. The Lord gave them bread from heaven.

What we have heard and know,
  and what our fathers have declared to us,
we will declare to the generation to come
  the glorious deeds of the LORD and his strength
  and the wonders that he wrought.   R.

He commanded the skies above
  and opened the doors of heaven;
he rained manna upon them for food
  and gave them heavenly bread.   R.

Man ate the bread of angels,
  food he sent them in abundance.
And he brought them to his holy land,
  to the mountains his right hand had won.   R.

READING II *Ephesians 4:17, 20–24*

Brothers and sisters: I declare and testify in the Lord that you must no longer live as the Gentiles do, in the futility of their minds; that is not how you learned Christ, assuming that you have heard of him and were taught in him, as truth is in Jesus, that you should put away the old self of your former way of life, corrupted through deceitful desires, and be renewed in the spirit of your minds, and put on the new self, created in God's way in righteousness and holiness of truth.

GOSPEL *John 6:24–35*

When the crowd saw that neither Jesus nor his disciples were there, they themselves got into boats and came to Capernaum looking for Jesus. And when they found him across the sea they said to him, "Rabbi, when did you get here?" Jesus answered them and said, "Amen, amen, I say to you, you are looking for me not because you saw signs but because you ate the loaves and were filled. Do not work for food that perishes but for the food that endures for eternal life, which the Son of Man will give you. For on him the Father, God, has set his seal." So they said to him, "What can we do to accomplish the works of God?" Jesus answered and said to them, "This is the work of God, that you believe in the one he sent." So they said to him, "What sign can you do, that we may see and believe in you? What can you do? Our ancestors ate manna in the desert, as it is written: *He gave them bread from heaven to eat.*" So Jesus said to them, "Amen, amen, I say to you, it was not Moses who gave the bread from heaven; my Father gives you the true bread from heaven. For the bread of God is that which comes down from heaven and gives life to the world."

So they said to him, "Sir, give us this bread always." Jesus said to them, "I am the bread of life; whoever comes to me will never hunger, and whoever believes in me will never thirst."

Practice of Hope

Jesus tells the crowd that meets him in Capernaum that he is the bread of life. We are reminded of the same each time we participate in Mass. ◆ The next time you go to Mass, pay particular attention during the Liturgy of the Eucharist. This part of the Mass begins when the bread and wine are brought forth to the altar and ends when the priest offers a short prayer after Communion. What words and actions stand out to you during the Liturgy of the Eucharist? Research answers to any questions you may have. ◆ While the bread and wine are processed to the altar, imagine you are also bringing yourself up as a gift. Pray about how the Bread of Life will transform and inspire you to "put away . . . your former way of life" (Ephesians 4:22) this week. ◆ The next time you attend Mass, invite a friend to share in "the food that endures for eternal life" (John 6:27) with you.

Download more questions and activities for families, initiation groups, and other adult groups at http://www.ltp.org/ahw.

Scripture Insights

Our readings begin with the worries of the Israelites who find themselves out of their element. Despite their desires to be their best selves in relationship with God, they are city people now in the Sinai wilderness, wondering what they have done. They question what the future may hold.

In the Gospel, John prepares us for the Bread of Life discourse by gathering those who witnessed the sign of the miraculous feeding of the crowd (6:1–15) and are now wondering about whether Jesus had crossed the sea by another miracle. Jesus' opening challenge to the crowd's superficiality insists that they work for food that endures for eternal life—nourishment that the Son of Man gives. The crux of this food's true gift is in the future. Facing the question of authentic faith in God's continual presence, Jesus further challenges them to be nourished by believing in the One sent by God.

The next stage opens with the crowd asking Jesus for a sign. As John often indicates, these crowds and religious leaders are locked into a closed system of religion. They affirm what God has done for them through Moses and show no inclination to look elsewhere. Jesus challenges them to transcend that limited understanding and seek the "true bread" that God continues to give from heaven. The crowd again intervenes, leading Jesus to identify himself as the true Bread of Life. He is the one sent by God who comes to do the will of God, to draw all who believe in him into eternal life, both here on earth and hereafter in heaven.

◆ John's Gospel demands that we open ourselves to the miraculous, to God working in the world now as we claim that God has worked in the past. How do you respond?

◆ Paul further counsels us to let go of old ways and embrace the truth of Christ and the renewal that Christ gives. What does this mean for you?

◆ Do you have practices that help you renew your spirit and put on the new self created in you by God's way of righteousness, holiness, and truth? If not, what might you do to fill this need?

READING I *1 Kings 19:4–8*

Elijah went a day's journey into the desert, until he came to a broom tree and sat beneath it. He prayed for death, saying: "This is enough, O LORD! Take my life, for I am no better than my fathers." He lay down and fell asleep under the broom tree, but then an angel touched him and ordered him to get up and eat. Elijah looked and there at his head was a hearth cake and a jug of water. After he ate and drank, he lay down again, but the angel of the LORD came back a second time, touched him, and ordered, "Get up and eat, else the journey will be too long for you!" He got up, ate, and drank; then strengthened by that food, he walked forty days and forty nights to the mountain of God, Horeb.

RESPONSORIAL PSALM
Psalm 34:2–3, 4–5, 6–7, 8–9 (9a)

R. Taste and see the goodness of the Lord.

I will bless the LORD at all times;
  his praise shall be ever in my mouth.
Let my soul glory in the LORD;
  the lowly will hear me and be glad. R.

Glorify the LORD with me,
  let us together extol his name.
I sought the LORD, and he answered me
  and delivered me from all my fears. R.

Look to him that you may be radiant with joy,
  and your faces may not blush with shame.
When the afflicted man called out,
    the LORD heard,
  and from all his distress he saved him. R.

The angel of the LORD encamps
  around those who fear him and delivers them.
Taste and see how good the LORD is;
  blessed the man who takes refuge in him. R.

READING II *Ephesians 4:30—5:2*

Brothers and sisters: Do not grieve the Holy Spirit of God, with which you were sealed for the day of redemption. All bitterness, fury, anger, shouting, and reviling must be removed from you, along with all malice. And be kind to one another, compassionate, forgiving one another as God has forgiven you in Christ.

So be imitators of God, as beloved children, and live in love, as Christ loved us and handed himself over for us as a sacrificial offering to God for a fragrant aroma.

GOSPEL *John 6:41–51*

The Jews murmured about Jesus because he said, "I am the bread that came down from heaven," and they said, "Is this not Jesus, the son of Joseph? Do we not know his father and mother? Then how can he say, 'I have come down from heaven'?" Jesus answered and said to them, "Stop murmuring among yourselves. No one can come to me unless the Father who sent me draw him, and I will raise him on the last day. It is written in the prophets: *They shall all be taught by God.* Everyone who listens to my Father and learns from him comes to me. Not that anyone has seen the Father except the one who is from God; he has seen the Father. Amen, amen, I say to you, whoever believes has eternal life. I am the bread of life. Your ancestors ate the manna in the desert, but they died; this is the bread that comes down from heaven so that one may eat it and not die. I am the living bread that came down from heaven; whoever eats this bread will live forever; and the bread that I will give is my flesh for the life of the world."

Practice of Faith

Spend time writing about how you have sought God out in the past: How have you glorified the Lord? With whom have you extolled the Lord's name? How have you called out to the Lord in affliction? How have you taken refuge in the Lord? Consider seeking God in a new way today. ◆ Last week's reading from the Letter to the Ephesians challenged us to recreate ourselves according to God's way and holiness. Today's second reading continues to guide us in how we might do that. St. Paul calls us to be kind, compassionate, and forgiving in our communities. ◆ The Church's social teaching adds to this guidance by helping us focus on specific ways we can live out holiness. Learn about this teaching at the United States Bishops' Conference website, usccb.org. At the website, go to the page for the Office of Justice, Peace & Human Development and, click on "Catholic Social Teaching" under "Resources & Initiatives." ◆ Choose one action on that page that will help you be living bread for others.

Download more questions and activities for families, initiation groups, and other adult groups at http://www.ltp.org/ahw.

Scripture Insights

In John's Gospel, Jesus is engaged in his "Bread of Life discourse" to gathering crowds following his Galilean signs at Passover. This festival celebrates God's power and presence among the Israelites during the Exodus and Sinai covenant. Covenantal symbolism ensues as Jesus presses his audience to be open to God acting in him now just as God acted in the past.

Jesus now proclaims, "I am the bread that came down from heaven" (John 6:41). He embodies God's gift of manna in the Sinai wilderness. The crowd questions how Jesus makes such claims when they know his origins. Jesus then reveals himself as the one who makes God known. Who Jesus is, and what he does to bring others to life, is possible because God is "the Father who sent me" (John 6:44). Because of Jesus' origins in God, he alone, much more than manna, makes God known and gives life both here and hereafter. Those who believe in Jesus, the Bread of Life, will not perish as did the manna and those who lived by it.

For Israel, the manna stopped when the people of God took possession of their land, but a new "bread from heaven" continued: the Law of Moses. Jesus insists that he is the "true" bread from heaven. He does not annul God's former gift but brings it to completion. He perfects God's gift to Israel in the Sinai covenant and gives life to all who partake of his offer of himself.

◆ In his worst moments of suffering Elijah lies down with hopes of never rising. After a rest, God gifts him with sustenance that revives his vocation. How do you recognize such sustenance in our world?

◆ Through the Letter to the Ephesians, Paul counsels us to imitate God and love as Christ loved. How does this resonate for you?

◆ John's first Gospel audience, people who must believe without seeing Jesus, are faced with a problem like ours today. Where do the people in the Gospel encounter the Son of Man who will give them the Bread of Life? Where do you?

READING I *Proverbs 9:1–6*

Wisdom has built her house,
    she has set up her seven columns;
she has dressed her meat, mixed her wine,
    yes, she has spread her table.
She has sent out her maidens; she calls
    from the heights out over the city:
"Let whoever is simple turn in here;
    to the one who lacks understanding,
        she says,
Come, eat of my food,
    and drink of the wine I have mixed!
Forsake foolishness that you may live;
    advance in the way of understanding."

RESPONSORIAL PSALM
Psalm 34:2–3, 4–5, 6–7 (9a)

R. Taste and see the goodness of the Lord.

I will bless the LORD at all times;
    his praise shall be ever in my mouth.
Let my soul glory in the LORD;
    the lowly will hear me and be glad. R.

Glorify the LORD with me,
    let us together extol his name.
I sought the LORD, and he answered me
    and delivered me from all my fears. R.

Look to him that you may be radiant with joy,
    and your faces may not blush with shame.
When the poor one called out, the LORD heard,
    and from all his distress he saved him. R.

READING II *Ephesians 5:15–20*

Brothers and sisters: Watch carefully how you live, not as foolish persons but as wise, making the most of the opportunity, because the days are evil. Therefore, do not continue in ignorance, but try to understand what is the will of the Lord. And do not get drunk on wine, in which lies debauchery, but be filled with the Spirit, addressing one another in psalms and hymns and spiritual songs, singing and playing to the Lord in your hearts, giving thanks always and for everything in the name of our Lord Jesus Christ to God the Father.

GOSPEL *John 6:51–58*

Jesus said to the crowds: "I am the living bread that came down from heaven; whoever eats this bread will live forever; and the bread that I will give is my flesh for the life of the world."

The Jews quarreled among themselves, saying, "How can this man give us his flesh to eat?" Jesus said to them, "Amen, amen, I say to you, unless you eat the flesh of the Son of Man and drink his blood, you do not have life within you. Whoever eats my flesh and drinks my blood has eternal life, and I will raise him on the last day. For my flesh is true food, and my blood is true drink. Whoever eats my flesh and drinks my blood remains in me and I in him. Just as the living Father sent me and I have life because of the Father, so also the one who feeds on me will have life because of me. This is the bread that came down from heaven. Unlike your ancestors who ate and still died, whoever eats this bread will live forever."

Practice of Faith

Even the Jews who themselves encountered Jesus struggled to "advance in the way of understanding" (Proverbs 9:6). It may still be difficult for us now to understand Jesus' words, but today's reading from Proverbs gives us some important insight: Wisdom invites us directly to eat her food and drink her wine. She declares that, despite any confusion we might experience with the Word of God, spending intentional time with God is the key to advancing in the way of understanding. ◆ This week, visit www.ignatianspirituality.com /ignatian-prayer/the-examen/ to learn more about the examen, a practice that helps us see God at work in our daily life. Dedicate time each evening to practice the examen to see how you recognized the Lord throughout the day. ◆ What is something you can do today to address one of your neighbors "in psalms and hymns and spiritual songs" (Ephesians 5:19)?

Download more questions and activities for families, initiation groups, and other adult groups at http://www.ltp.org/ahw.

Scripture Insights

John narrates the conclusion of Jesus' Bread of Life discourse, which he delivers during Passover. The festival celebrates God's power and presence among the Israelites during the Exodus and Sinai covenant. Covenantal symbolism has, thus, permeated Jesus' teaching as he challenges his audience to recognize God acting in him now as God has always done.

When the crowd grumbles about Jesus' origin and his ability to speak of it, he responds by further claiming his heavenly origin: "I am the living bread that came down from heaven." He then undertakes a new tactic by speaking about eating the bread he embodies, leading to a eucharistic application of all that was taught so far. Jesus claims his flesh is the living bread, the perfection of God's gift of manna in the wilderness. Using ceremonial imagery of eating and drinking the Eucharistic meal—and offering himself as that meal—Jesus challenges both crowds and disciples to be open to the ongoing revelation of God in him and eternal relationship with him.

Such talk of eating Jesus' flesh generates horrified responses. Jesus presses even further: he establishes the Son of Man, sent from the Father, whose flesh and blood sustains life, as the one in whom they abide forever. Jesus concludes the discourse in a synagogue in Capernaum by symbolically pointing to the Eucharist as their true encounter with the broken Body and the spilt Blood of Jesus. Here they are called to believe in the revelation of God through Jesus, leading to eternal life.

◆ John's Passover narrative comes full circle, from a feeding miracle to Jesus teaching that it is he who makes God known in the Eucharistic meal. How does this teaching resonate with you?

◆ Proverbs describes Wisdom as a hospitable hostess who welcomes all into her house to advance in understanding. How do you actualize such Wisdom in your life?

◆ The Letter to the Ephesians furthers Proverbs' call to forsake immediate gratification for the sustenance of the Holy Spirit. What is your method for responding positively to this call?

READING I *Joshua 24:1–2a, 15–17, 18b*

Joshua gathered together all the tribes of Israel at Shechem, summoning their elders, their leaders, their judges, and their officers. When they stood in ranks before God, Joshua addressed all the people: "If it does not please you to serve the LORD, decide today whom you will serve, the gods your fathers served beyond the River or the gods of the Amorites in whose country you are now dwelling. As for me and my household, we will serve the LORD."

But the people answered, "Far be it from us to forsake the LORD for the service of other gods. For it was the LORD, our God, who brought us and our fathers up out of the land of Egypt, out of a state of slavery. He performed those great miracles before our very eyes and protected us along our entire journey and among the peoples through whom we passed. Therefore we also will serve the LORD, for he is our God."

RESPONSORIAL PSALM *Psalm 34:2–3, 16–17, 18–19, 20–21 (9a)*

R. Taste and see the goodness of the Lord.

I will bless the LORD at all times;
   his praise shall be ever in my mouth.
Let my soul glory in the LORD;
   the lowly will hear me and be glad.   R.

The LORD has eyes for the just,
   and ears for their cry.
The LORD confronts the evildoers,
   to destroy remembrance
      of them from the earth.   R.

When the just cry out, the LORD hears them,
   and from all their distress
      he rescues them.
The LORD is close to the brokenhearted;
   and those who are crushed
      in spirit he saves.   R.

Many are the troubles of the just one,
   but out of them all the LORD delivers him;
he watches over all his bones;
   not one of them shall be broken.   R.

READING II *Ephesians 5:21–32*

Shorter: Ephesians 5:2a, 25–32

Brothers and sisters: Be subordinate to one another out of reverence for Christ. Wives should be subordinate to their husbands as to the Lord. For the husband is head of his wife just as Christ is head of the church, he himself the savior of the body. As the church is subordinate to Christ, so wives should be subordinate to their husbands in everything. Husbands, love your wives, even as Christ loved the church and handed himself over for her to sanctify her, cleansing her by the bath of water with the word, that he might present to himself the church in splendor, without spot or wrinkle or any such thing, that she might be holy and without blemish. So also husbands should love their wives as their own bodies. He who loves his wife loves himself. For no one hates his own flesh but rather nourishes and cherishes it, even as Christ does the church, because we are members of his body.

> For this reason a man shall leave his father
>   and his mother and be joined to his wife,
>   and the two shall become one flesh.

This is a great mystery, but I speak in reference to Christ and the church.

GOSPEL *John 6:60–69*

Many of Jesus' disciples who were listening said, "This saying is hard; who can accept it?" Since Jesus knew that his disciples were murmuring about this, he said to them, "Does this shock you? What if you were to see the Son of Man ascending to where he was before? It is the spirit that gives life, while the flesh is of no avail. The words I have spoken to you are Spirit and life. But there are some of you who do not believe." Jesus knew from the beginning the ones who would not believe and the one who would betray him. And he said, "For this reason I have told you that no one can come to me unless it is granted him by my Father."

As a result of this, many of his disciples returned to their former way of life and no longer accompanied him. Jesus then said to the Twelve, "Do you also want to leave?" Simon Peter answered him, "Master, to whom shall we go? You have the words of eternal life. We have come to believe and are convinced that you are the Holy One of God."

Practice of Charity

How often, after hearing the Word of God, have you found yourself saying, as did many of Jesus' disciples, "This is hard; how can I accept it?" Following the Holy One of God is a great mystery, one that comes with many challenges. As we hear in the Book of Joshua, we can choose either to serve the Lord or serve other gods such as wealth, prestige, or some worldly desire. ◆ Today, light a candle and spend intentional time reflecting on your actions from this past week. Did you serve God or were your actions in service of a different objective? Which god did you serve? What keeps you from singular focus on the Lord? ◆ Following Jesus requires wholehearted dedication to serving others. Whom do you resist serving? How can you better serve that person?

Download more questions and activities for families, initiation groups, and other adult groups at http://www.ltp.org/ahw.

Scripture Insights

In his final act as prophetic leader of God's people, Joshua brought the tribes together to renew the Sinai covenant. This action formed a league that was crucial for creating a unified people. When he recites Israel's history, Joshua begins with God's ancestral promises and culminates with a decision. Sinai's first commandment is reiterated in terms of service. God has already chosen Israel; Israel, as a tribal confederation, must now respond with their choice for God. By reaffirming the Sinai covenant, the people of this new generation render themselves participants in that same relationship.

In John's Gospel, Jesus has challenged the crowds to the very limits of their religious worldview. The enormity of the progression of Jesus' public challenge is reflected in the responses to it. Many disciples now falter: "This saying is hard; who can accept it?" (John 6:60). In rejecting Jesus, they assert that Moses, manna, and the Torah exhaust all possibilities for God's action and presence in their lives.

Jesus then challenges the Twelve directly. This is the first time that Jesus' inner circle of twelve disciples is identified, and their number is mentioned three times, both in the context of acceptance and in Judas' ultimate rejection. Recognizing that Jesus is "the Holy One of God," essential to authentic believing, Peter takes this initial lead and responds on behalf of the disciples by making a public confession of their growing belief in and determination to follow Jesus.

◆ Joshua challenges God's people to declare where they stand, even in unsettled times. What might be a similar situation today? Could you respond with such conviction?

◆ All of John 6 leads to a turning point as we witness the mass exodus of disciples and crowds, Peter's declaration of who Jesus is, and the foreshadowed end of the Son of Man's earthly mission. Where would you stand?

◆ Ephesians calls for extreme mutuality in all our societal relationships. How do you manifest solidarity with the "other" in various relationships?

Prayer before Reading the Word

In humility and service, O God,
your Son came among us
to form a community of disciples
who have one Father in heaven,
and one teacher, the Messiah.
Let your Spirit make our hearts
docile to the challenge of your Word,
and let the same mind be in us
that was in Christ Jesus.
We ask this through our Lord Jesus Christ,
     your Son,
who lives and reigns with you
in the unity of the Holy Spirit,
God, for ever and ever. Amen.

Prayer after Reading the Word

To the last as to the first, O God,
you are generous and more than just,
for as high as the heavens are above the earth,
so high are your ways above our ways
and your thoughts above our thoughts.
Open our hearts to the wisdom of your Son,
fix in our minds his sound teaching,
that, without concern for the cost of discipleship,
we may work without ceasing
for the coming of your kingdom.
We ask this through our Lord Jesus Christ,
     your Son,
who lives and reigns with you
in the unity of the Holy Spirit,
God, for ever and ever. Amen.

Weekday Readings

September 2: *1 Corinthians 2:1–5; Luke 4:16–30*
September 3: *1 Corinthians 2:10b–16; Luke 4:31–37*
September 4: *1 Corinthians 3:1–9; Luke 4:38–44*
September 5: *1 Corinthians 3:18–23; Luke 5:1–11*
September 6: *1 Corinthians 4:1–5; Luke 5:33–39*
September 7: *1 Corinthians 4:6b–15; Luke 6:1–5*

September 9: *1 Corinthians 5:1–8; Luke 6:6–11*
September 10: *1 Corinthians 6:1–11; Luke 6:12–19*
September 11: *1 Corinthians 7:25–31; Luke 6:20–26*
September 12: *1 Corinthians 8:1b–7, 11–13; Luke 6:27–38*
September 13: *1 Corinthians 9:16–19, 22b–27; Luke 6:39–42*
September 14: Feast of the Exaltation of the Holy Cross
Numbers 21:4b–9; Philippians 2:6–11; John 3:13–17

September 16: *1 Corinthians 11:17–26, 33; Luke 7:1–10*
September 17: *1 Corinthians 12:12–14, 27–31a; Luke 7:11–17*
September 18: *1 Corinthians 12:31—13:13; Luke 7:31–35*
September 19: *1 Corinthians 15:1–11; Luke 7:36–50*
September 20: *1 Corinthians 15:12–20; Luke 8:1–3*
September 21: Feast of St. Matthew, Apostle and Evangelist
Ephesians 4:1–7, 11–13; Matthew 9:9–13

September 23: *Proverbs 3:27–34; Luke 8:16–18*
September 24: *Proverbs 21:1–6, 10–13; Luke 8:19–21*
September 25: *Proverbs 30:5–9; Luke 9:1–6*
September 26: *Ecclesiastes 1:2–11; Luke 9:7–9*
September 27: *Ecclesiastes 3:1–11; Luke 9:18–22*
September 28: *Ecclesiastes 11:9—12:8; Luke 9:43b–45*

September 30: *Job 1:6–22; Luke 9:46–50*
October 1: *Job 3:1–3, 11–17, 20–23; Luke 9:51–56*
October 2: *Job 9:1–12, 14–16; Matthew 18:1–5, 10*
October 3: *Job 19:21–27; Luke 10:1–12*
October 4: *Job 38:1, 12–21; 40:3–5; Luke 10:13–16*
October 5: *Job 42:1–3, 5–6, 12–17; Luke 10:17–24*

October 7: *Galatians 1:6–12; Luke 10:25–37*
October 8: *Galatians 1:13–24; Luke 10:38–42*
October 9: *Galatians 2:1–2, 7–14; Luke 11:1–4*
October 10: *Galatians 3:1–5; Luke 11:5–13*
October 11: *Galatians 3:7–14; Luke 11:15–26*
October 12: *Galatians 3:22–29; Luke 11:27–28*

October 14: *Galatians 4:22–24, 26–27, 31—5:1; Luke 11:29–32*
October 15: *Galatians 5:1–6; Luke 11:37–41*
October 16: *Galatians 5:18–25; Luke 11:42–46*
October 17: *Ephesians 1:1–10; Luke 11:47–54*
October 18: Feast of St. Luke, Evangelist
2 Timothy 4:10–17b; Luke 10:1–9
October 19: *Ephesians 1:15–23; Luke 12:8–12*

October 21: *Ephesians 2:1–10; Luke 12:13–21*
October 22: *Ephesians 2:12–22; Luke 12:35–38*
October 23: *Ephesians 3:2–12; Luke 12:39–48*
October 24: *Ephesians 3:14–21; Luke 12:49–53*
October 25: *Ephesians 4:1–6; Luke 12:54–59*
October 26: *Ephesians 4:7–16; Luke 13:1–9*

October 28: Feast of Sts. Simon and Jude, Apostles
Ephesians 2:19–22; Luke 6:12–16
October 29: *Ephesians 5:21–33; Luke 13:18–21*
October 30: *Ephesians 6:1–9; Luke 13:22–30*
October 31: *Ephesians 6:10–20; Luke 13:31–35*
November 1: Solemnity of All Saints
Revelation 7:2–4, 9–14; 1 John 3:1–3; Matthew 5:1–12a
November 2: Commemoration of All the Faithful
Departed
Wisdom 3:1–9; Romans 5:5–11 or Romans 6:3–9;
John 6:37–40

November 4: *Philippians 2:1–4; Luke 14:12–14*
November 5: *Philippians 2:5–11; Luke 14:15–24*
November 6: *Philippians 2:12–18; Luke 14:25–33*
November 7: *Philippians 3:3–8a; Luke 15:1–10*
November 8: *Philippians 3:17—4:1; Luke 16:1–8*
November 9: Feast of the Dedication of the Lateran Basilica
Ezekiel 47:1–2, 8–9, 12; 1 Corinthians 3:9c–11, 16–17;
John 2:13–22

November 11: *Titus 1:1–9; Luke 17:1–6*
November 12: *Titus 2:1–8, 11–14; Luke 17:7–10*
November 13: *Titus 3:1–7; Luke 17:11–19*
November 14: *Philemon 7–20; Luke 17:20–25*
November 15: *2 John 4–9; Luke 17:26–37*
November 16: *3 John 5–8; Luke 18:1–8*

November 18: *Revelation 1:1–4; 2:1–5; Luke 18:35–43*
November 19: *Revelation 3:1–6, 14–22; Luke 19:1–10*
November 20: *Revelation 4:1–11; Luke 19:11–28*
November 21: *Revelation 5:1–10; Luke 19:41–44*
November 22: *Revelation 10:8–11; Luke 19:45–48*
November 23: *Revelation 11:4–12; Luke 20:27–40*

November 25: *Revelation 14:1–3, 4b–5; Luke 21:1–4*
November 26: *Revelation 14:14–19; Luke 21:5–11*
November 27: *Revelation 15:1–4; Luke 21:12–19*
November 28: *Revelation 18:1–2, 21–23; 19:1–3, 9a;*
Luke 21:20–28
November 29: *Revelation 20:1–4, 11—21:2; Luke 21:29–33*
November 30: Feast of St. Andrew, Apostle
Romans 10:9–18; Matthew 4:18–22

READING I *Deuteronomy 4:1–2, 6–8*

Moses said to the people: "Now, Israel, hear the statutes and decrees which I am teaching you to observe, that you may live, and may enter in and take possession of the land which the LORD, the God of your fathers, is giving you. In your observance of the commandments of the LORD, your God, which I enjoin upon you, you shall not add to what I command you nor subtract from it. Observe them carefully, for thus will you give evidence of your wisdom and intelligence to the nations, who will hear of all these statutes and say, 'This great nation is truly a wise and intelligent people.' For what great nation is there that has gods so close to it as the LORD, our God, is to us whenever we call upon him? Or what great nation has statutes and decrees that are as just as this whole law which I am setting before you today?"

RESPONSORIAL PSALM
Psalm 15:2–3, 3–4, 4–5 (1a)

R. The one who does justice will live in the
    presence of the Lord.

Whoever walks blamelessly and does justice;
  who thinks the truth in his heart
  and slanders not with his tongue.   R.

Who harms not his fellow man,
  nor takes up a reproach against his neighbor;
by whom the reprobate is despised,
  while he honors those who fear the LORD.   R.

Who lends not his money at usury
  and accepts no bribe against the innocent.
Whoever does these things
  shall never be disturbed.   R.

READING II
James 1:17–18, 21b–22, 27

Dearest brothers and sisters: All good giving and every perfect gift is from above, coming down from the Father of lights, with whom there is no alteration or shadow caused by change. He willed to give us birth by the word of truth that we may be a kind of firstfruits of his creatures.

Humbly welcome the word that has been planted in you and is able to save your souls.

Be doers of the word and not hearers only, deluding yourselves.

Religion that is pure and undefiled before God and the Father is this: to care for orphans and widows in their affliction and to keep oneself unstained by the world.

GOSPEL *Mark 7:1–8, 14–15, 21–23*

When the Pharisees with some scribes who had come from Jerusalem gathered around Jesus, they observed that some of his disciples ate their meals with unclean, that is, unwashed, hands.—For the Pharisees and, in fact, all Jews, do not eat without carefully washing their hands, keeping the tradition of the elders. And on coming from the marketplace they do not eat without purifying themselves. And there are many other things that they have traditionally observed, the purification of cups and jugs and kettles and beds.—So the Pharisees and scribes questioned him, "Why do your disciples not follow the tradition of the elders but instead eat a meal with unclean hands?" He responded, "Well did Isaiah prophesy about you hypocrites, as it is written:

This people honors me with their lips,
    but their hearts are far from me;
in vain do they worship me,
    teaching as doctrines human precepts.

You disregard God's commandment but cling to human tradition." He summoned the crowd again and said to them, "Hear me, all of you, and understand. Nothing that enters one from outside can defile that person; but the things that come out from within are what defile.

"From within people, from their hearts, come evil thoughts, unchastity, theft, murder, adultery, greed, malice, deceit, licentiousness, envy, blasphemy, arrogance, folly. All these evils come from within and they defile."

Practice of Charity

Our faith is one of transformation. Simply praying or attending Mass is not enough; selflessly honoring God with our lips and our actions is critical to bringing our hearts close to the Lord. ◆ When you hear the Word today, what does it compel you to do? What action can you take today to become a doer of the Word? ◆ The psalm proclaims that doing justice is required to live in the presence of the Lord. Visit the United States Conference of Catholic Bishops' Committee for Domestic Justice and Human Development website (www.usccb .org/committees/domestic-justice-and-human -development). Scroll down to the "Happening Now" section on the main page. Spend time this week learning about timely events and how you can get involved, such as by contacting your government representatives or donating goods or time to a local charity. How can you do justice?

Download more questions and activities for families, initiation groups, and other adult groups at http://www.ltp.org/ahw.

Scripture Insights

The title Deuteronomy is derived from the Greek words *deuteros* (second) and *nomos* (law) and indicates that this book is a second telling of the "law," (a translation of the Hebrew word *torah*). The book presents Moses' final teaching to the Israelites gathered on the plains of Moab. By reviewing their history, Moses prepares them to reenter Canaan, land promised them by God. He counsels them to keep the Lord's commandments. The rest of Deuteronomy details the statutes and ordinances, which concern ethics and how to act in community in covenant with God.

The remaining readings take the first as foundational and detail what behavior right relationship with God engenders. Psalm 15 refers to walking the walk we talk in how we behave and treat others. The letter of James discusses how our action must be grounded in love and in the truth of our tradition. James, more than any other New Testament author, exhorts us to action: to live out our faith in what we do in this world.

Mark culminates this teaching in a dynamic reinterpretation of Torah. Jesus and his disciples engage Pharisees, teachers of the Sinai covenant, in a question about proper behavior. Jesus takes the opportunity to address empty ritual. By contrast, he teaches that we must work toward manifesting the kingdom of God on earth.

◆ How does the deuteronomic call to live and act close to God reinforce the notion of living as if God is our authority?

◆ The letter of James challenges us to "be doers of the word and not hearers only" (James 1:22). How is it misguided to only live an internalized faith? In what ways might you accept this challenge?

◆ Mark summons us to reinterpret our moral elitism and draw the largest possible pool of people into community and relationship with God. How might you bring such a summons to manifest the kingdom of God into your life?

READING I *Isaiah 35:4–7a*

Thus says the LORD:
Say to those whose hearts are frightened:
   Be strong, fear not!
Here is your God,
   he comes with vindication;
with divine recompense
   he comes to save you.
Then will the eyes of the blind be opened,
   the ears of the deaf be cleared;
then will the lame leap like a stag,
   then the tongue of the mute will sing.
Streams will burst forth in the desert,
   and rivers in the steppe.
The burning sands will become pools,
   and the thirsty ground, springs of water.

RESPONSORIAL PSALM
Psalm 146:6–7, 8–9, 9–10 (1b)

R. Praise the Lord, my soul!
   or: Alleluia.

The God of Jacob keeps faith forever,
   secures justice for the oppressed,
   gives food to the hungry.
The LORD sets captives free. R.

The LORD gives sight to the blind;
   the LORD raises up those who were
     bowed down.
The LORD loves the just;
   the LORD protects strangers. R.

The fatherless and the widow the LORD sustains,
   but the way of the wicked he thwarts.
The LORD shall reign forever;
   your God, O Zion, through all generations.
     Alleluia. R.

READING II *James 2:1–5*

My brothers and sisters, show no partiality as you adhere to the faith in our glorious Lord Jesus Christ. For if a man with gold rings and fine clothes comes into your assembly, and a poor person in shabby clothes also comes in, and you pay attention to the one wearing the fine clothes and say, "Sit here, please," while you say to the poor one, "Stand there," or "Sit at my feet," have you not made distinctions among yourselves and become judges with evil designs?

Listen, my beloved brothers and sisters. Did not God choose those who are poor in the world to be rich in faith and heirs of the kingdom that he promised to those who love him?

GOSPEL *Mark 7:31–37*

Again Jesus left the district of Tyre and went by way of Sidon to the Sea of Galilee, into the district of the Decapolis. And people brought to him a deaf man who had a speech impediment and begged him to lay his hand on him. He took him off by himself away from the crowd. He put his finger into the man's ears and, spitting, touched his tongue; then he looked up to heaven and groaned, and said to him, "*Ephphatha!*"—that is, "Be opened!"—And immediately the man's ears were opened, his speech impediment was removed, and he spoke plainly. He ordered them not to tell anyone. But the more he ordered them not to, the more they proclaimed it. They were exceedingly astonished and they said, "He has done all things well. He makes the deaf hear and the mute speak."

Practice of Charity

Today we are reminded that we are called to serve everyone we encounter, especially those whom society casts out and ignores. Who is the "poor person in shabby clothes" (James 2:2) you meet on a regular basis? Do you treat them as you would someone with gold rings and fine clothes? ◆ Visit the Catholic Charities website (www.catholic charitiesusa.org/find-help/) to find your local Catholic Charities agency. Learn more about the work they are doing to serve those who are in need in your community; dedicate time to serve with them this week. ◆ Jesus says to the deaf man in Decapolis, "Be opened!" (Mark 7:34). Immediately the deaf man hears. How is Jesus telling you to "be opened"? Spend time reflecting on how you can figuratively open your ears and your heart to listen to how God may be speaking to you. ◆ Write your reflections down and bring them with you the next time you go to Mass. Lift them up in prayer; ask God to help you hear God's voice.

Download more questions and activities for families, initiation groups, and other adult groups at http://www.ltp.org/ahw.

Scripture Insights

This week's readings are powerful calls to attend to those who are the most marginalized in our societies. All four selections indicate that God is particularly interested in and concerned for those who need God most, what the Church has deemed God's "preferential option for the poor." Isaiah sends comfort to those who find themselves living in fear. Water, the power over which the Scriptures assign to God alone, symbolizes God's sustaining the faithful in even the direst situations this world might impose. Psalm 146 likewise extols God's justice for the oppressed.

James' letter to the early Christian communities is known for his challenge to the rich. In our passage he focuses on God's impartiality in welcoming people from all social strata into relationship. He further suggests that the marginalized in this world are especially close to God. They are rich in faith and equal heirs in the kingdom of God. This message is especially powerful in a particularly hierarchical and classist society.

Mark continues this sort of teaching in his Gospel account of Jesus encountering a man limited in both hearing and speaking in the Gentile region of the Decapolis. Jesus, like the scriptural teachings about God, shows partiality for neither class nor ethnicity as he interacts with one who needs him and has been brought to him in faith.

◆ The Scriptures challenge Christians to work for justice for all people, regardless of race, gender, class, or ethnicity. What more can you do to work for justice?

◆ James summons us to cross social and class boundaries to welcome the "other" into our churches, our community, and our hospitable gatherings. How might you rise to this challenge?

◆ Do you believe in miracles? If not, why not? If so, what do they look like in your twenty-first-century context? Are there ways that we can better recognize God's miraculous activity in our lives and in the world around us?

READING I   *Isaiah 50:4c–9a*

The Lord GOD opens my ear that I may hear;
    and I have not rebelled,
    have not turned back.
I gave my back to those who beat me,
    my cheeks to those who plucked my beard;
my face I did not shield
    from buffets and spitting.

The Lord GOD is my help,
    therefore I am not disgraced;
I have set my face like flint,
    knowing that I shall not be put to shame.
He is near who upholds my right;
    if anyone wishes to oppose me,
    let us appear together.
Who disputes my right?
    Let that man confront me.
See, the Lord GOD is my help;
    who will prove me wrong?

RESPONSORIAL PSALM
Psalm 116:1–2, 3–4, 5–6, 8–9 (9)

R. I will walk before the Lord,
    in the land of the living.
  or: Alleluia.

I love the LORD because he has heard
    my voice in supplication,
because he has inclined his ear to me
    the day I called. R.

The cords of death encompassed me;
    the snares of the netherworld seized upon me;
    I fell into distress and sorrow,
and I called upon the name of the LORD,
    "O LORD, save my life!" R.

Gracious is the LORD and just;
    yes, our God is merciful.
The LORD keeps the little ones;
    I was brought low, and he saved me. R.

For he has freed my soul from death,
    my eyes from tears, my feet from stumbling.
I shall walk before the LORD
    in the land of the living. R.

READING II   *James 2:14–18*

What good is it, my brothers and sisters, if someone says he has faith but does not have works? Can that faith save him? If a brother or sister has nothing to wear and has no food for the day, and one of you says to them, "Go in peace, keep warm, and eat well," but you do not give them the necessities of the body, what good is it? So also faith of itself, if it does not have works, is dead.

Indeed someone might say, "You have faith and I have works." Demonstrate your faith to me without works, and I will demonstrate my faith to you from my works.

GOSPEL   *Mark 8:27–35*

Jesus and his disciples set out for the villages of Caesarea Philippi. Along the way he asked his disciples, "Who do people say that I am?" They said in reply, "John the Baptist, others Elijah, still others one of the prophets." And he asked them, "But who do you say that I am?" Peter said to him in reply, "You are the Christ." Then he warned them not to tell anyone about him.

He began to teach them that the Son of Man must suffer greatly and be rejected by the elders, the chief priests, and the scribes, and be killed, and rise after three days. He spoke this openly. Then Peter took him aside and began to rebuke him. At this he turned around and, looking at his disciples, rebuked Peter and said, "Get behind me, Satan. You are thinking not as God does, but as human beings do."

He summoned the crowd with his disciples and said to them, "Whoever wishes to come after me must deny himself, take up his cross, and follow me. For whoever wishes to save his life will lose it, but whoever loses his life for my sake and that of the gospel will save it."

Practice of Charity

Today, we struggle with Peter as we ponder where following Jesus might lead us. The passage from the letter of James reminds us that our faith must inspire us to act in a very specific way: our actions must focus on radically following Christ and dedicating ourselves to justice. Jesus openly speaks to his disciples about the suffering he will endure, which reminds us that the cost of discipleship is great. Following God's call to act justly can be scary. ◆ Spend time resting in peace knowing that God opens your ears so that you may hear God's call. Ask God to help you pinpoint one action you can take today to open your heart so that you can think as God does. ◆ Who is someone who inspires you to deny yourself and follow Jesus? Reach out to them this week for a conversation about what you are hearing God say to you.

Download more questions and activities for families, initiation groups, and other adult groups at http://www.ltp.org/ahw.

Scripture Insights

The prophet Isaiah begins our readings by modeling the powerful results of listening to God, even when we least expect to hear his voice. If we open ourselves while amid conflict, God's counsel may become apparent. This revelation could be direct and clear but, far more likely, it will come in some unexpected manner embedded in our culture. As the psalmist declares, the souls of those who heed the voice of God are freed from death, but our lives must be committed, in the name of the Lord, to the living.

In his letter, James' most famous declaration that faith without works is dead has been contentious in the tradition. Some even suggest that James contradicts our most prolific New Testament author, Paul. But this is not so. When Paul speaks of works, he refers to keeping the Torah prescribed in the Sinai covenant. Christians are now justified by faith, not by works. When James speaks of works, he refers to active efforts for social justice. Both authors agree that these goals are essential to authentic faith.

The turning point of Mark's Gospel comes when the question that has pervaded the first half of the text is finally answered: Who is Jesus? After detailing popular speculation, Peter speaks on behalf of the disciples and calls Jesus the messiah Jesus accepts this title, then immediately begins to redefine what it means to be the messiah by foretelling his suffering at the hands of the authorities, and his vindication. This is difficult to hear, but Jesus challenges us to heed God's plan.

◆ In what ways do you live out your faith with works?

◆ Peter objects to suffering and rejection being part of Jesus' messianic mission rather than kingship and sovereignty. How does such an objection ring true to you?

◆ Jesus, in contradiction to all messianic and even societal expectations, embraces suffering that leads to vindication and further, salvation for others. What might this mean for your life and attempts to listen to God?

READING I *Wisdom 2:12, 17–20*

The wicked say:
  Let us beset the just one, because
        he is obnoxious to us;
    he sets himself against our doings,
  reproaches us for transgressions of the law
    and charges us with violations
        of our training.
  Let us see whether his words be true;
    let us find out what will happen to him.
  For if the just one be the son
        of God, God will defend him
    and deliver him from the hand of his foes.
  With revilement and torture let us put the
        just one to the test
    that we may have proof of his gentleness
    and try his patience.
  Let us condemn him to a shameful death;
    for according to his own words,
        God will take care of him.

RESPONSORIAL PSALM
Psalm 54:3–4, 5, 6–8 (6b)

R. The Lord upholds my life.

O God, by your name save me,
  and by your might defend my cause.
O God, hear my prayer;
  hearken to the words of my mouth. R.

For the haughty have risen up against me,
  the ruthless seek my life;
  they set not God before their eyes. R.

Behold, God is my helper;
  the Lord sustains my life.
Freely will I offer you sacrifice;
  I will praise your name, O LORD, for its
    goodness. R.

READING II *James 3:16—4:3*

Beloved: Where jealousy and selfish ambition exist, there is disorder and every foul practice. But the wisdom from above is first of all pure, then peaceable, gentle, compliant, full of mercy and good fruits, without inconstancy or insincerity. And the fruit of righteousness is sown in peace for those who cultivate peace.

Where do the wars and where do the conflicts among you come from? Is it not from your passions that make war within your members? You covet but do not possess. You kill and envy but you cannot obtain; you fight and wage war. You do not possess because you do not ask. You ask but do not receive, because you ask wrongly, to spend it on your passions.

GOSPEL *Mark 9:30–37*

Jesus and his disciples left from there and began a journey through Galilee, but he did not wish anyone to know about it. He was teaching his disciples and telling them, "The Son of Man is to be handed over to men and they will kill him, and three days after his death the Son of Man will rise." But they did not understand the saying, and they were afraid to question him.

They came to Capernaum and, once inside the house, he began to ask them, "What were you arguing about on the way?" But they remained silent. They had been discussing among themselves on the way who was the greatest. Then he sat down, called the Twelve, and said to them, "If anyone wishes to be first, he shall be the last of all and the servant of all." Taking a child, he placed it in their midst, and putting his arms around it, he said to them, "Whoever receives one child such as this in my name, receives me; and whoever receives me, receives not me but the One who sent me."

Practice of Hope

How often do we find ourselves hoping to be thanked for doing a good deed or recognized for an accomplishment? Jesus reminds the disciples that placing a desire for recognition over the desire to serve breeds jealousy and selfishness. Our good deeds and accomplishments must always point to God. This takes a lot of effort and daily dedication to turn to God. ◆ Each day this week, hold in your prayer someone who models service. How does this person humbly help others? How do their actions point to God's goodness? How do they challenge you to a life of service to others? ◆ Consider an issue with which one of your neighbors or someone in your community struggles. What is something you can do to assist them and relieve their burden? How can you center that act of service on gratitude, humility, and Jesus' call to serve?

Download more questions and activities for families, initiation groups, and other adult groups at http://www.ltp.org/ahw.

Scripture Insights

The Book of Wisdom speaks in the voice of the ungodly as it calls us to put the just one to the test. Although sarcasm is at play here, such discernment nonetheless remains relevant in our time. True wisdom would have us prove the intentions and abilities of those who make promises—especially if they include greatness and luxury. The psalmist confirms that God is our helper and defender. God wants us to be our best selves, but that may not be what the prevailing culture extols either popularly or politically.

James affirms that jealousy and selfish ambition lead to disorder, but justice and uprightness cultivate peace and community. Wisdom is indeed pure and merciful and combats inconstancy and insincerity. Therefore, we must seek wisdom and work for the common good to receive the strength and passion to empower our diverse vocations.

Mark's Gospel recounts what interpreters often call the second passion prediction. Jesus gave the first in Mark 8 and the third and final prediction will come in Mark 10. Here, Jesus expands on his initial teaching about his impending sacrificial death and resurrection with a concern for his disciples' understanding. They don't get it, so he explains by using the metaphor of a child. If you receive the least—like a child—it is as though you receive Jesus, and if you receive Jesus, it is as though you have received God. Such childlike openness allows us to accept God working in our lives in unexpected ways—sometimes in sacrifice and other times in resurrected vindication.

◆ How do you respond when the Scriptures challenge you in unexpected ways? Are you able to dwell in discomfort to learn new things?

◆ James challenges us to overturn cultural expectations and live. How might you learn to ask, in genuine faith, for God's help?

◆ Put yourself in the place of Jesus' disciples— longing for a messiah in David's line who will bring sovereignty to your nation. How might you respond to his sacrificial intentions and his summons to receive others openly?

READING I *Numbers 11:25–29*

The LORD came down in the cloud and spoke to Moses. Taking some of the spirit that was on Moses, the LORD bestowed it on the seventy elders; and as the spirit came to rest on them, they prophesied.

Now two men, one named Eldad and the other Medad, were not in the gathering but had been left in the camp. They too had been on the list, but had not gone out to the tent; yet the spirit came to rest on them also, and they prophesied in the camp. So, when a young man quickly told Moses, "Eldad and Medad are prophesying in the camp," Joshua, son of Nun, who from his youth had been Moses' aide, said, "Moses, my lord, stop them." But Moses answered him, "Are you jealous for my sake? Would that all the people of the LORD were prophets! Would that the LORD might bestow his spirit on them all!"

RESPONSORIAL PSALM
Psalm 19:8, 10, 12–13, 14 (9a)

R The precepts of the Lord give joy to the heart.

The law of the LORD is perfect,
  refreshing the soul;
the decree of the LORD is trustworthy,
  giving wisdom to the simple. R.

The fear of the LORD is pure,
  enduring forever;
the ordinances of the LORD are true,
  all of them just. R.

Though your servant is careful of them,
  very diligent in keeping them,
yet who can detect failings?
  Cleanse me from my unknown faults! R.

From wanton sin especially, restrain your servant;
  let it not rule over me.
Then shall I be blameless and innocent
  of serious sin. R.

READING II *James 5:1–6*

Come now, you rich, weep and wail over your impending miseries. Your wealth has rotted away, your clothes have become moth-eaten, your gold and silver have corroded, and that corrosion will be a testimony against you; it will devour your flesh like a fire. You have stored up treasure for the last days. Behold, the wages you withheld from the workers who harvested your fields are crying aloud; and the cries of the harvesters have reached the ears of the Lord of hosts. You have lived on earth in luxury and pleasure; you have fattened your hearts for the day of slaughter. You have condemned; you have murdered the righteous one; he offers you no resistance.

GOSPEL *Mark 9:38–43, 45, 47–48*

At that time, John said to Jesus, "Teacher, we saw someone driving out demons in your name, and we tried to prevent him because he does not follow us." Jesus replied, "Do not prevent him. There is no one who performs a mighty deed in my name who can at the same time speak ill of me. For whoever is not against us is for us. Anyone who gives you a cup of water to drink because you belong to Christ, amen, I say to you, will surely not lose his reward.

"Whoever causes one of these little ones who believe in me to sin, it would be better for him if a great millstone were put around his neck and he were thrown into the sea. If your hand causes you to sin, cut it off. It is better for you to enter into life maimed than with two hands to go into Gehenna, into the unquenchable fire. And if your foot causes you to sin, cut it off. It is better for you to enter into life crippled than with two feet to be thrown into Gehenna. And if your eye causes you to sin, pluck it out. Better for you to enter into the kingdom of God with one eye than with two eyes to be thrown into Gehenna, where 'their worm does not die, and the fire is not quenched.'"

Practice of Faith

Jesus calls his disciples to seriously consider the ways they sin, the ways they choose to move away from God. His intense imagery in today's Gospel according to Mark challenges us to reflect on how we are (or are not) radically rejecting sin and temptation. ◆ The second reading invites you to consider what wealth you are storing up and withholding from the world. Your wealth may be money, but it could also be a talent you have hidden, time you have not given, kindness you have not shared, or something else. How can you give of your luxury and pleasure to enter right relationship with God and with your community? ◆ Schedule a time to go to confession this week. Before celebrating the sacrament of penance, make sure you dedicate time for prayer. For a structured guide to examine your conscience, visit: https://www.usccb.org/prayer-and-worship/sacraments-and-sacramentals/penance/examination-conscience-in-light-of-catholic-social-teaching.

Download more questions and activities for families, initiation groups, and other adult groups at http://www.ltp.org/ahw.

Scripture Insights

The Book of Numbers gives instruction on being open to God working in the world even in and among unexpected people. Today's text introduces Joshua, a key figure in the development of the Israelites. But here Joshua is still learning. Moses teaches that God works as God wills and expresses his desire that we were all prophets. A prophet is one who speaks for God in human language to human beings.

The psalmist concurs in his own way. God's law (Torah) is perfect in its wisdom, especially in its prescriptions for our treatment of one another. James expounds upon this when he gives his harshest condemnation of the rich. In his experience, the rich are focused only on their own gain in this life. They store their treasures at the expense of employees who struggle to get by. James declares their reward to be limited while the faithful have much more for which to hope.

In Mark, Jesus teaches that all those who share the Good News must be accepted and lauded. He further explains that true models are those who give freely and do not prevent others from seeking right relationship with God. Consequences for those who lead people astray are dire. Jesus as Christ, Son of God and Son of Man, wants all to encounter God in truth.

◆ Joshua becomes a significant leader of God's people. Here we see his early struggle to learn what it means to lead. Does this give you hope in your vocation?

◆ James challenges the rich in his time and does not believe that they are able to be genuine, giving, and active in their faith lives. Many Christians find themselves quite comfortable in our contemporary society. How might this reading challenge us? Other Christians identify more with those who suffer in the current social order. How might this inspire us?

◆ In Mark, Jesus challenges us to be open to God working in and through unlikely people and places. Are there paths you can take in your life to rise to this challenge?

READING I *Genesis 2:18–24*

The LORD God said: "It is not good for the man to be alone. I will make a suitable partner for him." So the LORD God formed out of the ground various wild animals and various birds of the air, and he brought them to the man to see what he would call them; whatever the man called each of them would be its name. The man gave names to all the cattle, all the birds of the air, and all wild animals; but none proved to be the suitable partner for the man.

So the LORD God cast a deep sleep on the man, and while he was asleep, he took out one of his ribs and closed up its place with flesh. The LORD God then built up into a woman the rib that he had taken from the man. When he brought her to the man, the man said:

"This one, at last, is bone of my bones
    and flesh of my flesh;
this one shall be called 'woman,'
    for out of 'her man' this one
      has been taken."

That is why a man leaves his father and mother and clings to his wife, and the two of them become one flesh.

RESPONSORIAL PSALM
Psalm 128:1–2, 3, 4–5, 6 (see 5)

R. May the Lord bless us all the days of our lives.

Blessed are you who fear the LORD,
  who walk in his ways!
For you shall eat the fruit of your handiwork;
  blessed shall you be, and favored. R.

Your wife shall be like a fruitful vine
  in the recesses of your home;
your children like olive plants
  around your table. R.

Behold, thus is the man blessed
  who fears the LORD.
The LORD bless you from Zion:
  may you see the prosperity of Jerusalem
  all the days of your life. R.

May you see your children's children.
  Peace be upon Israel! R.

READING II *Hebrews 2:9–11*

Brothers and sisters: He "for a little while" was made "lower than the angels," that by the grace of God he might taste death for everyone.

For it was fitting that he, for whom and through whom all things exist, in bringing many children to glory, should make the leader to their salvation perfect through suffering. He who consecrates and those who are being consecrated all have one origin. Therefore, he is not ashamed to call them "brothers."

GOSPEL *Mark 10:2–16*

Shorter: Mark 10:2–12

The Pharisees approached Jesus and asked, "Is it lawful for a husband to divorce his wife?" They were testing him. He said to them in reply, "What did Moses command you?" They replied, "Moses permitted a husband to write a bill of divorce and dismiss her." But Jesus told them, "Because of the hardness of your hearts he wrote you this commandment. But from the beginning of creation, *God made them male and female. For this reason a man shall leave his father and mother and be joined to his wife, and the two shall become one flesh.* So they are no longer two but one flesh. Therefore what God has joined together, no human being must separate." In the house the disciples again questioned Jesus about this. He said to them, "Whoever divorces his wife and marries another commits adultery against her; and if she divorces her husband and marries another, she commits adultery."

And people were bringing children to him that he might touch them, but the disciples rebuked them. When Jesus saw this he became indignant and said to them, "Let the children come to me; do not prevent them, for the kingdom of God belongs to such as these. Amen, I say to you, whoever does not accept the kingdom of God like a child will not enter it." Then he embraced them and blessed them, placing his hands on them.

Practice of Faith

Initially, today's readings seem to speak only to married couples or those discerning marriage; however, there is much that all of us—married or not—can glean from these passages. In Genesis, we are taken through a part of a story of God creating a "suitable partner" for man. ◆ What does it mean to be a "suitable partner," or a suitable member of a community? What is one change you can make this week that will make you a more suitable neighbor? ◆ Though we don't hear it proclaimed in the first reading, we know that God creates humans in God's image and likeness. This means we are innately communal beings, yearning for opportunities to be in right relationship with our partners, friends, colleagues, neighbors, and others. ◆ This week, spend time reflecting on what it means to be made in God's image. What does this call you to do; how does this call you to act?

Download more questions and activities for families, initiation groups, and other adult groups at http://www.ltp.org/ahw.

Scripture Insights

God declares that it is not good for humans to be alone. We need partners to form community. In the creation account, the human encountered all created animals before God created the woman as the counterpart to the man. This is an etiology (origin story) for the custom of marriage. In a larger context, it is the foundation for the human need for community and partnership, regardless of gender identification. We do not all achieve partnership in this world, but Genesis 2 says this is what God desires for us. This passage teaches how human beings need community. Some men seek wives, but all of us seek love and acceptance to express our true selves.

Hebrews confirms the reality of suffering even as it celebrates a life beyond such challenges. As Jesus brought many to glory through his suffering, he led to salvation all who live in his name. Suffering for cultural mores and missteps will not be the end of anyone's story. Christ consecrates all in our shared origin, "in the image and likeness of God" (Genesis 1:26–28), and we are called to live likewise.

In Mark, Jesus reinterprets the Torah. He desires community and communion eternally. For many of us, Jesus' teaching on divorce is difficult—more stringent than the Torah and evoking many questions. Exploring the details of Jesus' teaching, we see that he desires continued community and communion. He wants us to put this first and foremost in all of our decisions. The kingdom of God belongs to those who accept it just as children embrace those who care for them. We must discern carefully and prayerfully what that means for each of us.

◆ How might you be open to the human need for community? Is there someone you know who doesn't easily fit in but still needs community?

◆ Are there segments of the population in your sphere who still need community? How might you help?

◆ How should we minister to and accept those who are divorced in our community?

135

READING I *Wisdom 7:7–11*

I prayed, and prudence was given me;
    I pleaded, and the spirit of wisdom came
      to me.
I preferred her to scepter and throne,
and deemed riches nothing in comparison
      with her,
    nor did I liken any priceless gem to her;
because all gold, in view of her, is a little sand,
    and before her, silver is to be accounted mire.
Beyond health and comeliness I loved her,
and I chose to have her rather than the light,
    because the splendor of her
      never yields to sleep.
Yet all good things together came
    to me in her company,
    and countless riches at her hands.

RESPONSORIAL PSALM
Psalm 90:12–13, 14–15, 16–17 (14)

R. Fill us with your love, O Lord, and we will
    sing for joy!

Teach us to number our days aright,
    that we may gain wisdom of heart.
Return, O LORD! How long?
    Have pity on your servants! R.

Fill us at daybreak with your kindness,
    that we may shout for joy
      and gladness all our days.
Make us glad, for the days when you afflicted us,
    for the years when we saw evil. R.

Let your work be seen by your servants
    and your glory by their children;
and may the gracious care of the LORD
      our God be ours;
    prosper the work of our hands for us!
Prosper the work of our hands! R.

READING II *Hebrews 4:12–13*

Brothers and sisters: Indeed the word of God is living and effective, sharper than any two-edged sword, penetrating even between soul and spirit, joints and marrow, and able to discern reflections and thoughts of the heart. No creature is concealed from him, but everything is naked and exposed to the eyes of him to whom we must render an account.

GOSPEL *Mark 10:17–30*

Shorter: Mark 10:17–27

As Jesus was setting out on a journey, a man ran up, knelt down before him, and asked him, "Good teacher, what must I do to inherit eternal life?" Jesus answered him, "Why do you call me good? No one is good but God alone. You know the commandments: *You shall not kill; you shall not commit adultery; you shall not steal; you shall not bear false witness; you shall not defraud; honor your father and your mother.*" He replied and said to him, "Teacher, all of these I have observed from my youth." Jesus, looking at him, loved him and said to him, "You are lacking in one thing. Go, sell what you have, and give to the poor and you will have treasure in heaven; then come, follow me." At that statement his face fell, and he went away sad, for he had many possessions.

    Jesus looked around and said to his disciples, "How hard it is for those who have wealth to enter the kingdom of God!" The disciples were amazed at his words. So Jesus again said to them in reply, "Children, how hard it is to enter the kingdom of God! It is easier for a camel to pass through the eye of a needle than for one who is rich to enter the kingdom of God." They were exceedingly astonished and said among themselves, "Then who can be saved?" Jesus looked at them and said, "For human beings it is impossible, but not for God. All things are possible for God." Peter began to say to him, "We have given up everything and followed you." Jesus said, "Amen, I say to you, there is no one who has given up house or brothers or sisters or mother or father or children or lands for my sake and for the sake of the gospel who will not receive a hundred times more now in this present age: houses and brothers and sisters and mothers and children and lands, with persecutions, and eternal life in the age to come."

Practice of Faith

At first glance in today's Gospel, it may seem as if Jesus is saying that those who are economically wealthy cannot inherit eternal life. However, gaining "wisdom of heart," as the psalmist says, takes careful observation of our day-to-day actions. ◆ Each night this week, spend thirty minutes reflecting on and writing about your day. What consumed your time? What activities or tasks pulled you away from God? After looking back on your day, consider how you can eliminate the things that keep you from God. If you cannot give something up, such as work or a certain necessary responsibility, what can you do to invite God into those moments when you might lack wisdom of heart? How can you ask the Lord to fill you with his love so you can sing for joy? ◆ Regardless of your financial status, we are called to give to the poor. How can you give to someone this week?

Download more questions and activities for families, initiation groups, and other adult groups at http://www.ltp.org/ahw.

Scripture Insights

The reading from the Book of Wisdom tells us that genuine continuous prayer gives us the spirit of wisdom and insight into what God wills for the good of all. We are called to prudence, care, and thought for the future. The riches imparted far exceed the glitter and gold valued by the world. The psalmist confirms this teaching in terms of the joyous prosperity that comes from working with our hands. Ultimately, the psalmist extols the forging of hopeful endurance in our life's plans.

The reading from Hebrews reminds us that God's word is true, but nonetheless sharp—sharper than any double-edged sword—such that it cuts to the depths of our hearts. Naked and exposed before God, we are called to more than we could ever imagine—eternal life through our faithful action in the world.

The Gospel of Mark recounts Jesus' encounter with a questioning man. With love and compassion, Jesus challenges the man to keep the commandments and even more, to live in service to the poor and marginalized. Mark tells us that the man's face fell, but nothing more. Perhaps he rose to the occasion? We are left to wonder. Jesus' challenge yields various other responses, all equally dismayed and concerned. Jesus doubles down with the well-known image of a camel traversing a needle's eye as easier than entrance of the rich into the kingdom of God. The rewards of such a high bar, however, are profound: dwelling in eternal union with God.

◆ Our readings challenge us to seek wisdom and blossom with her gifts. How does this manifest in your life today? How might you strive to do more to live prudently as God calls you?

◆ Hebrews teaches that we cannot conceal ourselves from God. How might this be concerning? How might this inspire you to live in service to others?

◆ How do you envision the rich young man's story resolving? Did he rise to Jesus' challenge and serve those in need? How might you respond to a similar summons?

READING I *Isaiah 53:10–11*

The LORD was pleased to crush him in infirmity.

If he gives his life as an offering for sin,
    he shall see his descendants in a long life,
    and the will of the LORD shall
      be accomplished through him.

Because of his affliction
    he shall see the light in fullness of days;
through his suffering, my servant
      shall justify many,
    and their guilt he shall bear.

RESPONSORIAL PSALM
Psalm 33:4–5, 18–19, 20, 22 (22)

R. Lord, let your mercy be on us, as we place
    our trust in you.

Upright is the word of the LORD,
    and all his works are trustworthy.
He loves justice and right;
    of the kindness of the LORD
      the earth is full. R.

See, the eyes of the LORD are upon those who
    fear him,
    upon those who hope for his kindness;
to deliver them from death
    and preserve them in spite of famine. R.

Our soul waits for the LORD,
    who is our help and our shield.
May your kindness, O LORD, be upon us
    who have put our hope in you. R.

READING II *Hebrews 4:14–16*

Brothers and sisters: Since we have a great high priest who has passed through the heavens, Jesus, the Son of God, let us hold fast to our confession. For we do not have a high priest who is unable to sympathize with our weaknesses, but one who has similarly been tested in every way, yet without sin. So let us confidently approach the throne of grace to receive mercy and to find grace for timely help.

GOSPEL *Mark 10:35–45*

Shorter: Mark 10:42–45

James and John, the sons of Zebedee, came to Jesus and said to him, "Teacher, we want you to do for us whatever we ask of you." He replied, "What do you wish me to do for you?" They answered him, "Grant that in your glory we may sit one at your right and the other at your left." Jesus said to them, "You do not know what you are asking. Can you drink the cup that I drink or be baptized with the baptism with which I am baptized?" They said to him, "We can." Jesus said to them, "The cup that I drink, you will drink, and with the baptism with which I am baptized, you will be baptized; but to sit at my right or at my left is not mine to give but is for those for whom it has been prepared." When the ten heard this, they became indignant at James and John. Jesus summoned them and said to them, "You know that those who are recognized as rulers over the Gentiles lord it over them, and their great ones make their authority over them felt. But it shall not be so among you. Rather, whoever wishes to be great among you will be your servant; whoever wishes to be first among you will be the slave of all. For the Son of Man did not come to be served but to serve and to give his life as a ransom for many."

Practice of Charity

As James and John ask Jesus to bestow on them great honor (who doesn't want to be honored with Jesus, even just a little bit?), Jesus graciously reminds them that greatness comes from being the servant of all. ◆ Learn about radical service, including how the Church is working to serve those living in poverty and those experiencing socioeconomic distress, at the Catholic Campaign for Human Development website: https://www.usccb.org/committees/catholic-campaign-human-development. ◆ Think about someone who has gone above and beyond for you. How can you hold them in your prayer this week? What is something you can do to express your gratitude for them and the example they have set? ◆ Who is someone in your immediate circle with whom you struggle, perhaps someone with whom you become indignant easily? How can you support them this week?

Download more questions and activities for families, initiation groups, and other adult groups at http://www.ltp.org/ahw.

Scripture Insights

Across Isaiah chapters 40—55, the prophet presents four poems that characterize God's servant who suffers on behalf of humankind. Our reading is from the final song of this "Suffering Servant." We learn that although God crushes the servant with pain, God's plan is ultimately accomplished through him. Indeed, the suffering of God's Chosen One produces an offering of reparation and atonement that brings light and justifies all whose sins he bears.

The Letter to the Hebrews teaches that, as God's chosen high priest, Jesus is the one who has been tested in every way, the one who, without sin, bears the sins of all humankind. His ability to sympathize with all our weaknesses, yet work through and rise above them, allows us the prospect of the same. Through the model of Christ, we strive to be our best selves, knowing that God's mercy will be with us even when we fail, because we eagerly seek God's good for all creation.

Mark's Gospel follows Jesus' third prediction of his passion (Mark 10:32–34). There he tells his disciples that in Jerusalem he will be arrested by Jewish authorities who condemn and hand him over to death, then after three days he will rise from the dead. Jesus is thus presented as God's Suffering Servant. Zebedee's sons, however, show they still expect a kingly Davidic messiah whose privileged advisors they desire to be. Jesus redirects them, teaching that his true disciples serve others as he does by sacrificing himself. Though they have a lot to learn here, these imperfect disciples grow to stand strong and share the Good News. We are likewise called to grow by overcoming societal norms and live by bringing to light God's will in the world.

◆ Isaiah indicates that we can find light through the darkness of pain. Might this be possible?

◆ How might we integrate the second reading's teaching of Christ as our exalted model into the reality of this world and its challenges?

◆ In Mark, Jesus shocks his disciples by describing himself as God's Son whose mission is to serve with abandon. How might we do likewise in our lives?

READING I *Jeremiah 31:7–9*

Thus says the LORD:
Shout with joy for Jacob,
    exult at the head of the nations;
    proclaim your praise and say:
The LORD has delivered his people,
    the remnant of Israel.
Behold, I will bring them back
    from the land of the north;
I will gather them from the ends of the world,
    with the blind and the lame in their midst,
the mothers and those with child;
    they shall return as an immense throng.
They departed in tears,
    but I will console them and guide them;
I will lead them to brooks of water,
    on a level road, so that none shall stumble.
For I am a father to Israel,
    Ephraim is my first-born.

RESPONSORIAL PSALM
Psalm 126:1–2, 2–3, 4–5, 6 (3)

R. The Lord has done great things for us; we are
    filled with joy.

When the LORD brought back the captives of Zion,
  we were like men dreaming.
Then our mouth was filled with laughter,
  and our tongue with rejoicing.   R.

Then they said among the nations,
  "The LORD has done great things for them."
The LORD has done great things for us;
  we are glad indeed.   R.

Restore our fortunes, O LORD,
  like the torrents in the southern desert.
Those that sow in tears
  shall reap rejoicing.   R.

Although they go forth weeping,
  carrying the seed to be sown,
they shall come back rejoicing,
  carrying their sheaves.   R.

READING II *Hebrews 5:1–6*

Brothers and sisters: Every high priest is taken from among men and made their representative before God, to offer gifts and sacrifices for sins. He is able to deal patiently with the ignorant and erring, for he himself is beset by weakness and so, for this reason, must make sin offerings for himself as well as for the people. No one takes this honor upon himself but only when called by God, just as Aaron was. In the same way, it was not Christ who glorified himself in becoming high priest, but rather the one who said to him:
  You are my son:
    this day I have begotten you;
just as he says in another place:
  You are a priest forever
    according to the order of Melchizedek.

GOSPEL *Mark 10:46–52*

As Jesus was leaving Jericho with his disciples and a sizable crowd, Bartimaeus, a blind man, the son of Timaeus, sat by the roadside begging. On hearing that it was Jesus of Nazareth, he began to cry out and say, "Jesus, son of David, have pity on me." And many rebuked him, telling him to be silent. But he kept calling out all the more, "Son of David, have pity on me." Jesus stopped and said, "Call him." So they called the blind man, saying to him, "Take courage; get up, Jesus is calling you." He threw aside his cloak, sprang up, and came to Jesus. Jesus said to him in reply, "What do you want me to do for you?" The blind man replied to him, "Master, I want to see." Jesus told him, "Go your way; your faith has saved you." Immediately he received his sight and followed him on the way.

Practice of Faith

Today's readings highlight the joy of sight and the joy that comes with following Jesus. Though we may "go forth weeping" (Psalm 126:6) or stumble along the way, we indeed carry seeds that we must choose to sow with those same tears. Jesus is our companion as we work to reap joy. ◆ Bartimaeus chooses courage as he tells Jesus he wants to see. Jesus heals him, and Bartimaeus can see both physically and spiritually. In your prayer this week, take courage and talk to Jesus: What is preventing you from seeing? How can this conversation with Jesus help you recognize what you need to do to be filled with the joy of the Lord? ◆ After your conversation with Jesus, commit to an action you can take to move toward healing, to gain clear vision.

Download more questions and activities for families, initiation groups, and other adult groups at http://www.ltp.org/ahw.

Scripture Insights

In 538 BC, the Kingdom of Judah was overrun, and God's people were deported to all parts of the Babylonian Empire. The Israelites wondered how this could happen and if they would ever return to their homeland and traditions of culture and worship. Jeremiah and the psalmist affirm God's power and plan to restore the faithful. Present suffering is not the end. The faithful ultimately dwell in peaceful union with God.

The Letter to the Hebrews expresses a particular understanding of Jesus Christ as a priest in the line of Aaron and Melchizedek. Aaron is Moses' brother who is God's prophet and founder of Israel's high priests (Exodus 4:14–31; 28:1–43). Melchizedek, meaning "my just king," appears in Genesis as a mysterious holy figure to whom our founding father Abraham bowed and gave tithe (14:17–24). The second reading presents Jesus as just such a high priest in intimate relationship with God, who acts in service on behalf of the people.

The Gospel reading meets Jesus and his disciples leaving Jericho on their journey to Jerusalem to celebrate the Passover and experience Jesus' passion. As they depart amid a crowd, they encounter Bartimaeus, blind and begging, on the roadside. Intuiting who Jesus is and his mission, Bartimaeus resists those who would silence him and cries out to Jesus to intercede with God on his behalf. Although the ensuing miracle involves the regaining of physical sight, Bartimaeus already has all the sight that he needs to know who Jesus is and how God is calling him to live. The miracle is for those who crowd around, blind to God's call in their lives. Bartimaeus' faith will astound and convince them.

◆ What does it mean for you to know that God is the One who restores all people into union through relationship to himself?

◆ Those who are physically blind may well not need the bumbling attempts of physically sighted people to "restore" them. What might the physically sighted learn from them?

◆ How might Bartimaeus be a model of faith?

READING I *Deuteronomy 6:2–6*

Moses spoke to the people, saying: "Fear the LORD, your God, and keep, throughout the days of your lives, all his statutes and commandments which I enjoin on you, and thus have long life. Hear then, Israel, and be careful to observe them, that you may grow and prosper the more, in keeping with the promise of the LORD, the God of your fathers, to give you a land flowing with milk and honey.

"Hear, O Israel! The LORD is our God, the LORD alone! Therefore, you shall love the LORD, your God, with all your heart, and with all your soul, and with all your strength. Take to heart these words which I enjoin on you today."

RESPONSORIAL PSALM *Psalm 18:2–3, 3–4, 47, 51 (2)*

R. I love you, Lord, my strength.

I love you, O LORD, my strength,
  O LORD, my rock, my fortress,
    my deliverer. R.

My God, my rock of refuge,
  my shield, the horn of my salvation,
    my stronghold!
Praised be the LORD, I exclaim,
  and I am safe from my enemies. R.

The LORD lives! And blessed be my rock!
  Extolled be God my savior;
You who gave great victories to your king
  and showed kindness to your anointed. R.

READING II *Hebrews 7:23–28*

Brothers and sisters: The levitical priests were many because they were prevented by death from remaining in office, but Jesus, because he remains forever, has a priesthood that does not pass away. Therefore, he is always able to save those who approach God through him, since he lives forever to make intercession for them.

It was fitting that we should have such a high priest: holy, innocent, undefiled, separated from sinners, higher than the heavens. He has no need, as did the high priests, to offer sacrifice day after day, first for his own sins and then for those of the people; he did that once for all when he offered himself. For the law appoints men subject to weakness to be high priests, but the word of the oath, which was taken after the law, appoints a son, who has been made perfect forever.

GOSPEL *Mark 12:28b–34*

One of the scribes came to Jesus and asked him, "Which is the first of all the commandments?" Jesus replied, "The first is this: *Hear, O Israel! The Lord our God is Lord alone! You shall love the Lord your God with all your heart, with all your soul, with all your mind, and with all your strength.* The second is this: *You shall love your neighbor as yourself.* There is no other commandment greater than these." The scribe said to him, "Well said, teacher. You are right in saying, 'He is One and there is no other than he.' And 'to love him with all your heart, with all your understanding, with all your strength, and to love your neighbor as yourself' is worth more than all burnt offerings and sacrifices." And when Jesus saw that he answered with understanding, he said to him, "You are not far from the kingdom of God." And no one dared to ask him any more questions.

Practice of Charity

A scribe tests Jesus, asking him about God's law. Jesus identifies the commandments: to love God with all of one's being and to love one's neighbor as oneself. This Sunday, we are invited to reflect on how we embody these commandments. Though to the point and seemingly simple, living these commandments can be a challenge in our daily lives; it is important to reflect on how we can be careful to observe them. ◆ This week, consider what it means to love God with all your heart, all your soul, all your mind, and all your strength. How can you show your love for God in each of those ways? ◆ Through the commandment to love our neighbors, we can love God. At the end of each evening, say a prayer for those you struggle to love. How can you invite God into difficult relationships?

Download more questions and activities for families, initiation groups, and other adult groups at http://www.ltp.org/ahw.

Scripture Insights

Deuteronomy 6 expresses the essence of Israel's covenant relationship with God. Moses calls God's people to embody the decrees that will bear fruit for generations to come. Foundational to this relationship of faith and vocation is love. The relationship of faith is vertical: between the individual and God. The relationship of vocation is between people: the individual and all humankind. Both types of relationship begin and end with loving God with the entirety of one's mind, body, and soul. Our love for God, ourselves, and others makes possible community—living in unity with God and one another. The genius of God acting in covenant relationship with creation and God's chosen people is this love that sustains all modes of being—biological, psychological, sociological, political, scientific, and religious.

Mark pointedly builds upon this understanding of covenant relationship. Leaders query Jesus' understanding of these commandments. Jesus responds first with who God is, then with our response to God and, finally, in our relationship to one another. Jesus grounds his teaching in the Scripture from Deuteronomy. The coming of Jesus as the Christ, God's anointed one, to redeem and restore all humankind to himself is well grounded in who God always is: one who desires to dwell in covenant relationship with creation.

The Scriptures challenge us to ground the new in the old. We must also recognize the old for its historically contextualized veracity and move into the new. Christians, by definition, live in the new covenant, written by the one ultimate redeeming sacrifice of Jesus Christ, who makes covenant relationship possible for all who believe. This is eternal. We are still discovering all the different modes of being. Let us be open to God's teaching.

◆ How do you embody God's first commandment (Deuteronomy 6)?

◆ Are you open to the question-and-answer dialogue in which Jesus participates in Mark 12?

◆ What might it mean to be open to God's continual teaching through modes of being?

READING I *1 Kings 17:10–16*

In those days, Elijah the prophet went to Zarephath. As he arrived at the entrance of the city, a widow was gathering sticks there; he called out to her, "Please bring me a small cupful of water to drink." She left to get it, and he called out after her, "Please bring along a bit of bread." She answered, "As the LORD, your God, lives, I have nothing baked; there is only a handful of flour in my jar and a little oil in my jug. Just now I was collecting a couple of sticks, to go in and prepare something for myself and my son; when we have eaten it, we shall die." Elijah said to her, "Do not be afraid. Go and do as you propose. But first make me a little cake and bring it to me. Then you can prepare something for yourself and your son. For the LORD, the God of Israel, says, 'The jar of flour shall not go empty, nor the jug of oil run dry, until the day when the LORD sends rain upon the earth.'" She left and did as Elijah had said. She was able to eat for a year, and he and her son as well; the jar of flour did not go empty, nor the jug of oil run dry, as the LORD had foretold through Elijah.

RESPONSORIAL PSALM
Psalm 146:7, 8–9, 9–10 (1b)

R. Praise the Lord, my soul!
  or: Alleluia.

The LORD keeps faith forever,
  secures justice for the oppressed,
  gives food to the hungry.
The LORD sets captives free. R.

The LORD gives sight to the blind;
  the LORD raises up those
    who were bowed down.
The LORD loves the just;
  the LORD protects strangers. R.

The fatherless and the widow he sustains,
  but the way of the wicked he thwarts.
The LORD shall reign forever;
  your God, O Zion, through all generations.
    Alleluia. R.

READING II *Hebrews 9:24–28*

Christ did not enter into a sanctuary made by hands, a copy of the true one, but heaven itself, that he might now appear before God on our behalf. Not that he might offer himself repeatedly, as the high priest enters each year into the sanctuary with blood that is not his own; if that were so, he would have had to suffer repeatedly from the foundation of the world. But now once for all he has appeared at the end of the ages to take away sin by his sacrifice. Just as it is appointed that human beings die once, and after this the judgment, so also Christ, offered once to take away the sins of many, will appear a second time, not to take away sin but to bring salvation to those who eagerly await him.

GOSPEL *Mark 12:38–44*

Shorter: Mark 12:41–44

In the course of his teaching Jesus said to the crowds, "Beware of the scribes, who like to go around in long robes and accept greetings in the marketplaces, seats of honor in synagogues, and places of honor at banquets. They devour the houses of widows and, as a pretext recite lengthy prayers. They will receive a very severe condemnation."

He sat down opposite the treasury and observed how the crowd put money into the treasury. Many rich people put in large sums. A poor widow also came and put in two small coins worth a few cents. Calling his disciples to himself, he said to them, "Amen, I say to you, this poor widow put in more than all the other contributors to the treasury. For they have all contributed from their surplus wealth, but she, from her poverty, has contributed all she had, her whole livelihood."

Practice of Faith

Jesus challenges us to consider how we might be like the scribes, who led a community and were complicit in the suffering and poverty of their neighbors. It is indeed admirable that the widow generously donates to the treasury, despite her poverty. The Scriptures do not condone living in poverty, but rather encourage us to ask ourselves how we give from our surplus. ◆ In your prayer today, share with God what you have given: your time, money, gifts, or talents. Are you giving from your surplus, like the rich people in today's Gospel? ◆ We are called to join the Lord in working for justice for the oppressed. Learn more about poverty in the United States here: www.poverty usa.org/poverty-quiz. ◆ Find an action you can take this week: challenge yourself to give as the widow does.

Download more questions and activities for families, initiation groups, and other adult groups at http://www.ltp.org/ahw.

Scripture Insights

The mighty power of a living, ever-present God is in evidence in this week's readings. Both the prophet Elijah and the widow he encounters in Zarephath mark their lives by God's presence. Elijah responds in kind to her faith and hospitality as she gives to him despite her dire need. God works through them both as they provide for each other. The true miracle of the never-empty jar is the relationship that emerges and the lives that bloom.

On a more universal level, the psalmist reminds us that God who brings two people in need together also secures justice, renders liberation, and sustains all humankind. The author of Hebrews affirms that God brings salvation to all humankind through the sacrifice of Christ as the offering that atones for sin for all time. That said, these authors uphold God's presence for individuals. Indeed, God has particular concern for those with whom society often dispenses, such as immigrants, people who are poor, and others bowed down by the weight of this world.

In Mark's Gospel, Jesus continues this teaching. At this point, Jesus and his disciples have traveled to Jerusalem and Jesus knows his time is short. Here in the temple area, Jesus warns those coming to him to beware of those who lord their power over people, those whose greed is insatiable. Jesus has already taught that true leadership is manifest through service. Now he exposes the emptiness and impotence of those who are more concerned with status than where they stand in relationship with God and fellow human beings. Teaching in the line of Elijah, Jesus upholds the woman who gives from her need all that she has in the hope of new life.

◆ What might it mean to live in relationship with God as if your jug will never run dry?

◆ How do you perceive God as one who works for global justice and meets individual need?

◆ Jesus calls us to give from our poverty. How does that resonate with you?

READING I *Daniel 12:1–3*

In those days, I, Daniel,
  heard this word of the Lord:
"At that time there shall arise
  Michael, the great prince,
  guardian of your people;
it shall be a time unsurpassed in distress
  since nations began until that time.
At that time your people shall escape,
  everyone who is found written in the book.

"Many of those who sleep in the dust of the
    earth shall awake;
  some shall live forever,
  others shall be an everlasting horror
    and disgrace.

"But the wise shall shine brightly
  like the splendor of the firmament,
and those who lead the many to justice
  shall be like the stars forever."

RESPONSORIAL PSALM
Psalm 16:5, 8, 9–10, 11 (1)

R. You are my inheritance, O Lord!

O LORD, my allotted portion and my cup,
  you it is who hold fast my lot.
I set the LORD ever before me;
  with him at my right hand
    I shall not be disturbed. R.

Therefore my heart is glad and my soul rejoices,
  my body, too, abides in confidence;
because you will not abandon my soul
    to the netherworld,
  nor will you suffer your faithful one
    to undergo corruption. R.

You will show me the path to life,
  fullness of joys in your presence,
  the delights at your right hand forever. R.

READING II *Hebrews 10:11–14, 18*

Brothers and sisters: Every priest stands daily at his ministry, offering frequently those same sacrifices that can never take away sins. But this one offered one sacrifice for sins, and took his seat forever at the right hand of God; now he waits until his enemies are made his footstool. For by one offering he has made perfect forever those who are being consecrated.

Where there is forgiveness of these, there is no longer offering for sin.

GOSPEL *Mark 13:24–32*

Jesus said to his disciples: "In those days after
    that tribulation
  the sun will be darkened,
    and the moon will not give its light,
  and the stars will be falling from the sky,
    and the powers in the heavens will
      be shaken.
"And then they will see 'the Son of Man coming in the clouds' with great power and glory, and then he will send out the angels and gather his elect from the four winds, from the end of the earth to the end of the sky.

"Learn a lesson from the fig tree. When its branch becomes tender and sprouts leaves, you know that summer is near. In the same way, when you see these things happening, know that he is near, at the gates. Amen, I say to you, this generation will not pass away until all these things have taken place. Heaven and earth will pass away, but my words will not pass away.

"But of that day or hour, no one knows, neither the angels in heaven, nor the Son, but only the Father."

Practice of Hope

From listening to Jesus in today's Gospel, we can learn the importance of paying attention. Jesus encourages his disciples to learn from the growth of the fig tree. In a similar way, we can see the ways God is present in our lives each day, encouraging us to be like the wise who "shine brightly / . . . / and those who lead the many to justice" (Daniel 12:3). ◆ Sometime this week, go outside to take a walk. Challenge yourself to silence potential distractions, such as technology. As you walk, take note of your surroundings. Can you feel or notice God's presence? ◆ Today's psalm expresses a great deal of love and trust in God: the psalmist proclaims that with the Lord "at my right hand I shall not be disturbed" (Psalm 16:8). ◆ Aside from your walk, spend intentional time in prayer throughout the week to cultivate a relationship with God that radiates delight and trust.

Download more questions and activities for families, initiation groups, and other adult groups at http://www.ltp.org/ahw.

Scripture Insights

Daniel 12 reveals the climax of God's work in history. In apocalyptic form, the passage comforts the afflicted through imagery of heavenly battle and earthly recompense. The author reassures the faithful of the integrity of creation and God's fidelity to his covenanted people by confirming both God's sovereignty and the justice through which God works in creation. For the first time, an unmitigated claim for individual resurrection is made; but this too is part and parcel of God's righteous plan. Creation has a purposeful beginning, middle, and end. Science affirms the finiteness of nature; faith affirms that it has a purpose. God's purposes determine the course of every aspect of creation. What is new in Daniel 12 is the notion that those who hold these tenets can transcend death.

God's presence is unfailing. And yet, God is not in the business of protecting people from pain. We are to act wisely, turn others to righteousness, and wait. Pain triggers responses to one another in a way that the absence of pain could not facilitate. What God offers is struggle, endurance, and guidance for those who reach for the One who is in control. Perfection or success in human terms is not guaranteed; God's justice and recompense that transcend the earthly realm are. At the appointed time, God breaks into human history and yanks his people back on the track of the divine plan for creation.

The times and the details will always remain veiled. What Daniel 12 declares without apology is that God acts. And in the end, our recompense is just.

With his final speech in Mark 13, Jesus stands firmly in the line of Daniel.

◆ The apocalypticism of Daniel forges a new path in Judaism that is foundational to Christianity. How does this comfort and challenge you?

◆ The psalmist declares faith as the path to life. How do you see this in your life?

◆ In Mark, Jesus affirms his identity as the Son of Man in the line of Daniel. How does this impact your understanding?

READING I *Daniel 7:13–14*

As the visions during the night continued, I saw
  one like a son of man coming,
    on the clouds of heaven;
  when he reached the Ancient One
    and was presented before him,
  the one like a Son of man received dominion,
      glory, and kingship;
  all peoples, nations,
    and languages serve him.
His dominion is an everlasting dominion
    that shall not be taken away,
    his kingship shall not be destroyed.

RESPONSORIAL PSALM
Psalm 93:1, 1–2, 5 (1a)

R. The Lord is king; he is robed in majesty.

The LORD is king, in splendor robed;
  robed is the LORD and girt about with
    strength. R.

And he has made the world firm,
  not to be moved.
Your throne stands firm from of old;
  from everlasting you are, O LORD. R.

Your decrees are worthy of trust indeed;
  holiness befits your house,
  O LORD, for length of days. R.

READING II *Revelation 1:5–8*

Jesus Christ is the faithful witness, the firstborn
of the dead and ruler of the kings of the earth. To
him who loves us and has freed us from our sins
by his blood, who has made us into a kingdom,
priests for his God and Father, to him be glory and
power forever and ever. Amen.

  Behold, he is coming amid the clouds,
    and every eye will see him,
    even those who pierced him.
  All the peoples of the earth will lament him.
  Yes. Amen.

"I am the Alpha and the Omega," says the
Lord God, "the one who is and who was and who
is to come, the almighty."

GOSPEL *John 18:33b–37*

Pilate said to Jesus, "Are you the King of the Jews?"
Jesus answered, "Do you say this on your own or
have others told you about me?" Pilate answered,
"I am not a Jew, am I? Your own nation and the
chief priests handed you over to me. What have
you done?" Jesus answered, "My kingdom does
not belong to this world. If my kingdom did belong
to this world, my attendants would be fighting to
keep me from being handed over to the Jews. But
as it is, my kingdom is not here." So Pilate said to
him, "Then you are a king?" Jesus answered, "You
say I am a king. For this I was born and for this I
came into the world, to testify to the truth. Everyone who belongs to the truth listens to my voice."

Practice of Hope

Today we celebrate the Solemnity of Our Lord Jesus Christ, King of the Universe, the last Sunday of our liturgical year. There is much we can continue to learn about who Jesus is and thus who we are called to become, as we hear him testify to the truth even in the face of being handed over to Pilate for torturous persecution. ◆ Jesus reminds Pilate that the kingdom is not yet here. How can you work to continue to bring forth the kingdom on earth today? What is an action you can take this week to proclaim the truth you have learned from Jesus? ◆ Let us reflect on how we have journeyed with our Lord Jesus Christ, King of the Universe, throughout this past liturgical year. How have you pierced Jesus? How have you actively seen him in your daily life? How have you brought the humble, service-oriented truth Jesus proclaims to those around you? Bring these reflections to your prayer.

Download more questions and activities for families, initiation groups, and other adult groups at http://www.ltp.org/ahw.

Scripture Insights

The apocalyptic vision presented in Daniel 7 is the foundation for Jesus' Gospel claims to be the Son of Man. Daniel is characterized, through the court tales of Daniel 1—6, as a faithful sage through whom God reveals Godself. In Daniel 7, he begins to receive God's plan for humankind, including seeing "one like a son of man" (Daniel 7:13). In contemporary Jewish idiom, this refers to a human being. Daniel sees one such person in relation to God, presented as the Ancient One, whose kingship is eternal. Jesus takes this on as a title to represent his self-understanding in relationship to God and he is the Christ, God's anointed one.

John's Gospel presents Pilate interrogating Jesus on the charges at stake for the Roman Empire: kingship and sedition. The heart of the Roman trial is the question of truth. Kingship in the political sense is Pilate's only concern. Jesus parries and prods Pilate to take a stand. Speaking of his kingdom, and strongly so, Jesus declares his kingship beyond that of Pilate or any political system. Not of the world, it is nonetheless witnessed in the world. Pilate pursues the question and indeed Pilate will say four times in the coming scenes that Jesus is king (John 18:39; 19:14, 15, 19). Jesus modifies the title and lays bare the real issue at stake: truth. All accusations come down to this. Jesus, however, continues to fulfill his mission, bearing witness to the truth even on trial.

◆ Are you familiar with Daniel 7? Have you understood its significance for the Gospels? How does this impact you?

◆ Pilate's dismissal of the knowledge of truth while standing before its embodiment influences the rest of Jesus' story. Authentic believing in Jesus is based on openness to his word as the revelation of God. This is Jesus' final challenge and Pilate refuses to recognize God's revelation in him, but nonetheless seeks neutrality by acting as if Jesus' challenge has nothing to do with him. Can this attempt at neutrality stand?

◆ How do these readings call the faithful to stand for truth in their everyday lives?